PROGRESSION IN SECONDARY DRAMA

by

Andy Kempe and Marigold Ashwell

Heinemann Educational Publishers
Halley Court, Jordan Hill, Oxford, OX2 8EJ
a division of Reed Educational & Professional Publishing Ltd
Heinemann is a registered trademark of Reed Educational & Professional Publishing Ltd

OXFORD MELBOURNE AUCKLAND
JOHANNESBURG BLANTYRE GABARONE
IBADAN PORTSMOUTH NH (USA) CHICAGO

First published 2000

ISBN 0 435 18595 0

04 03 02 01
10 9 8 7 6 5 4 3 2

Typeset by TechType, Abingdon, Oxon
Printed and bound in Great Britain by Biddles Ltd.

Acknowledgements

The publishers gratefully acknowledge the following for permission to reproduce copyright material. Every
effort has been made to trace copyright holders but if they have inadvertently overlooked any they will be
pleased to make the necessary arrangements as soon as possible.

Extracts: pp18-19 extract from National Literacy Strategy: Framework for teaching, DfEE 1988, © HMSO;
pp 23-24 extract from 'Inspecting subjects and aspects 11-18 English – Drama' February 1999, published by
OFSTED; p 42 extract from Starting drama teaching by Michael Fleming, published by David Fulton, 1994;
p 42 extract from 'Progression and continuity in the teaching of Drama' by Michael Fleming, published in
Drama Magazine, the Journal of National Drama, Vol 7, No 1, November 1999; pp 74-75 extract from
'The Old Man and His Grandson', from World of Fairy Tales by Michael Foreman, published by Pavillion
Books Ltd, reprinted by permission of Pavillion Books Ltd.; p 106-9 extract from Ancient Mariner by Michael
Bogdanov. Reprinted with permission of Curtis Brown on behalf of Michael Bogdanov; p 116 extract from
'A Case of Murder' by Vernon Scannell. Reprinted by permission of the author; p 116 extract from 'Night
Mail' by WH Auden, published by Faber & Faber Ltd; pp 120-1 'FX' from Robinduck by Roger McGough
© Roger McGough. Reprinted by permission of Peters Fraser and Dunlop Ltd on behalf of Roger McGough;
pp 122-3 'The Car Trip' by Michael Rosen from The Hypnotiser published by HarperCollins, 1998. © Michael
Rosen. Reprinted by permission of Peters Fraser and Dunlop Ltd on behalf of Michael Rosen; pp 126-8
'Children's Games' by William Carlos Williams, from Collected Poems Vol II, published by Carcanet Press Ltd.
Reprinted with permission from Carcanet Press Ltd; p 131 'Charlotte O'Neill's Song' by Fiona Farrell,
published in Cutting Edge, 1987. Reprinted by permission of Auckland University Press, New Zealand and
Fiona Farrell; p 161 extract from Waiting for Godot by Samuel Beckett, published by Faber and Faber Ltd.
Reprinted by permission of Faber and Faber Limited and Grove Atlantic Inc.; p 163 extract from The National
Health by Peter Nichols, published by Faber and Faber Ltd. Reprinted with permission of Faber and Faber Ltd.;
p 164 extract from Loot by Joe Orton, published by Methuen. Reprinted by permission of Methuen
Publishing Ltd.; p 165 extract from No Orchids for Miss Blandish by Robert David MacDonald, published by
Oberon Books Ltd.; p 166 extract from The Widowing of Mrs Holroyd by DH Lawrence. Reprinted by
permission of Laurence Pollinger Ltd and the Estate of Frieda Lawrence Ravagli; p 184 extract from Rainbow's
Ending by Noel Greig © Noel Greig. Copyright agent: Alan Brodie Representation Ltd.; p 185 extract from
Under Milk Wood by Dylan Thomas, published by JM Dent. Reprinted with permission of David Higham
Associates Ltd.; p 187 extract from Staying Up by Robert Swindells, published by Transworld Publishers, a
division of The Random House Group Ltd. © Robert Swindells, 1998. All rights reserved; pp 192-3 extract
from The Weir by Conor McPherson, published by Nick Hern Books; p 218 extract from Superscripts – Stone
Cold by Joe Standerline, published by Stanley Thornes, 1999; p 219 extract from The Birthday Party by Harold
Pinter, published by Faber and Faber Ltd. Reprinted with permission of Faber and Faber Ltd.; p 221 extract
from Two Weeks with the Queen by Mary Morris, adapted from the novel by Morris Gleitzman and published
by Currency Press, Sydney, 1993. Reprinted with permission of Currency Press; pp 224 and 249 extracts from
Oh What a Lovely War by Theatre Workshop. Reprinted with permission of Methuen Publishing Ltd.; pp 256,
258-62 extracts from The Colour of Justice by Richard Norton Taylor, published by Oberon Books, 1999.
Reprinted by permission of Oberon Books; pp 268-71 extract from 'I will be haunted by the look Ruth Ellis
gave me as the hangman led her off to die' by Ruki Sayid, from The Mirror, 27 November 1999.

Illustrations: p 93 The Art Archive; p 98 Bill Brandt, Hulton Getty; p 100 AKG, London; p 102 Kharbine
Tapabor, Paris, Bridgeman Art Library; p 125 AKG London.

Contents

Foreword

Drama in secondary schools continues to grow in popularity. Numbers of candidates at all levels continue to rise and results are often among the best in the school. A school with a thriving drama department that values drama as part of its profile is, more often than not, an over-subscribed school.

In most subject areas the National Curriculum guides and directs the business of the classroom. It determines structures of assessment, and is the measure with which a school judges its success – and by which it is judged. Specialist drama teachers, however, have not been provided with such complete structures and some have understandably felt uncertainty regarding what criteria should be employed in organising and evaluating their work.

By reflecting the well-established patterns of National Curriculum planning and assessment, *Progression in Secondary Drama* provides drama teachers with a structure for participating fully in the discourses of the new century's school curriculum. The authors suggest a framework in which teachers can plot and assess the knowledge, skills and understanding their students gain in drama lessons while preserving the principles of student autonomy and creativity that have always been such a powerful hallmark of drama in schools.

The National Literacy Strategy is increasingly resulting in a greater awareness of drama forms and processes in pupils arriving in Year 7 and there is now an exciting opportunity for drama teachers to complement and build on this knowledge and experience. The innovative approach promoted by *Progression in Secondary Drama* recognises this potential and suggests ways in which drama might be developed and realised in the practical environment of the secondary drama lesson.

In this book, Andy Kempe and Marigold Ashwell offer the teacher a splendidly eclectic portfolio of material for class projects. At the same time the book, which is fully compatible with the wide-ranging demands of the National Curriculum, takes care to organise ideas for a curriculum framework which is progressive; that is, pupils progress through it. Eschewing jargon, this work should be welcomed as just the kind of book to help secondary drama teachers plan, execute and evaluate their work in the context of the structures of the whole school curriculum.

Dr David Hornbrook
Performing Arts Inspector, Further Education Funding Council

Acknowledgements

Many of the ideas and strategies explored in this book have developed as a result of the creativity and reflections of a host of practitioners. The authors would especially like to acknowledge the influence of teacher colleagues, especially those in Berkshire, past PGCE students at the University of Reading, Trading Faces and Oxfordshire Touring Theatre Company on their thinking and practice. Specific thanks for ideas and techniques described in this book must go to Karen Allen, Alastair Black, Noreen Boylan, David Condon, Jacqui Crooks, Anne Fenton, Mike Harrison, John Hertrich (HMI), Rick and Jan Holroyd, David Rhys Jones, John Kane, Allan Lindsay, Ron Price, Madonna Stinson, Shelley Upton and Professor Brian Watkins. A very special thank you must also be made to Dr Helen Nicholson for reading early manuscripts and making incisive yet always supportive comments on the developing work, Nick Ashwell, Sarah Bergson and Cathy Wardale.

Introduction

It would be convenient if the title of this book, *Progression in Secondary Drama,* would speak for itself. However, language is altogether too slippery for that. Although the words of a language remain largely the same, the context in which they are used is forever changing. The meanings words appear to hold in one context are carried forward to new situations with the result that language is never value free. The *Oxford English Dictionary*'s definition of the word 'progression', for example, suggests simply a series or succession. But what would be the implications of designing a drama curriculum based on such a bland definition? Would simply setting students a 'series' of tasks represent progress in our practice as teachers or move students towards greater knowledge and understanding of drama? Does not 'progression' in the context of education somehow imply 'getting better' at something? Of course, an acceptance of the term 'better' is contingent upon the values one holds within a given context. And knowing whether or not someone or something has actually 'got better' is dependent upon the way those values are translated into assessable criteria.

If trying to communicate through the written word alone is such a complex business, consider how much more complex communication is when it also involves the sounds of words and the pace, volume and tone at which they are spoken. Add the visual impact made by the speaker and consider how what they are wearing, how they are gesturing and where they are in relation to their audience may also communicate meaning. In addition, consider the effect any background sounds and images could have on the audience. Communicating through the language of drama involves being able to consciously manipulate and interpret combinations of sound, movement, light and space. The context in which drama communicates is always unique. One of its defining features is that it exists in a moment in time. The exact conditions surrounding the way any performance is received can never be wholly replicated.

Recognising the complexity of drama as a means of communicating suggests that it is not possible to teach the subject without specialist training and support. This book sets out to help those who already have a sound understanding of the subject formulate ways of shaping a curriculum that will ensure students progress in it. The intention of the book is to help teachers structure series of tasks purposefully, in order to help students learn the language of drama and become progressively better at using and understanding it.

If the expectation is that students should get better at drama when they study it in school, we need to be clear what that actually implies. In the first section of this book the nature of drama as a subject in the curriculum is explored and, by way of an example of how assessing progression is contingent upon context, the criteria currently applied in the English education system are outlined. Section Two offers a detailed framework for planning, monitoring and assessing progression. The model emphasises the need to use the assessment of students as an aid to improve planning, rather than allowing the curriculum to be driven by the need to assess. In Section Three a wide range of resources and practical ideas is used to demonstrate how progression may be achieved in practice. Each chapter in this section explores a particular facet of the art form of drama and shows how a unit of work may be devised to address specific learning outcomes in that area.

Drama is now established as part of the curriculum. Students are introduced to it at the very start of their school life and many continue their studies in it through to the end of their formal education. A great many secondary schools boast excellent specialist facilities in drama and many are rightly proud of the specialist staff they have. There continues to be a need to introduce more teachers to the specialist knowledge and expertise required to teach drama effectively in the secondary school. It is also the case, however, that many drama teachers are ready to move on themselves in order to find more effective ways of ensuring that their students similarly progress in their knowledge, understanding and skills. We hope that this book will make a contribution to that movement.

Andy Kempe
Marigold Ashwell

1
Progression in the drama curriculum

1.1
The drama curriculum

Planning for, assessing and reporting on progression in drama requires a clear concept of what the purpose of teaching the subject is and what students learn in it. This chapter explores:

- what drama involves and what claims have been made for it as a crucial part of the education of young people
- what the subject actually looks like in schools and how it may be seen as an art form in its own right
- how the drama curriculum can be focused by seeing it as encompassing three related modes of activity – Creating, Performing and Responding.

1 Aims and claims for drama education

Questioning the claims

The place of drama in the school curriculum has been defended by claims that it:

- promotes self-expression
- builds self-confidence
- enhances creativity
- encourages co-operation.

However, many teachers other than those using drama might claim that their work was serving similar purposes. Perhaps these seem fine and laudable aims for all teachers, but it is difficult, both logistically and philosophically, to assess achievement in them and thus be able to monitor students' progress towards them. There is no logic in seeing such aims as being the preserve of the drama curriculum. In practice, though, drama can be seen to involve a whole host of activities which may contribute to students' development in these areas. For example:

- physical and mental games
- role-plays

- discussions
- simulation activities
- physical, mental and vocal warm-up activities
- trust activities
- movement and dance work.

In drama students may be involved in:

- creating dramatic situations and evolving characters by exploring their situation and feelings
- using improvisations to discover effective ways of communicating a dramatic story
- experiencing dramatic situations at first hand and reflecting on how they would personally respond to the events and characters being depicted
- interacting with each other during the process of making drama, to discover how the same situation may be perceived in different ways
- regarding the drama class as a laboratory for the dissection and investigation of human experience, rather than as a workshop for the manufacture and re-creation of other people's plays.

Such a curriculum is driven by the individual drama student's interactions with their peers. However, without critically reviewing the work done in the drama studio in the light of a greater cultural context, drama students may find themselves drawing on a limited knowledge and understanding of dramatic forms and what the craft of drama involves. While students' personal and social development should be a factor in any educational enterprise, without access to a diet of different types of drama and insights into how they are created, performed and received, students' work can seem thin and repetitive. Thus, a broader view needs to be taken of what should be included in the drama curriculum if students are to make progress in it.

A broader view

In order to help students enrich their work and see it in a broader cultural, historical and aesthetic context, the drama curriculum needs to be specifically concerned with the knowledge, skills and concepts of the art form. This involves:

- introducing students to a wide range of dramatic texts and forms and encouraging an interpretation of them
- helping students understand the cultural and historical context in which drama originates and is performed
- experimenting with different ways of performing and recording drama

- introducing different performance styles and matching these to the texts studied
- teaching students how to speak and move with fluency and clarity of intention
- improvising around the central themes of a stimulus in order to gain greater insight into its dramatic potential
- working towards a formal presentation of a drama
- reviewing how students' own explorations of ideas in drama match the ideas of other practitioners and commentators
- teaching students how to respond critically to written texts of plays and to both live and recorded performances from a variety of cultures, genres and styles.

Clarifying the basic aims

Broadening the drama curriculum in this way empowers students by providing an awareness of the part drama plays in shaping and reflecting the world in which they live. It makes the student an active agent in interpreting what drama communicates and in using these findings to inform new acts of communication. The aims of such a curriculum could thus be expressed as being:

1 **To develop students' critical awareness:**

   Through the recognition and appreciation of their own ideas, students come to see themselves as active agents in the creative process. Their confidence as dramatic artists is enhanced as they realise that they have the ability to spot the dramatic potential of a situation or character, give an idea dramatic form, and understand how drama is open to different interpretations. An education in drama prepares students to be critically aware members of a society in which drama plays an important part. Through its investigation of human issues drama is clearly concerned with personal and moral education.

2 **To enable students to understand the social context of their work:**

   Drama is a social art form. It involves people working together in order to communicate with others. Moreover, it is principally concerned with exploring social issues, that is, how and why people respond to specific situations. Through interacting with each other in the exploration and presentation of dramatic ideas, the students' acceptance of other views, and the formulation of their own positions on social issues, will contribute to their all-round appreciation of what society is and how it might be developed. The links between drama, social education and ethical citizenship are strong.

3 **To extend the students' engagement with drama as an expression of culture:**

By drawing from a wide range of resources and involving the students themselves in research, the drama teacher is able to contribute to the development of the students' knowledge of subjects across the whole curriculum. History, literature, current affairs and the world of art are all rich resources for exploration through drama. Drama in its literary and performative forms cannot be divorced from its cultural and historical context. Plays and performances from different times and places can teach a great deal about the society that generated them and so offer contrasts and new insights into contemporary culture. Drama offers the opportunity of experiencing events in a direct way. It engages and appeals to thought and feeling and can thus be a powerful motivator for further investigation and discussion.

4 **To provide students with a practical understanding of the craft of drama:**

Introducing students to the work of professional writers, directors, designers and actors or to different types and styles of drama from a wide range of cultural traditions facilitates a greater understanding of the different constituent elements of drama. The purpose is to heighten students' own practical engagement with every aspect of the art form. Most particularly, it is to kindle and fuel the flame of imagination that lies at the heart of art.

It is difficult to see these four aims as being independent of each other. Rather, they work together to create an holistic experience.

The role of the teacher

Shaping and delivering an eclectic and useful curriculum implies an active role for the teacher. Rather than simply being the one who offers the stimulus and constraints with which students must work, or being the arbiter of what is worth studying and how to perform, the teacher becomes the one who:

- offers a range of resources that have dramatic potential
- can move the exploration on by offering new alternatives or helping the students find and keep a focus
- asks questions which will challenge the students' perceptions and intentions
- sometimes plays a central role within the developing drama in order to heighten the students' felt experience and give them new situations to respond to in their playing of dramatic roles

- interacts with the class as a fellow researcher rather than directing the outcomes.

What is sought here is a balance by which teachers give students insights into the world of drama beyond the classroom, while establishing the classroom itself as the crucible from which new and unique work springs. Such a project will involve critically reviewing existing forms and conventions of drama in order, ultimately, to help students craft and perform their own drama. In this way students progress from dependence to autonomy.

2 Four faces of drama in schools

There are very few schools where there is little or no drama to be seen. However, the manner in which students come across drama varies from school to school, though four of these means may be fairly clearly identified. Within each there are implications and opportunities for students to progress towards the aims defined above.

As a complement to work across the curriculum

Activities that relate to drama are quite often used in other areas of the curriculum. For example, in some schools personal and social education has a separate time on the timetable and the teacher may use dramatic activities to explore issues as part of the programme. Role-play is sometimes used to prepare young people for specific situations such as interviews, or to review incidents that seem important to the group. In the humanities, students may acquire a greater empathy and awareness of the implications of events and decisions. Role-play may also be used to help foster communication skills in both mother tongue and foreign languages by offering new contexts within which to speak and listen.

While the dynamic nature of the activity may constitute an effective and appealing teaching strategy, what the students are progressing towards is a greater knowledge and understanding of the subject in hand. Any furtherance of their ability to create, perform or respond to a drama may be negligible and will obviously be difficult to monitor and record in this context.

Another way of considering drama in cross-curricular terms is to regard the skills fostered by working with the art form as being transferable to other situations. Suzi Clipson-Boyles (1998) notes how creating, performing and responding to drama enhances a number of assessable skills which are pertinent to the whole curriculum. She

LIVERPOOL HOPE UNIVERSIT

identifies, for example, how drama involves acquiring and manipulating a number of the Key Skills which form part of the rationale of the National Curriculum in England. For example:

- communication (using the spoken and written word along with space, movement and gesture)
- working with others (planning, problem-solving, working collaboratively)
- improving own learning and performance (researching, trying out ideas, evaluating personal contribution to the drama process and performance)
- problem-solving (finding creative solutions to problems, interpreting different stimuli and employing different resources)
- reasoning (considering drama in its context, identifying what needs to be done and how effects will be achieved)
- enquiry (deconstructing images, questioning conventions, researching and experimenting with alternative ways of doing things)
- creative thinking (interpreting character, content and context, designing technical solutions to practical problems)
- evaluation (watching, listening, recognising personal emotional and intellectual responses and using these to inform a consideration of the needs of an audience).

As a framework for the curriculum

The tension implicit in a dramatic fiction can be used to motivate the students in a broad range of curriculum areas. Organising the whole curriculum around a central dramatic problem poses a number of challenges for students who may become deeply embroiled in solving situations from the perspective of a given role. However, where so many elements are prescribed, such an approach is not without challenges for the teacher as a planner of the curriculum either. Accommodating all the demands of an imposed curriculum content can make the drama feel unwieldy and simply be too taxing on the teacher's imagination and organisational abilities.

Working in this way uses drama as the 'engine' which drives the curriculum, but it is difficult to ascertain what progress the students make in their understanding of, and capacity to manipulate and interpret, the art form. Certainly, it would be difficult to incorporate a range of performance styles in such a framework in any kind of systematic way.

In the presenting of plays

Most schools, in all phases of education, periodically (if not regularly) offer students the chance to present drama. Such performances range from the class assembly to ambitious productions of the classics, well known musicals or contemporary theatre. The school play is often genuinely a whole school event, which generates tremendous excitement and satisfaction. The performers may work from a script or devise original pieces. In some schools, members of staff play acting parts themselves or take responsibility for some of the backstage and technical tasks. The presentation of a play may be the means by which a school celebrates itself and demonstrates its own culture.

The school play has been called 'an exemplar of differentiated teamwork' (*The Challenge for the Comprehensive School*, D. Hargreaves, 1982, Routledge and Kegan Paul), a description that signals that no matter what the ability of the individual, everyone can play some part in the making and presenting of the project. Although not all young people relish the thought of being placed in the limelight or taking the responsibility of remembering and delivering lines, many enjoy being involved somehow. The production and operation of lighting and sound effects, designing and building the set and producing posters and programmes are all aspects of production which require negotiation, explanation and notation. The theatre is increasingly offering splendid opportunities to teach students new ways of using modern technologies.

The possibilities for differentiating work around the production of a school play are considerable. While some groups are improvising, writing or rehearsing scenes, others may be at the computer producing the programme. Groups may be selecting and recording music for the sound track or helping to design and create the set, producing the lighting plot or using tape or video recorders to interview each other about their involvement in the production. Meanwhile, a teacher of a class not directly involved in the production might take a class to the hall or studio to demonstrate and explain how the project is taking shape. They may, for example, relate the story or talk about the author and context in which the play was written. They may choose to use the script and narrative as the basis for improvisations around the play's main themes, or as a means of exploring how scripts are realised.

Over the course of their time in school, students may experience an increasingly broad and varied number of activities and responsibilities via the production of plays, while the choice of plays may offer new challenges and areas of knowledge. Many teachers are highly successful in using productions to provide a context for working in the three modes of activity of creating, performing and responding and recording students' progress accordingly.

As a subject in its own right

To speak of the possibility of students progressing in drama admits that drama is a clearly identifiable subject with its own corpus of knowledge and specific skills. In England, drama is a separate strand of the National Curriculum for English at all four key stages, and in Wales, it is compulsory up to key stage 3. Attempting to fulfil the demands of the orders from behind the desks of the English classroom, though, is problematic. Drama activities are specifically identified under Attainment Target (AT)1: *Speaking and Listening*. Dramatic literature is also studied alongside poetry and the novel under AT2: *Reading*. But unlike poetry and the novel, the written text of a play does not wholly fulfil the writer's intention. Plays are written to be performed, and without considering the way drama communicates through a wide range of visual and aural images the potential of a play is considerably devalued. Similarly, as part of AT3: *Writing*, it is expected that students will be given the opportunity to write in a variety of dramatic forms and here again, some knowledge of how drama works in practice is essential. While the National Curriculum for English thus poses a number of challenges for some English specialists, it should be clear that drama specialists in schools have a vital contribution to make in meeting the requirements.

In many secondary schools drama is taught as a subject in its own right up to the compulsory school-leaving age. Around 90,000 candidates take a GCSE in Drama in England and Wales. This represents about 20 per cent of the cohort. The number of candidates in England and Wales who go on to take the higher A level examination in either Drama, Theatre Studies or Performing Arts continues to rise at a rate of around 9 per cent each year.

Given its recognition as a subject in its own right, there is clearly a need for teachers who have a depth of knowledge in drama and a range of specialist skills appropriate to teaching it. In drama, progression involves learning how to appreciate and make increasingly sophisticated use of spatial, audible and visual signs to communicate meaning. Some of these signs are employed by and enhance the work of the actors (for example, the use of movement, voice, gesture, costume and make-up). Other signs are outside the actor's domain. Set and lighting design and the use of music and other sounds, for example, all contribute to the layering of meanings in drama. These elements constitute the language of drama. Like any language, it can be taught and students can get better at it. The clearer a teacher's own view of what the language is, how it works, and the way it has been employed and adapted in different contexts, the more likely it is that the drama curriculum will provide students with a structured, coherent and effective learning experience. Planning such a curriculum demands some kind of framework into which students' achievements can be placed and built on.

③ Three modes of activity in drama

One such framework considers the students' work in the three inter-related modes of activity of creating, performing and responding. Although these modes of activity are frequently interwoven in any given drama experience, recognising their individual features can help with the planning of a programme in drama which has both breadth and depth. It also assists in the identification of individual students' strengths and so helps pinpoint areas for further development.

Creating drama

'Creating drama' might include activities as seemingly disparate as having a new idea to writing or directing a play. Sometimes people do have the most extraordinarily inspirational ideas, the origins of which are impossible to determine. More often, though, they have ideas in response to some sort of stimulus. This implies that creating drama involves:

- researching
- discussing
- questioning
- thinking
- sharing and shaping ideas
- experimenting.

The main focus of creating is experimenting with the shaping of ideas that emerge from the group. Most students will have played with symbols to represent meaning from a young age, but they may not have developed an explicit understanding of how this relates to drama. Neither would they necessarily have developed the aesthetic awareness to manipulate the elements of drama consciously, in order to create and convey meanings. An effective drama curriculum is one that fosters the students' aesthetic awareness and develops their ability to use form to articulate ideas.

The realisation of ideas in drama involves the selective use of visual and aural sign systems. There is a technical side to creativity, as well as a purely imaginative one. 'Technical' does not relate simply to designing and building stage sets or focusing lights, but also to finding the words a character might say in a given situation, or conveying a feeling through movement or gesture. It is here that creating drama becomes closely connected with the dimension of 'performing drama'.

'Creating drama' may be seen as encompassing all those activities which involve generating and shaping ideas in order to capture and express meanings in an active way.

Performing drama

One of the elements of drama that distinguishes it from other art forms is the way in which it uses, and indeed exists in, time. Drama is a 'temporal art form'. This in itself has implications, for no form of writing or electronic recording can fully capture the live dramatic event. It is because of this that a clear understanding of the notion of 'text' is important.

The written text

The word 'text' often refers simply to that which is written. The script of a play is a written text, and one that most people are quite familiar with in terms of what it looks like and how it can be read. But drama communicates through other things besides words. It is therefore helpful to regard the term 'text' as referring to anything holding a meaning that becomes apparent when considered by someone looking at it. Given this wider view of 'text', one can see that storyboards, pictograms and even sequences of shapes and colours might be used as 'texts' for drama.

In music, teachers talk of 'notation' to cover the variety of ways in which the actual sounds made in music can be recorded on paper. David Hornbrook (1990) has illustrated how, in drama, there are many ways of recording or notating the action of a play. Certainly, one way is to write down what is said, but film-makers, for example, often use simple cartoons to make a 'storyboard' of the action and so show more clearly what is happening.

The electronic text

In addition to the written text, teachers of drama will doubtless realise the importance of the electronic text, that is, drama recorded by sound or video equipment. The point of recognising this type of text is that while it clearly records a performance in one way, it doesn't actually capture the same elements that an audience perceives in a live performance. Anyone who has seen the same play in the theatre and then on television will be aware that the camera behaves in a more selective way than the human eye. The dynamics between an audience and the actors on a stage is very different from that which exists between a person and a television screen. The electronic text of drama has a huge impact on our lives. More and more young people are becoming adept at handling video recording equipment; but how critically aware are they of the way in which television, film and video mediate and dramatise the real world? An education in drama can give young people more control over, and understanding of, this all-pervasive and highly influential phenomenon.

The performance text

The word 'performance', like the word 'text', is loaded with connotations, many of which are somewhat unhelpful. The thought of a performance in a school might, in its most negatively stereotyped form, conjure up images of students stumbling through lines and bumping nervously into the scenery while watching parents, teachers and friends are at once delighted with the effort but sceptical of the artistic quality.

Most of us have a strong sense of what we look like and sound like to others; we are an audience to our own 'performance' in any social setting. In drama, this capacity to be our own audience is used to change and make the performance clearer and judge more objectively the meaning and potency of what others may perceive is being communicated. In the context of drama education, 'performance' encompasses the work of a group who have been given time to prepare and then share their ideas through some kind of enactment. It includes the activity that happens after a teacher says, 'Stop! Show us that bit again.' It includes the spontaneous role-play that would occur when a teacher enters the drama in role as a different character and the students react accordingly. It would also include the use of lighting, sound effects and music to convey a change in atmosphere or create a new level of meaning. In fact, it includes any activity that involves people presenting dramatic ideas to an audience (for example, other members of the participating group) for whatever purpose (for example, to entertain invited guests, or to explore more deeply a fictitious situation).

Performance can be electronically recorded or notated through words, sketches and diagrams. When it is, its meaning inevitably changes because key elements of drama such as time and space are being used in a different way.

'Performing drama' may thus be seen as the physical process of imparting meaning to an audience through the dramatic form.

- **Responding to drama**

Responding to drama might simply be what is happening when one says 'I liked that'.

Of course, one might be responding to a number of things about the drama when this is said. We could be responding to the content of the drama, that is, the storyline or the characters or the theme. Or we could be responding to the form, that is, the way the story was told, the way the characters were portrayed or the way the theme was symbolised. Responses could be at a purely emotional level:

> 'It moved me/it didn't move me.'
> 'It was good to watch.'

Or they could be intellectualised:

> 'I thought it made a good point about . . . '
> 'It was interesting the way you did that . . . '

Responses to drama do not always have to be verbal. One way of capturing a response would be to draw a favourite character in a way that demonstrates what was engaging or exciting about them. This might be a particularly appropriate response for very young students to make. Other approaches might include drawing a kind of graph to show how the play built tension, or ascribing colours or patterns to characters to show different character traits. It can be particularly productive to ask students to represent through one art form what has been experienced in another. Asking 'If this person was a colour, what colour would they be? If they were a line, would they be a squiggly line, or a jagged line or a curvy line?' would be to employ a device frequently used by professional actors to articulate and embody insights into a dramatic character.

Sometimes an audience's response has more to do with the people playing in the drama rather than either its form or content, and perhaps in the teacher's case this should always be so. When teachers respond to a piece of drama they want to assess what development the students have made both in the ideas they have come up with and in the way they have used them. Just as this evaluation of personal performance is important for the teacher's assessment of progress, it is also important for students to be able to evaluate fairly their own and each other's work. This implies that they need to see their own work in a context and have something to compare it with, hence the need to introduce students to dramas from other times and different cultures.

While it clearly isn't appropriate to compare students' work against that of professionals, it is fair to consider what they did this term against what they did last term. One measure of progression would be the students' ability to understand what is meant by evaluation in drama, and be increasingly able to use criteria effectively when they evaluate their own work at all stages of its development. Progression is also, of course, recognisable in the way that students evaluate the work of others. To achieve this, students need constantly to be asked about their own work and taught how to ask questions of themselves, of each other and of the dramas they experience through television, film and theatre.

Responding to drama involves expressing an understanding of what the drama is saying and how it is saying it.

4 An holistic approach

The way in which students engage with these three modes of activity is informed by other factors. Their own feelings and their actual ability or desire to express those feelings are factors, as is their existing knowledge, and experience becomes part of the equation along with the cultural context in which they are working. This includes both the wider culture outside the school and the social dynamics of the class itself.

Progression in drama involves attending to the three activities of creating, performing and responding. Not all the students will be equally proficient in each of the activities – why should we expect them to be? Planning a drama curriculum that provides them all with the chance of reaching their maximum potential demands a balance in opportunities to create, perform and respond. Monitoring and assessing progression demands an assessment scheme that recognises the relationship between these activities and weights them accordingly. An holistic approach to planning and teaching drama is one that takes account of the many facets of the art form of drama experience and seeks to foster an understanding and appreciation of the way they work together to create unique experiences.

Although schools currently have the opportunity to design their own programmes of study in drama, the drama curriculum is not entirely free of externally imposed demands and constraints. This chapter outlines:

- the different requirements that schools need to meet in terms of teaching drama
- the criteria used to inspect the way in which schools monitor and record students' progress in drama.

① Formal requirements for the teaching of drama

In the absence of formal, separate programmes of study for drama, schools have the opportunity to devise their own schemes of work in the subject. Such autonomy represents a tremendous opportunity to construct a curriculum that is innovative, draws on the teachers' own areas of expertise and reflects the needs of any particular cohort of students. Such freedom, however, also carries the weighty responsibility of ensuring that breadth and balance are achieved and that a number of externally imposed requirements are met within the scheme.

Schools offering examination courses in drama will need to ensure that the detailed criteria of the syllabuses are addressed in their schemes of work. Special attention needs to be paid to the relationship between drama and, where these apply, the National Curriculum for English and the National Literacy Strategy. Teachers will also doubtless be mindful of the need to demonstrate how their design of a drama curriculum will satisfy other outside agencies, such as school inspectors.

Dealing with these pressures need not divert the teacher from the task of helping students progress in their knowledge, understanding and skill in the three dimensions of drama. In fact, a review of the English curriculum and the Framework for Inspection of Schools in England reveals close links between the three modes of activity outlined in the previous chapter, and the formally stated requirements. What the teacher has to do is map the proposed content of the drama curriculum against both the formal requirements and what they perceive the students to need at any given point.

Outlined below are the required expectations for drama in the curriculum in England and insights into how drama is inspected by the Office for Standards in Education (Ofsted). While these are formal requirements that must be met in England, they may also serve as useful checks and balances for drama teachers in other educational systems.

In the National Curriculum for English the place of drama has been clarified and extended. 'Drama' appears as a separate heading within the attainment target for *Speaking and Listening* while in both *Reading* and *Writing* it is clear that students should also engage in and be taught about drama in its written form. The range of drama activities and skills delineated in the National Curriculum Orders corresponds closely to the National Literacy Strategy *Framework for teaching*. For many reasons, it will doubtless remain the case that students arriving at the secondary school drama room for the first time in Year 7 will have had a wide variety of experiences in the subject. However, it is becoming increasingly untenable for students entering secondary education to have no knowledge or understanding of the subject at all, as the following summaries should demonstrate.

② Drama in the National Curriculum for English

The inclusion of drama in the English curriculum is a statutory requirement in England and drama activities are identified at each key stage. Drama appears most prominently within the programme of study for *Speaking and Listening* and it is also explicitly mentioned in the attainment targets for both *Reading* and *Writing*. The purpose of the Orders is to delineate the minimum students can expect to be taught. There is no prescription as to exactly how the curriculum should be taught, or by whom. In the case of drama, therefore, schools would be wise to address these requirements by co-ordinating the work of their English and drama departments. Utilising the strengths of teachers in a co-ordinated way will of course help schools use limited time and facilities more effectively and ensure that students do not repeat elements of the curriculum unnecessarily.

KEY STAGE	DRAMA ACTIVITIES	LEARNING OUTCOMES
KS 1	At Key Stage 1 students need to be given opportunities to take part in drama activities such as: • working in role • presenting drama and stories to each other • responding to performances.	The skills that should be taught at this stage include how to: • use language and actions to convey situations, characters and emotions • create and sustain roles individually and when working with others • comment constructively on drama they have watched or in which they have participated.
KS 2	At Key Stage 2 students' knowledge and understanding of drama are developed through activities such as: • improvisation and working in role • scripting and performing • responding to performances.	Through these activities students are taught how to: • create, adapt and sustain different roles, individually and in groups • use character, action and narrative to convey story, themes, emotions and ideas in plays they devise and script • use dramatic techniques to explore characters and issues (for example, hot-seating, flashback) • evaluate their own and others' contributions to the overall effectiveness of performances.
KS 3 and 4	At Key Stages 3 and 4 students are expected to participate in a wide range of drama activities and be able to evaluate their own and others' contributions such as: • improvisation and working in role • devising, scripting and performing in plays • discussing and reviewing their own and others' performances. Within AT2: Reading students should have the opportunity to read: • two plays by Shakespeare • drama by major playwrights • recent and contemporary drama written for young people and adults • drama by major writers from different cultures and traditions. As a part of their study for AT3: Writing students should learn how to write in a range of forms including playscripts.	Through these activities students are taught how to: • use a variety of dramatic conventions to explore ideas, issues and meanings • use different ways to convey action, character, atmosphere and tension when they are scripting and performing plays (for example, through dialogue, movement and pace) • appreciate how the structure and organisation of scenes and plays contribute to dramatic effect • evaluate critically performances of dramas that they have watched or in which they have taken part.

It is difficult to see how these requirements could be met without getting students up from behind their desks and trying things out in practice. It is also clear that drama involves more than just acting. Being able to read, write and reflect on drama is an important part of the National Curriculum for English. While many drama activities can be organised in the classroom with minimal disruption, how much more effective could the learning be if the students were to work with a drama teacher in a specially designed space?

③ Drama in the National Literacy Strategy

The National Literacy Strategy recognises that speaking and listening are an essential part of literacy. In the *Framework for Teaching* (1998), which sets out the expectations for literacy work in primary schools, there are clear references to drama as an element of literature. Most of the references to drama and drama-related skills appear in the strand Text Level Work.

What follows on the next page is a series of extracts from the *Framework for Teaching*. The numbers in the right-hand column refer to the paragraphs relating to the phase. Because the National Literacy Strategy in the lower secondary years is founded on this work, drama and English teachers in secondary schools will need to be familiar with it in order to ensure that the work they plan provides students with opportunities to progress further in these areas of skills and knowledge.

Year	Term	Text Level Work
Reception		12 to experiment with writing in a variety of play, exploratory and role-play situations 15 to use writing to communicate in a variety of ways, incorporating it into play and everyday classroom life
1	1	5 to describe story settings and incidents and relate them to own experience and that of others 7 to re-enact stories in a variety of ways e.g. through role-play, using dolls or puppets
	2	8 to identify and discuss characters e.g. appearance, behaviour or qualities, to speculate about how they might behave; to discuss how they are described in the text; and to compare characters from different stories or plays 9 to become aware of character and dialogue e.g. by role-playing parts when reading aloud stories or plays with others
	3	5 to re-tell stories, to give the main points in sequence and to pick out significant incidents 6 to prepare and re-tell stories orally, identifying and using some of the more formal features of story language
2	1	3 to be aware of the difference between spoken and written language through comparing oral recounts with text; make use of formal elements in re-telling
	2	6 to identify and describe characters, expressing own views and using words and phrases from texts 14 to write character profiles e.g. simple descriptions, posters, passports, using key words and phrases that describe or are spoken by characters in the text
3	1	3 to be aware of the different voices in stories using dramatised readings, showing differences between the narrator and different characters used e.g. puppets to present stories 4 to read, prepare and present playscripts 5 to recognise the key differences between prose and playscript e.g. by looking at dialogue, stage directions, layout of text in prose and playscripts 14 to write simple playscripts based on own reading and oral work
	2	4 to choose and prepare poems for performance, identifying appropriate expression, tone, volume and use of voices and other sounds 5 rehearse and improve performance, taking note of punctuation
4	1	1 to investigate how settings and characters are built up from small details and how the reader responds to them 2 to identify the main characteristics of key characters, drawing on the text to justify views, and using the information to predict actions 5 to prepare, read and perform playscripts; compare organisation of scripts with stories – how are settings indicated, storylines made clear?

Year	Term	Text Level Work
		6 to chart the build-up of a play scene e.g. how scenes start, how dialogue is expressed, and how scenes are concluded 13 to write playscripts e.g. using known stories as a basis
	2	2 to understand how settings influence events and incidents in stories and how they affect characters' behaviour
	3	1 to identify social, moral or cultural issues in stories e.g. the dilemmas faced by characters or the moral of a story, and to discuss how the characters deal with them; to locate evidence in the text
5	1	3 to investigate how characters are presented, referring to the text: • through dialogue, action and description • how the reader responds to them (as victims, heroes etc.) • through examining their relationships with other characters 5 to understand dramatic conventions including: • the conventions of scripting (e.g. stage directions, asides) • how character can be communicated in words and gesture • how tension can be built up through pace, silences and delivery 15 to write new scenes or characters into a story, in the manner of the writer, maintaining consistency of character and style 18 write own playscript, applying conventions learned from reading; include production notes 19 to annotate a section of playscript as a preparation for performance, taking into account pace, movement, gesture and delivery of lines and the needs of an audience 20 to evaluate the script and the performance for their dramatic interest and impact
	3	4 to read, rehearse and modify performance of poetry 11 to use performance poems as models to write and to produce poetry in polished forms through revising, redrafting and presentation
6	1	1 to compare and evaluate a novel or play in print and the film/TV version e.g. treatment of the plot and characters, the differences in the two forms, e.g. in seeing the setting, in losing the narrator 9 to prepare a short section of story as a script e.g. using stage directions, location/setting
	2	13 to parody a literary text, describing stock characters and plot structure, language etc.

❹ The inspection of drama by Ofsted

In England every aspect of the curriculum is regularly inspected by the government agency Ofsted. Notwithstanding the analysis of the relationship between drama and English given above, Ofsted recognises that no clear rationale regarding that relationship was used to inform the National Curriculum. Inspectors have thus been encouraged to identify each school's approach to the subject and inspect it accordingly.

Consequently, an Ofsted internal report and analysis of the situation ('the HMI report') compiled by one of Her Majesty's Inspectors, himself a specialist adviser for English and Drama for Ofsted, suggested that drama might be identified as:

- serving the needs of the National Curriculum Programmes of Study for English
- a 'natural' part of the English curriculum
- a practical artistic subject in its own right in which the emphasis lies in making, performing and responding to drama
- a part of an expressive arts programme
- a vehicle for work in a number of other subjects
- contributing to the students' personal, social, moral and spiritual development
- an examination subject
- an extra-curricular activity.

Ofsted regards such a range of provision as a strength rather than a problem but this is not necessarily a widely held view. Those concerned with drama might reasonably ask how it is justified that some young people have the opportunity to study drama as a subject in its own right yet others do not. The HMI report recognises this and goes on to say *'schools need to have, but inspectors do not always find, a clear rationale which describes the approach to drama, including ways in which it meets the requirements for English; [and a] student's entitlement to drama in various forms and **notions of progression**'* (emphasis in original).

While Ofsted specifies the importance of including drama within the three attainment targets for English, it recognises that many English teachers feel uneasy teaching some aspects of the subject and *'sometimes lacked the skills and/or confidence to teach drama or to include it in their lessons'*. The implication here is clearly that English and Drama departments might draw profitably on each other's strengths to ensure that the formal requirements are met, and the students' best interests served, without compromising subject identities.

In the first six years or so of Ofsted inspections, drama was often not inspected at all or was, at best, given a brief and vague paragraph at the end of the report on English. This resulted in frustration for many drama teachers who found positive comments about drama being one of the school's strengths even though the subject had not been inspected by a drama specialist and no analysis of progression, attainment and the quality of provision was given. Most important of all, if there were weaknesses in identifying and monitoring progression, this was rarely highlighted and probably no opportunity for discussion and feedback was provided. The HMI report on the inspection of drama is evidence of a significant move forward from this situation. It highlights the fact that there was more evidence of drama being seen as a separate subject during 1998–9 than in previous years.

The HMI report draws on *The Arts Inspected* (1998), saying that where attainment and progress were judged to be good, the factors contributing to this included the installation of a system for assessing students' progress and attainment, and clearly relating standards achieved to a well-articulated scheme of work. The HMI report notes how, among a range of factors at work where attainment and progress were unsatisfactory, objectives tended to be unclear, progression in the short and long term was poor and non-specialist teachers were uncertain about standards to be aimed at.

'Evidence gathered from inspections in recent years showed that high standards of drama were characterised by the ability of students to:

- take on and sustain convincingly one or a number of roles;
- explore how individuals or groups in a specific situation behave, handle conflict, try out different solutions to a problem by using dramatic play as a way of testing relationships and making sense of the world;
- deepen their understanding of themselves, issues and texts;
- improve their communication skills;
- learn about and use dramatic concepts which underpin drama. For example, fiction, character, plot, setting, symbols and dramatic conventions governing the use of time, space and both oral and visual language;
- acquire techniques such as improvisation, simulation, tableau, thought tracking, forum theatre and hot-seating;
- make effective use of available resources and spaces;
- develop a critical approach to their own drama and to performance by others, whether in the theatre, on television or in other settings.'

HMI internal report

The HMI report advises inspectors on what they need to do when inspecting drama. This includes being familiar with, for example, the Arts Council publication 'Drama in Schools' (1992) which first proposed that drama involved the three modes of activities *Making, Performing and Responding*. It suggests that inspectors should:

- ask for a policy document and/or scheme of work which clarifies aims and approaches
- look for some degree of progression
- judge students' standards of attainment in terms of creating and performing, responding and appreciating and appraising
- use clear criteria including the degree to which students:
  - use imagination with belief and feeling
  - respond sensitively to their own work and that of others
  - create drama with conviction and concentration
  - use appropriately and effectively a range of dramatic skills, techniques and conventions to express ideas and feelings
  - recall, record and evaluate their own work and that of others.

As this was an internal document for Ofsted, it is not provided for all inspectors. What is available, and what it complements, is the guidance that is provided within *Inspecting Subjects and Aspects 11–18*, published by Ofsted in 1999, where specific guidance for drama is given within the English section (pages 23–4). These statements, which first appeared within the original 'Framework for Inspection', parallel many of the drama statements within the English Curriculum and connect with the rationale and framework for the drama curriculum that are offered in this book.

Ofsted Guidance on the Inspection of Drama

The following guidance is taken from *Inspecting Subjects and Aspects 11–18*, where drama has its own heading within the section on English.

Drama

- Judge drama as part of National Curriculum English and, if it is so taught, as a subject in its own right.

  Drama may be offered to pupils age 14 to 16, alongside the other arts. It is an increasingly popular GCSE and A-level subject.

- Also assess how drama is used as a method of learning in other subjects.
- For pupils aged 11 to 16, assess drama within two main categories:
  - making and presenting drama;
  - appreciating and appraising it.
- Pay particular attention to how well pupils:
  - use imagination, with belief and feeling;
  - create drama with conviction and concentration;
  - respond sensitively to their own work and that of others;
  - use a range of dramatic skills, techniques, forms and conventions to express ideas and feelings effectively;
  - grasp and use dramatic concepts effectively, recalling, recording and evaluating their own work and that of others.
- When **in lessons**, expect to see evidence of:
  - co-operation in creating and communicating effective drama;
  - the use of drama to widen experience of English, especially through the use of speaking and listening and purposeful learning;
  - the integration of language skills for a creative purpose;
  - the contribution of drama to the pupils' social and moral development and understanding.
  - **Observe** assemblies and extra-curricular activities such as drama groups and performances.

Continued on next page

Pupils' response to performance will extend the evidence of what they know, understand and can do. You need to recognise, though, that it is sometimes the more committed pupils who undertake these activities.

■ Use **records** and **recordings**, including sound or video recordings and photographs, as evidence of previous attainment, from which to gauge progress.

■ Study pupils' drama logs as evidence of understanding, response and personal development.

■ Use teachers' records as a source of evidence about previous attainment, especially if they are kept for drama and not just for speaking and listening.

2

Planning and assessing progression in drama

2.1

Planning for progression

Planning a curriculum that is exciting, eclectic, draws on the teacher's personal strengths and interests, and is tailored to suit the perceived needs of the students presents quite a challenge. Questions need to be asked: where to start, what to do next, where to aim? Finding answers that suit the unique situation of any school is dependent on a clear view of progression and its practical implications.

This chapter:

- provides a definition of progression based on a number of key principles
- proposes a process for planning a drama curriculum which adheres to those principles.

1 Progress and progression

Progress and progression are two separate but related aspects of the acquisition of knowledge, understanding, skills and attitudes.

Progress concerns the development made by each individual student. Teachers have been made increasingly aware of the need to monitor, assess and record each student's progress but there is by no means any consensus on how this is best done. Clearly, progress must be registered against some sort of criteria. In the arts, the exact nature of these criteria has often been a subject of heated debate relating to the perceived learning outcomes of teaching in, through or about the arts.

Progression implies that the activities undertaken over a whole course of study result in a greater depth and breadth of students' knowledge, skill and understanding. To achieve this the work needs to have a structure and sequence, so that students constantly face new challenges and new material. This does not, of course, negate the concept of the 'spiral curriculum' in which students may revisit knowledge and skills and apply them to new and more demanding contexts. One measure of progression may be seen as an increased ability to manipulate a certain skill or articulate a particular perception as a part of the process of acquiring new insights and practical knowledge.

Any definition may be debated and disputed and no doubt the definitions above will be. Even when a working definition of progression is found to be broadly acceptable, other questions arise:

- Should drama teachers be more concerned about monitoring students' progress in terms of their ability to manipulate drama as an art form in itself, or in terms of their ability to use the form to explore a given content such as, for example, an environmental or social issue?
- What do drama teachers consider to be essential in terms of knowledge and understanding, skills and attitudes?
- Can drama teachers ensure that the spiral curriculum does not result in students simply repeating the same tasks and topics, or practising the same skills, as they move up through the school?
- Is progression best taken to mean the acquisition of new skills and attitudes, or an increasing ability to understand, use and reflect on what already exists?
- What would represent student progression in drama to you in the context of your school?

② Structuring the drama curriculum

Structuring the curriculum in order to ensure that students progress in drama implies establishing certain principles upon which practicalities will depend. Part of the problem with structuring a curriculum is that no one order of activities or topics necessarily presents itself.

1 Consider the following list of topics commonly explored through drama. To what extent could units of work focused on these issues be put in an order which ensures a logical progression?

- bullying
- homelessness
- HIV awareness
- evacuees
- uncovering local history
- protesting against a new road
- the plight of Amazonian Indians.

Is any one of these necessarily more challenging than any other?

2 Or consider these areas of knowledge in drama. Could units of work focusing on these be put in an order which ensures a logical progression?

- Greek drama
- naturalism
- comedy
- tragedy
- melodrama
- Shakespeare and the Jacobeans
- ritual
- *commedia dell'arte*
- documentary theatre.

3 What about these dramatic skills? Can you imagine whole units of work focusing on these being in an order which ensures a logical progression?

- mime
- mask
- physical theatre
- monologue
- spontaneous improvisation
- set design
- direction
- script writing
- rehearsing from a script
- creating dramatic tension
- using light and sound.

4 Are any of these explorative strategies qualitatively more difficult than the others? What would a unit of work focused on any one of these look like?

- still images
- hot-seating
- slow motion
- thought tracking
- storyboards
- narrating
- role-play
- role on the wall
- flashback.

5 In what order would you introduce students to the following list of elements of drama?

- pace
- tension
- timing
- movement
- rhythm
- symbols
- use of levels
- use of space
- vocal tone
- climax/anticlimax
- contrasts (sound/silence, movement/stillness).

The question is, can any of the above be tackled in isolation? Even if they could, what would be the point?

A notion that makes these questions misguided, if not entirely redundant, is the way in which content and form are interwoven in the subject of drama. Any one unit may therefore offer students a matrix of opportunities to develop insights into a given content, while acquiring or honing formal skills.

It is not inconceivable that a drama teacher might consider all the areas of study noted above and proclaim that, through their secondary school course in drama, the students would have done all of these things and more. To achieve such a breadth and balance the teacher will almost certainly have refined a way of identifying exactly what students are bringing with them when they arrive in secondary school, and have a programme which effectively builds on this.

Through a consideration of these sorts of issues, drama teachers become better able to identify their own philosophy of teaching the subject in the particular context of their school. Arriving at such a point enables the teacher to formulate a policy statement that can be shared with other stakeholders in the education of any given cohort of students.

❸ From policy to practice

The first stage of plotting the inter-related processes of planning and assessing lies in designing a clear policy for the drama that will happen in the school. The policy statement for drama, as for any other subject, does not need to be long. It certainly should not be loaded with complex specialist terminology, but should rather be accessible to anyone interested in discovering what the school is trying to achieve.

Attempting to justify the inclusion of drama in the curriculum by making reference to vague, overarching and often highly questionable aims, only serves to reinforce negative attitudes towards the subject. What do statements such as 'Drama gives young people the opportunity to express themselves' really mean? Is it always a good thing for people to express themselves? Teachers frequently encounter students whose 'self' appears to need controlling or modifying rather than being openly expressed! Similarly, it is one thing to claim that 'Drama gives students self-confidence' but quite how one assesses 'self-confidence' is more of a problem. What sort of god-like powers do drama teachers have to make judgements about the 'self', and what might the effects on the 'self' be if their comments were less than complimentary?

Conversely, the statement that 'Studying and performing dramatic literature is an essential element in the development of cultural awareness' sounds grand and laudable but what is the ultimate outcome of such an awareness? The preservation of cultural icons and traditions? In whose interests is it to retain the values and status quo of past and existing cultures? Is simply being 'aware' of past and existing cultures enough, or should education strive to furnish the next generation with the means of changing it?

The use of broad yet ultimately dubious aims have led to drama education being mistrusted and derided as, variously, woolly or essentially conservative. It is helpful, therefore, for schools to be able to present a thoughtful and detailed policy statement that avoids using any language with which the staff themselves are not fully confident. Schools are increasingly aware of the value of having a clear policy for every subject taught. These policies need to be regularly updated to take account of new initiatives, constraints and opportunities in the individual context of the school.

Many schools already have a policy for drama and most have a scheme of work. There is no definitive way of setting out either a policy or a scheme of work but the commentary on page 30 aims to clarify the purpose of having such documents and how they may be used to their fullest potential. The approach proffered here is not intended as exemplar material but as a basic model that can be adapted and used to inform and develop existing planning methods.

The policy

A policy for drama would sensibly contain the same sort of information expected for any subject taught in the school. It could, for example, state the principal aims of the subject, relating these as far as possible to the overall cultural, aesthetic, social and moral outcomes to which the school aspires. The policy statement might usefully identify provision relating to access, equal opportunities, health and safety arrangements and give a brief explanation of the kinds of activities in which students will engage in their drama lessons. In describing how the subject will be taught and assessed, the headings Creating, Performing and Responding could be used. These headings can then form the basis of unit and lesson plans, reports and departmental records.

Underpinning the policy statement should be an attempt to provide clear and concise answers to two fundamental questions:

- How does the school ensure that students experience a range of drama activities that lead them to progress in their knowledge, skill and understanding of the subject?
- How is the student's progress in the subject monitored, when are students assessed and how are records maintained and used to inform planning?

These are central issues as they identify how the subject provides opportunity for students to reach their potential, and how their progress will be communicated to the students themselves and others to whom the school is accountable.

A specimen policy statement is shown in the left-hand column of the following table. A commentary on the different parts of the statement is given in the right-hand column.

DRAMA DEPARTMENT POLICY STATEMENT	COMMENTARY
As a part of the whole school curriculum, students will be provided with a rich and diverse experience of the historical, cultural and practical aspects of the art form of drama.	Drama is an integral part of the students' entitlement to an education in the arts.
Drama classes will be taught in specially equipped teaching spaces by staff who are either subject specialists in their own right, or who have undertaken additional training in the teaching of drama.	Drama is a discrete art form that requires specialist teaching and specialist teaching rooms.

DRAMA DEPARTMENT POLICY STATEMENT	COMMENTARY
The breadth and balance of the drama curriculum will ensure that students are taught how to create, perform and respond to drama by working with a variety of stimuli from different sources and traditions.	Drama contributes to the development of a broad spectrum of knowledge, skills and understanding. It introduces students to different literary, technical, cultural and aesthetic dimensions of the human experience.
It will be made clear to the students what they are learning in drama and why. They will be shown how the knowledge and skills addressed in the drama curriculum are relevant to adult life in our society.	There is no inherent conflict between drama as a means of learning subjects from other areas of the curriculum and as a form requiring the acquisition of specific skills. A good scheme of work should work towards specific learning objectives both in the subject matter (content) and in the skills required to effectively communicate that content (form).
The drama curriculum will give students new insights into the world and the means to communicate their personal response to issues in creative and effective ways.	Drama is concerned with communication. To do this successfully one must have something worth communicating, a purpose for doing so, and the appropriate skills to do so effectively.
Students will keep a working notebook of their progress as evidence of the work they have undertaken and what they feel they are achieving. The notebook will contribute to and provide evidence of their development as independent critical thinkers.	Challenging and questioning students' assumptions underpin the best work in drama. Self-evaluation and critical reflection are therefore an essential ingredient in all drama work.
Students will be taught the skills involved in different aspects of drama. The art of the playwright, director, designer, technician and critic will be as much a part of the student's experience of drama as the art of the actor.	Drama is not just about acting. It offers students the opportunity to learn through actively researching, discovering, experiencing, experimenting and evaluating. The process of such learning involves creating, performing and responding to a wide range of dramatic activities.
Students' progress in creating, performing and responding to drama will be monitored and recorded twice each term and reported on twice each year.	Regular monitoring of students' progress in drama is needed in order to plan future work effectively. Students benefit from having their achievements recognised and new targets set.
Students will be given frequent opportunities to watch and learn from peers and professionals. Every possible opportunity to invite professionals into the school will be taken and every student will be given the opportunity to make at least one visit to a theatre at each key stage as part of the drama programme.	The students' own work in drama should be supplemented by experience of professional theatre. This will include studying a broad range of plays, seeing performances and learning about the technical aspects of modern theatre production.
Drama is a way of expressing the real concerns people have about themselves and the society in which they live. It is also a way of celebrating culture and belief. The drama that students experience in this school is just one thread in a vast tapestry. Students will be encouraged to wonder about the implications of such an idea.	Drama does not exist in a cultural or academic vacuum. Students should have access to diverse cultural experiences and be given the opportunity to reflect on, develop and articulate social values and beliefs. Drama develops the way students think and feel about themselves, each other and the world in which they live.

The scheme of work

The values expressed in the policy for drama will be reflected in a scheme of work that shows how breadth and depth are actually achieved in the drama curriculum. The purpose of the scheme of work is to outline what aspects of the subject will be covered at what points and by what means. Outlining the drama curriculum in this way helps avoid repetition and enables the drama department to use their work to complement other curriculum areas where this is appropriate and

Units of work – Extracts from summary of scheme for Key Stage 3 and 4

	UNIT 1	UNIT 2	UNIT 3
YEAR 7	Introducing drama Focus/aims • introduce drama as an art form in its own right • establish sound working relationships within the group • baseline assessment.	Movement, mime and circus	Creating meaning through signs Focus/aims • introduce semiotics • recognise and use dramatic potential • extend understanding of drama skills, concepts and techniques.
YEAR 8	Living news	Forum theatre Focus/aims • prepare for and use forum theatre to develop and focus drama • understand the purpose of forum theatre.	The mask
YEAR 9	Crime and punishment	Technical theatre (sound, lighting, costume, make-up)	Telling tales Focus/aims • consider ways that theatre practitioners use a range of skills, techniques and concepts to engage an audience • explore and realise in performance the dramatic potential of an original story.
YEAR 10	Introduction to GCSE course	Semiotics Focus/aims • extend and apply understanding of semiotics • prepare for improvisation as part of GCSE examination work.	Performing scripts 1 (group projects)
YEAR 11	Theatre production and design	Displaced	*Final Cargo:* script work Focus/aims • prepare for independent work on realising a script in performance • prepare for devising scripts and productions based on a specific theme.

Section 2 • Planning and assessing progression in drama

helpful to students. The content of the drama curriculum as outlined in the scheme will be underpinned by a clear conception of what knowledge, skills and understanding the students should be capable of achieving at any given stage in their school drama career. An increasing number of drama departments make use of the kind of progression charts shown on pages 38–41 to inform their scheme of work.

There are different ways of setting out a scheme of work. The example included here shows how the practical units explored in Section Three may fit into a scheme of work that covers the whole of Key Stages 3 and 4 (ages 11–16).

Unit 4	Unit 5	Unit 6	Unit 7
Pantomime	*Rainbow's Ending*: script work	Hauntings and mysteries (including scenes from Shakespeare)	*The Rime of the Ancient Mariner* Focus/aims • identify, explore and realise the dramatic potential of a visual stimulus.
Working with the voice Focus/aims • understand and use the voice effectively • consider how images can be translated through different art forms.	Physical theatre	Melodrama	Storytelling and the oral tradition
Shakespeare (set text for KS3)	Evacuees	From soap to politics	*Commedia dell'arte* Focus/aims • extend knowledge of dramatic genre • apply new knowledge in performance.
Street theatre	Dig where you stand (research project)	*Antigone*: script work Focus/aims • introduction to performing Greek drama • extend understanding of and practice in heightening dramatic tension.	Documentary theatre
Performing scripts 2 (small group projects)	Playwrights and directors (research project)	Images of men and women	Community theatre (whole-group project)

As can be seen from the examples, the unit titles and the specific aims for each unit are recorded. A unit may focus on a theme, the study of a play, an historical event, a particular style or genre, the exploration of a complex issue, a research project or a combination of these. What is more important is the aims of each unit, as it is these that will govern what the teaching objectives will be. These aims should connect clearly back to the policy for drama and if used in combination with the strands identified on the progression chart, should ensure breadth and balance and provide a means of mapping the curriculum. The aims for those units described in this book have been included, but titles for other units are also presented in order to demonstrate a variety of contexts that might be used.

Units of work

It is through this matrix of units of work that it should be possible to see the detail of the scheme of work throughout a key stage or combination of key stages. The units detail the kinds of activities that will be employed to provide the students with the knowledge, skills and understanding being developed at each stage and these can be planned through using descriptors on the progression chart. Each unit of work provides the frame and focus of work over a series of lessons and the chart can be used to inform the planning of those units. Having gained some idea of the level of ability of the students, teachers can use the chart to determine what knowledge, skills and understanding they hope that students will achieve through each unit. If, for instance, there has been a particular focus in one unit of work on analysis of how effects were achieved in a performance, then teachers will need to consider what should be planned to build on this in the next unit. In practice, a unit might last just two or three lessons, or it might cover the work over a half term. The activities within the unit will draw on and explore different specific plays, genres, concepts and issues. The way these connect to the learning objectives will be made explicit within the unit planner.

The potential learning outcomes of any particular unit of work need to be identified if the lessons are to contribute to an overall scheme designed to facilitate progression. These are the objectives of the unit plan. This is certainly not to say that what a teacher states on the unit plan as the main objectives for learning will in fact be all that the students learn. It is probably true to say that teachers are never fully in control of what students learn any more than a director or actor is in complete control of the way an audience will interpret a piece of drama. Nevertheless, the purpose of stating objectives for learning is to allow the teacher to:

- focus on particular aspects of the students' work
- assess individual students' progress in these aspects
- determine from the students' work the appropriateness and efficacy of the unit for them
- evaluate the effectiveness of their own teaching
- inform and improve future planning and classroom practice.

Setting long lists of objectives for a unit of work may well look impressive on paper, but if it is not possible to make any kind of assessment of the actual learning outcomes they correspond to, simply writing them down is a futile activity.

Some departmental schemes of work offer a range of optional units appropriate to a given age or ability group. This can be a particularly effective way of ensuring that resources are used well and that different teachers working in the department can play to their own individual strengths.

One way of ensuring that units of work realise the intentions of the department's overall scheme is to record them on a unit planner. Examples of these are included at the end of each chapter in Section Three to show how the focus of that chapter might be translated into a discrete unit of work. The basic tenet for such a template is that it should record:

- the amount of time it is intended to spend on the work
- the year group/key stage for whom the work is designed
- the overall aim of the unit (e.g. *to introduce students to the historical context and performance style of Victorian melodrama*)
- the intended learning outcomes – that is, what the students should know, understand and be able to do at the end of the unit
- the activities and tasks to be undertaken
- the resources to be used
- the evidence that will be used to assess the achievement of individual students.

As teachers use the opportunities during the lessons to identify progress, they should focus on the evidence of learning identified within their planning. They will doubtless also be aware of other unplanned learning and may choose to record this too.

• Lesson plans

In writing individual lesson plans teachers work out in more detail the nature of the different activities which are intended to fulfil the objectives stated in the unit of work. In any one lesson it could be that just one objective is being addressed and there may be one activity that is particularly pertinent for informing assessment. For the teacher, the lesson plan also provides another chance to ask 'Why am I doing this particular activity? What is it I want the students to know, understand or be able to do as a result of it? How should I set it up?' Teachers are increasingly recognising that students often benefit from knowing what is being looked for in terms of their achievement. In response to this, teachers may share their objectives with students by telling them or writing them on the whiteboard for use as a reference point during the lesson.

Teachers need to respond appropriately in a lesson to what has previously happened. In other words, as a class proceeds through a unit of work it may become clear to the teacher that the students need additional support to achieve the intended outcomes. Conversely, it may well be that the students have started to work in ways that are far more interesting and have more potential for learning than the planned unit caters for. The teacher thus needs to have some flexibility from lesson to lesson to address the students' needs. Evaluating the way students responded to the work and assessing their achievement will help the teacher to reconsider the way that particular unit contributes to progression and where it should be placed in the scheme of work.

④ Mapping progress in the drama curriculum

• The progression chart

The idea of a progression chart is to provide a guide for teachers when plotting and monitoring the work that students do in drama within the scheme of work. It works as follows:

- by looking down the Strands and Levels columns, the teacher can check that the different units which make up the overall scheme of work do in fact offer the students a breadth and balance of experience
- by looking across the chart, the teacher can monitor progression in a particular dimension of drama.

The three areas of activity are broken down into strands which are explained in more detail below. Descriptors are suggested as possible levels of attainment within the strands and these can be tracked using the horizontal axis. The vertical axis tracks the three modes of activity. The sample chart shown on pages 38–41 demonstrates how progression in drama can be tracked from the start of Key Stage 1 through to Key Stage 4, and indeed beyond. This example is not intended to be prescriptive. Drama departments may wish to draw up their own charts in a way that reflects their particular values and focuses on the levels at which they expect their students to be working. It should also be stressed that these are not statutory descriptors, but they have been produced with specific reference to drama requirements in the English Curriculum, the National Literacy Strategy, key aspects of the various GCSE drama syllabuses and Ofsted's guidance on drama. All these have implications for what and how drama is taught throughout secondary education.

Using the baseline

Having established a baseline (see page 45) on entry to the secondary system, the teacher is in a good position to put in order the units of work that will be taught during Key Stage 3 (Years 7–9 in England) and Key Stage 4 (Years 10–11). Although *commedia dell'arte*, for example, may always have been taught in Year 9 in the past, if it is found that a new group have already covered this sort of work, repeating it will not be an effective use of precious time and resources. Baselining thus helps to identify an appropriate starting point for the drama curriculum and to guide how that curriculum proceeds. This will inevitably involve employing some kind of model for planning which recognises the whole gamut of learning that can result from working through the dramatic process of exploration, research, rehearsal and giving expression to content and form.

The progression chart that follows on pages 38–41 can be accessed at:

www.heinemann.co.uk/drama/progression/chart.html

It is available as a PDF file which you can print out as two A4 sheets or as a Word file. You will be able to customise the chart in Word if desired.

The word file can be accessed and can then be customised, if so desired, for users with Word.

To access either file you will need the following information:

User name: Progressionchart
Password: Prchart

Progression chart: Tracking skills, knowledge and understanding

STRANDS	LEVEL 1	LEVEL 2
CREATING		
responding to, researching and experimenting with stimulus material – the content and context	explore familiar themes and characters, e.g. responding to teacher in role to explore characters from stories and themes	respond to a variety of stimulus material including scripts of plays, artefacts, objects and images
working supportively and creatively with others	plan an imaginative play area with others	suggest how to present ideas in drama through experimenting with others
structuring and notating plays and performances	practise and develop ideas for acting out stories	structure simple scenes independently, making use of dialogue and improvising their own
making dramatic action through experimenting with and shaping the elements of drama – spoken language, space, sound, gesture, text etc.	use simple props and resources in creating drama	select and use props and resources to represent particular meanings
PERFORMING		
working supportively with others in performance	take part in small group and whole-class dramas	work sensitively with others in role in small-group and whole-class dramas
interpreting narrative and portraying character in performance	adopt a role and be able to answer questions in role	use language which is appropriate to the role
manipulating the different signs through which drama communicates meaning	use space, sound and movement which is appropriate for the drama	use space, sound and movement to communicate specific meaning
realising a range of genres, styles and forms including new forms for different purposes and addressing different audiences	present their own stories using more than one form of drama – puppets, using a narrator, etc.	contribute to a range of performances using different forms such as puppet and shadow theatre, tableau, dance/drama etc.
RESPONDING		
using the language and vocabulary of theatre when talking about plays and analysing plots and performances	use simple drama terms when talking about drama in which they have taken part or that they have seen	express what they liked about a performance, e.g. explaining why they liked a particular character or scene
using specific criteria to reflect on and evaluate their own and others' performances, and using these responses to adapt and improve work	express and describe their feelings in response to the drama (e.g. after the performance of a visiting theatre group)	reflect on their responses to their own drama, saying what they wanted to achieve and how it might be improved
understanding the content explored in the drama and identifying the relationship between it and the form used	recognise key moments in the drama and be able to say why they used a particular voice or movement in interpreting character	suggest alternative forms of action from those shown in the drama
making connections between different styles, traditions and genres, including live and recorded drama, and understanding the cultural/historical context of the drama	talk about dramas that they have seen, including TV drama, and make simple connections with situations in their own lives	recognise that there are different types of drama and make connections between some of them

in drama

LEVEL 3	LEVEL 4
work with others in researching the context of the drama (e.g a concept or an event in history)	explore and research factual contexts for drama (e.g. conservation, the law) and record and share findings, and discuss possible ideas for the drama
try different ways of exploring characters and narrative, responding to the techniques used by the teacher	develop each other's ideas when devising work based on scenes from novels, poems, or plays
record ideas for devised drama, considering appropriate starting points, key moments and endings	devise simple scripts through improvisation, understanding the use of stage directions and drama conventions
experiment with simple technical resources when creating drama – sound, light, costume	experiment with the elements of drama when developing work and be able to give and receive direction
support others when participating in drama for a formal audience (e.g. school assembly)	co-operate and work supportively with others in a performance for a public audience
maintain role throughout the scene that is being shared or performed	communicate character through the use of words, movement and gesture
begin to be able to sustain mood and atmosphere effectively in performances	show understanding of theatrical effects, e.g. in creating tension – sound, silence, stillness
engage confidently in a range of dramatic techniques structured by the teacher – forum drama, hot-seating, thought tracking etc.	perform drama that demonstrates understanding of the text (stimulus material) used, and begin to understand that form conveys content
using simple drama terms, discuss the effectiveness of the drama, e.g. the performance of a play by a well-known playwright	using a basic drama vocabulary, write a response to a drama performance
comment sensitively on how intended effects have been achieved and suggest ways that their own and others' work could be improved	be prepared to accept the comments and ideas of others following a performance, and use this to develop their work
in groups, reflect on the issues or themes that are being explored through the drama	connect the drama with other ways that the issue, theme or story could be explored in other art forms
recognise and identify different genres in drama such as soap, documentary and pantomime	recognise particular forms of cultural expression in drama such as carnival, ritual, street theatre, etc.

STRANDS	LEVEL 5	LEVEL 6
CREATING		
responding to, researching and experimenting with stimulus material – the content and context	in response to a range of stimulus material including scripts of plays, plan drama, and notate ideas which demonstrate imagination	in response to a wide range of textx experiment with original and different ways that feelings and responses can be presented in drama
working supportively and creatively with others	work co-operatively and sensitively with others in a group in creating drama	challenge the ideas of others sensitively; contribute appropriate ideas and extend those of others
structuring and notating plays and performances	explore issues and themes and write plays using the conventions of script writing	as part of a group, make an effective contribution to the writing of an imaginative short script
making dramatic action through experimenting with and shaping the elements of drama - spoken language, space, sound, gesture, text etc.	consider how images create meaning, and experiment with objects, physical imagery, gesture and space	work in a variety of small groups, showing understanding of how dramatic signs and symbols can be used to communicate meaning
PERFORMING		
working supportively with others in performance	work sensitively and supportively with others in a range of presentations and performances	contribute to the performance of a unified piece of work showing commitment to 'role' or character
interpreting narrative and portraying character in performance	using a range of skills participate in short extracts from plays including a play by Shakespeare	communicate convincing character through the effective use of spoken (signed) words, movement and gesture in a short scripted play by a professional playwright
manipulating the different signs through which drama communicates meaning	show awareness of audience using the space in original ways to communicate the intended meaning	apply different ideas to communicate mood and atmosphere in devised or scripted drama performances
realising a range of genres, styles and forms including new forms for different purposes and addressing different audiences	show basic understanding of the relationship between content and form	communicate the intentions of the playwright through effective use and thinking, e.g. of timing, space and language
RESPONDING		
using the language and vocabulary of theatre when talking about plays and analysing plots and performances	recognise and use a range of theatre terms and connect these with drama they see or in which they take part in and out of school	talk about the ways in which the drama did or did not engage the feelings of those watching
using specific criteria to reflect on and evaluate their own and others' performances, and using these responses to adapt and improve work	when creating and performing, reflect on their own and each others' drama work providing constructive responses and ideas for improving it	during the devising process, reflect on work and use responses to develop it further
understanding the content explored in the drama and identifying the relationship between it and the form used	reflect on different ways that the same content can be portrayed	reflect on whether the effects used were pertinent for the content of the drama
making connections between styles, traditions and genres, including live and recorded drama, and understanding its cultural/historical context	make connections between their drama and that of a wider dramatic culture, including TV drama	explain the characteristics of different types of drama

LEVEL 7	LEVEL 8	EXCEPTIONAL PERFORMANCE
collaborate, modify and adapt ideas as a result of reflection, research and experiment, and show understanding of the rehearsal process	research/record in working notebook the psychology and context of characters and experiment with how these can be realised /visualised in performance	demonstrate in working notebook thoroughness of research, knowledge and development of ideas with others and appropriateness of decisions taken
initiate and respond to ideas and participate in the organisation and direction of drama for a specific purpose and audience	solve problems in the devising process by offering solutions which demonstrate awareness of the skills of the group	be flexible enough to work in a variety of groups, showing sensitivity, commitment and initiative in achieving targets
interpret, shape and structure in imaginative ways, using a range of forms and styles	explore and use a range of genres, forms and styles in shaping their ideas for producing devised work	be prepared to take risks and interpret, shape and structure drama in consistently imaginative and effective ways
be able to work in the abstract and employ different concepts through the use of language, space, sound, gesture, text and form	independently make use of different techniques, skills, concepts and conventions when devising, interpreting and directing plays	organise the drama effectively, being selective and demonstrating a high level of understanding and purpose in the use of dramatic form
work responsibly and sensitively with others, maintain roles/ responsibilities in a short independently devised piece for another class	work effectively with others with increasing independence in performing plays for different purposes and audiences	participate effectively as part of an ensemble in a variety of plays produced independently, reproducing the performance with good control and an ability to think on feet when needed
participate effectively in a full length play, showing clear and imaginative interpretations of character, situation and narrative	show insight into the narrative and the motivation and behaviour of characters through the effective use of a range of drama skills, techniques and concepts	demonstrate excellent understanding of dramatic effect so that the audience is engaged throughout the performance
use a range of technical and other sound resources to enhance performances	use a range of techniques, skills and conventions and apply dramatic concepts to communicate meaning in appropriate ways, with insight	use the expressive potential of the elements of drama in communicating meaning of a range of texts
perform drama which demonstrates understanding of the relationship between form and content	perform drama which shows sound understanding of the way form can be used in original ways	perform drama which demonstrates insight, originality and inspiration in interpretation to the audience
analyse how plots and characters are portrayed in different dramas using appropriate terminology	use the language and conventions of theatre criticism when evaluating professional and amateur productions seen	write insightfully about productions as a whole, showing recognition and appreciation of the different forms, genres, styles and cultural traditions that they see
identify and analyse how effects were achieved, saying how they were intended and whether they were successful	in regular written evaluations, write clearly about their own contribution to the drama, using appropriate language and identifying why and how it could be improved	use criteria (agreed by the group and in line with requirements) to evaluate their contribution to a group performance, including the whole rehearsal process
consider how a drama about a particular theme or issue could be adapted for a different audience	critically evaluate how the organisation and structure of plays contribute to dramatic effect	discuss and, as a theatre critic, evaluate whether the play in performance was appropriate for the content
talk about and explain preferences in drama, making connections with different forms and cultural traditions	recognise the work of a range of playwrights and theatre artists	talk about a wide range of theatre, showing good supporting knowledge

LIVERPOOL HOPE UNIVERSIT

Principles of progression

A common model for curriculum planning draws on the work of Hirst (1974). In essence, this involves identifying objectives, choosing teaching strategies perceived as being the most likely to fulfil the objectives and then using some kind of test to determine the extent to which they have in fact been fulfilled. Drama teachers, like many others, have often planned activities and then considered the learning that emerged. Michael Fleming (1994) suggests that, in the arts especially, there are often very good reasons for this. He asks, 'Is the emphasis on planning for successful drama or on planning the learning which comes about as a result of the drama, and to what extent can these objectives be conceived separately? Is it the teacher's task to plan drama or should the aim be for students to acquire that ability?' One of the problems of adopting a single planning framework such as that suggested by Hirst is that it ignores the important learning that may occur beyond what the teacher actually predicted or planned for. There is a particular tension in the kind of rational planning fostered by the National Curriculum and other extant frameworks and planning in the arts in that the only learning that is deemed to be worthwhile in the former is that which is easily recognised and assessed. The contribution made by the learner in identifying what constitutes worthwhile learning is denied. In the case of the arts in particular, it is understandable that this kind of mechanistic approach is viewed with suspicion, as it appears to be against creativity and innovation. Learning in the arts does not necessarily follow a predictable linear sequence. Nevertheless, it is similarly apparent that the development of knowledge, skills and understanding is not simply a matter of chance: if it were, the consequent implication would be that drama teachers would never have to plan anything at all.

In considering the tensions that exist between emphasising *knowledge* and *skills* and recognising the value of drama in the development of *understanding*, Fleming (1999) concludes that learning about content emerges through handling the form of drama. He proposes that 'progression and continuity in teaching drama can only sensibly be described in terms of the knowledge and skills (broadly defined) which students need in order to "get better at drama". There is no necessary conflict here with the pursuit of "drama for understanding" when making drama. There is, however, likely to be a change of emphasis.'

To reiterate the rationale posited above:

- units of work may be focused on whatever range of themes and topics the teacher considers to be appropriate for the students given the local circumstances
- each unit should provide a context in which knowledge, understanding and skills may develop
- the purpose of the chart device suggested here is that activities may be planned in order to provide a breadth and depth of experience
- each statement builds on students' prior experience while at the same time ensuring that key aspects of learning in and about drama are covered over the period of time addressed by the scheme of work
- the statements on the chart are thus necessarily quite broad and should be flexible enough for teachers to use them as hooks on which they can place their planning, rather than prescriptions of exactly what to plan. They can also be customised on the chart available on the web (see page 37)
- this does not imply that the stated objectives of each unit simply repeat the words presented on the chart. Rather, each unit of work needs to identify the opportunities for learning that the teacher intends to provide for the students at that point in their drama education.

⑤ Tracing progression through using the chart

This kind of progression chart allows teachers to trace students' progression in the three modes of drama activity, creating, performing and responding. The complexities of each of these modes have been distilled into four separate strands of development although the chart recognises the holistic nature of drama. So, for example, aspects of creating can be found within strands of both performing and responding. The strands simply suggest different aspects of development in drama in a way that will provide teachers with a means of plotting the knowledge, skills and understanding being acquired by the students. The focus of each strand is as follows:

CREATING
- responding to, researching and experimenting with stimulus material – the content and context
- working supportively and creatively with others
- structuring and notating plays and performances
- making dramatic action through experimenting with and shaping the elements of drama – spoken language, space, sound, gesture etc.

PERFORMING

- working supportively with others in performance
- interpreting narrative and portraying character in performance
- manipulating the different signs through which drama communicates meaning
- realising a range of genres, styles and form including new forms for different purposes and addressing different audiences.

RESPONDING

- using the language and vocabulary of theatre when talking about plays and analysing plots and performances
- using specific criteria to reflect on and evaluate their own and others' performances, and using these responses to adapt and improve work
- understanding the content explored in the drama and identifying the relationship between it and the form used
- making connections between different styles, traditions and genres (including live and recorded drama) and understanding the cultural/historical context of the drama.

Students value the work they do in drama when their work is recognised and valued in return. In order to get better at and learn more about something, students need to know what they have already covered and achieved. To this end, both the nature of the work undertaken and the individual student's level of attainment need to be monitored and recorded in such a way that both teacher and student can build on prior achievement. This chapter:

- outlines a way of establishing a baseline upon which to plan for progression

- suggests a system for compiling a record of achievement which can be used to trace students' progress in drama

- proposes a number of 'level descriptors' against which students' progress can be matched.

1 Establishing a baseline at Key Stage 3

Before teachers can identify the progress that a student appears to be making in any of the strands plotted on a progression chart, they need to establish what the student knows, understands and can do at the start of the process. This is called the baseline. The information used to establish such a starting point might be drawn from a variety of sources.

When a student enters the secondary school, data should be available from the previous school in the form of individual profiles, records of achievement and Standard Attainment Test data. Some new students may have individual education plans that need to be taken into account when planning introductory work. If liaison is good, some teachers may have been able to visit the primary or middle feeder schools and observe students working in drama. Some secondary school drama departments plan special projects involving older students working with Year 6 students in the summer term. Planned and managed with care, such projects can be tremendously productive for all involved, allowing for some initial assessment and profiling of the new intake while providing new challenges for the more experienced group.

Many drama teachers may choose to spend the first couple of sessions establishing a relationship with a new group and helping them get to know each other. It is likely, and certainly desirable, that ground rules regarding expectations of behaviour and how to use the space be set, and an introduction given to the way drama is taught in the school. Given this agenda, it is probably not appropriate for baseline assessment activities to take place in the first lesson, though some assessment tasks can be woven into an introductory unit of work. An example of how this might be done is shown on page 52.

Once the teacher starts to teach and provide opportunities for learning, students should start to progress beyond the baseline. It is the early activities, therefore, that will provide the teacher with the clearest idea of where the members of the group are in terms of their experience of and aptitude in drama.

A practical approach to baseline assessment

One way of approaching baseline assessment is to set the new students an entirely practical task. The teacher might, for example, present the group with a small range of resources to serve as stimuli. Different types of printed texts, objects and artefacts may be used: anything that will engage the students and prompt the imagination. For example:

- a candle (with matches available to light it) and candle-holder
- an old ornate key
- an envelope with a dried rose or a feather in it
- a torn photograph
- a very short simple tale
- an extract from a play
- a clipping from a newspaper.

(It is very important that the reading level of printed resources is considered for this activity as it is the students' ability to work in drama that is being assessed, rather than their ability to read.)

The resources are displayed and the class is invited to work in groups of five or six. A student from each group selects an object on behalf of their group and once selected, the stimulus should not be changed. The groups are given ten minutes to create a short piece of drama (no more than three minutes long) which uses the stimulus in some way. The students are told that they have the freedom to present their drama as they want, but that their aim is to try to get as close as they can to what that object or extract means to them and to communicate that to an audience. It is important that the teacher gives no further guidance than this to avoid influencing the group's interpretation of the task. When the set time is up, each group is invited to perform. Those watching are asked to respond briefly to each presentation, saying what they liked and how and why the drama was effective.

The exact way in which teachers organise and manage an activity such as this is highly dependent upon the context. In co-educational schools it is productive to ask the students to work in mixed gender groups in this first instance. It may also be necessary to establish a few simple rules regarding appropriate audience behaviour. Teachers will certainly need to be tight with their use of time. Introducing this activity to a class of thirty students and allowing them to work in six groups of five to create, perform and respond to the drama, will probably take two lessons in most schools. What the teacher will learn about the students through the whole process of this activity is certainly worth this amount of time though taking any longer should be avoided.

Other ways of baselining

An alternative, or perhaps additional, way of gathering evidence of what new students already know, understand and can do would be to ask them to complete some kind of straightforward questionnaire in which they outline their previous experience of drama in and out of the school curriculum. Many students attend drama clubs, youth theatres or 'stage schools' in their own time. They may already have a good understanding of some aspects of drama through theatre visits or a particular interest in films or television drama. It may, of course, be very difficult for the teacher to take account of the disparate knowledge and experiences of individuals in their planning. Some aspects of the students' prior experiences may be tangential to or conflict with the stated aims of the department. Nevertheless, it is helpful for teachers to have a sound grasp of the context within which they are working. Discovering that very few students have ever seen live theatre may make the teacher target this as a priority in their planning.

Further evidence of students' background in drama might be gained through a host of quite engaging practical tasks completed either at school or home. New students might, for example, be provided with a photograph or drawing of the inside of a theatre, showing staging, lighting, actors, the auditorium, the cyclorama and so on. Words identifying everything on the photo are printed at the bottom of the page. Students are asked to use a ruler and pencil to link each word with the relevant fixture, person, resource or equipment. The activity is easy to mark and of course the same test could be used at a later date to identify an improvement in this aspect of subject-specific knowledge and vocabulary. Obviously, this kind of task only presents evidence of a very narrow type of knowledge and understanding but, when used in conjunction with other strategies, it can nevertheless give the teacher clear signals regarding what the curriculum should include in order to help the students progress in drama.

● Recording the baseline assessment

The three activities outlined above all strive to provide the teacher with different types of information regarding each individual student's knowledge, skill and understanding. The teacher's initial assessment of the students' responses to such a task may be recorded on a record sheet such as the one shown on page 54. This example is based on the programme of study for Key Stage 2 English and the Literacy Strategy, but also includes other statements that are particularly important in drama and recognises the expected attainment of students at the end of Key Stage 2.

② Monitoring students' progress

Drama teachers tend to have considerable leeway in what and how they teach within their subject area. Nevertheless, all teachers need to demonstrate how they have identified and employed criteria appropriate to the assessment of their students. Such criteria must be clear and relate to the intended learning outcomes of a unit of work. In any one unit it is likely that students will be progressing in their ability to create, perform and respond to drama though there may be a greater weighting on one mode of activity than on another. The key questions for teachers when monitoring students' progress and evaluating their part in facilitating learning must be:

- What performance indicators are there to suggest that the students are progressing? What can I see, hear or read that tells me what the students know, understand and can do?
- Have the activities provided opportunities for the learning I intended?

In practical terms, students' work can be monitored through:

- *Watching and listening closely when students are working with each other.* Through this the teacher will be able to gauge which students are having their own ideas and helping others shape theirs.

- *Regularly watching students present their work to each other.* This might range from brief spontaneous improvisations in which the teacher 'spotlights' a number of groups who simply carry on with their work for a few moments while the rest of the class observe, to more formal presentations when the class watches and then responds to a piece of work that has been rehearsed to a greater or lesser extent. This kind of monitoring will show how students are experimenting with the form to communicate characters and meaning.
- *Periodically setting practical tasks in which the students know that aspects of their work are being assessed.* Such tasks might range from a series of briefs for spontaneous improvisations, through extended role-plays to the prepared performance of devised or scripted work. These sorts of tasks help the teacher focus on how well members of the group are working together to realise drama and illustrate the students' developing understanding of, for example, structure, characterisation, genre and technology.
- *Establishing the importance of keeping a working notebook.* An increasing number of schools are introducing notebooks right at the start of the secondary school programme. A 'working notebook' is just that – a way of recording both a process and ideas to be pursued and developed further. There are just as many opportunities for setting homework in drama as in any other subject. Using the Internet and books to research aspects of theatre history, finding new resources for drama, designing sets using, for example, computer generated software, costume and masks etc., sketching out ideas for scenes in script form or as a storyboard are just a few of the things which students can undertake on their own and which will contribute to their knowledge and understanding of the art form. Having the notebook readily available in every drama lesson allows students to jot down ideas and responses while they are still 'hot'. In this way, the students are better able to recall and comment on the creative process than if they later try to recapture the way they did things, and why. Regularly checking the contents of such notebooks helps teachers assess the students' ability to research, record and respond to ideas.

❸ Recording progress

Having monitored students' progress in different modes of drama activity, the next obvious step is to record the findings. There are a number of possible systems for this. Whichever system is chosen, the purpose of formative assessment is to inform future planning and set new targets appropriate for any given individual or group of students.

At the end of any unit, the teacher can use the same structure for recording assessment as that which is used for baseline assessment. It can also provide the means of recording the learning that was unplanned, but which was achieved as a result of the activities. To monitor individual progress and set individual targets however, teachers can use the level descriptors shown on the chart. Those appropriate for each student can be discussed with individual students as part of individual pupil tracking.

As part of the discussion, students can productively be asked to identify indicative numbers for themselves as part of their self evaluation (1 – working towards the level; 2 – working at the level, and 3 – working beyond/above the level). The potential for dialogue with students should be clear. If the student has achieved the target well and the record sheet is used with the progression chart, the next target can be identified too. By having unit assessment sheets for every class taught and retaining these sheets in a clip file, it becomes possible for teachers to monitor the work very effectively.

Some schools may use 'the traffic light system' for monitoring, recording and target setting. Here the colour code of traffic lights is shown instead of numbers and both teachers and students can see where they are and what they can work towards. Students need to know and understand the purpose of their work and to be clear about how it will be assessed. Providing opportunities for students to have a hand in the assessment process themselves contributes to their development as independent reflective thinkers. They can only do this effectively, of course, if they know and understand the criteria. When the reflection process is used well students will find self-assessment more empowering than difficult. For instance, they may be told that one of the objectives of a unit is to consider the motivation of a dramatic character by improvising around a piece of text. As part of their reflection on how their work is developing, they are asked whether they feel they have done this effectively and to say how they know by giving a specific example. This might be done orally with the teacher, as written homework, or through a simple written questionnaire.

Many schools regularly ask students to complete a self-evaluation pro-forma in which they comment on their contribution to and development through a term's work. Introducing this kind of evaluative response and reflection in the lower secondary years enables students to contribute to their own summative assessment and prepares them for the more critically reflective aspects of their future work towards a public examination in drama. The students' own evaluations provide more evidence for the teacher when reflecting on the nature and appropriateness of units of work and should help in future planning. This sort of reflection can be recorded on a simple template such as the one shown on pages 56–7.

Unit planning sheet for drama

Unit title Introducing drama   **Time scale** 3 × 50 minutes or 2 hrs 30 mins

Key stage 3   **Year** 7

AIMS

- to introduce students to drama as an art form in its own right
- to establish sound working relationships within the group
- to inform baseline assessment.

SUGGESTED ACTIVITIES

- introduction to drama in the school – the Y7 course and ground rules for drama
- whole-class focus games – name games, e.g. 'names across the circle', 'By invitation only!', 'Dracula'
- prompting the imagination: 'Pass the pen', 'What's in the box?'
- group dynamics: points of balance, walking blind across circle
- brainstorm/identification of key drama activities and the basic skills, conventions and techniques (to be recorded)
- presentation (by teacher) of stimulus objects and texts.

Baseline assessment task

- group improvisation developing piece in response to stimulus object/text (any style of drama may be used)
- presentation of scenes
- observing groups responding to work that they see and reflecting on the work in which they have taken part.

EVIDENCE OF LEARNING (CREATING, PERFORMING, RESPONDING)

Creating Are students:

- co-operating and developing each other's ideas in structuring drama?
- demonstrating or sharing imaginative ideas?
- experimenting with language, sound, gesture and space?

Performing Are students:

- communicating meaning through the use of space, movement and gesture?
- sustaining their role?
- able to convey a simple dramatic narrative?

Responding Are students:

- watching and listening to each other with focus and attention?
- contributing imaginative ideas on how intended effects have been achieved?
- offering comments to develop their own and other people's work?
- using appropriate basic language vocabulary for drama?

By the end of the unit the students should know and understand:

- expectations and ground rules for drama
- the importance of listening, co-operating, negotiating and responding sensitively
- what some of the essential ingredients for drama are, including a basic drama vocabulary
- that meaning can be communicated through the use of sound, space, movement and gesture.

They should be able to:

- use imagination when creating and responding to stimulus material
- work effectively in a small group to devise and present a short piece of drama
- respond to their own and each other's work, identifying what was effective and how this was achieved.

RESOURCES

- stimulus materials – e.g. candlestick and holder, red rose, walking stick, goblet, Bible, white feather, spanner, extract from *Anansi* by Alistair Campbell, copy of *The Old Man and his Grandson* from Michael Foreman's *World of Fairy Tales*
- basic studio resources – staging, lighting, sound as available.

COMMENTS/EVALUATION POINTS

Levels 2–5

- unit to be used as part of process for developing baseline – see baseline assessment recording sheet for KS3.

KS3 Teacher baseline assessment record sheet

Key to completion 1 = working towards   2 = working at the level   3 = working above

	Sam Adams	Gemma Barnes	Meena Habib	Oliver Lawrence				Andrea Whittle	Iwan Williams	Sharda Wynant
Creating Students are										
developing each other's ideas in creating drama	2	1	1	2				3	2	2
cooperating and sharing imaginative ideas	3	1	1	1				2	2	3
devising and writing a simple, imaginative script through improvisation, using stage directions etc	2	2	2	1				3	1	1
experimenting with language, sound, gesture and space in creating drama	1	3	2	1				2	1	1
Performing Students are										
communicating meaning through the use of facial expression, movement, gesture	1	2	2	1				2	2	1
sustaining a role in a group performance	1	2	2	1				3	2	2
using the space to communicate meaning	1	2	1	1				2	2	1
conveying simple dramatic narrative	2	1	1	2				2	1	1
Responding Students are										
using a basic dramatic vocabulary when talking about performances seen	2	1	2	2				2	1	1
suggesting ways that their own and others' work could be improved	2	1	1	1				2	1	2
commenting on how intended effects have been achieved	1	1	2	1				3	1	1
watching and listening to each other with focus and attention	3	1	1	2				1	1	3

Year 7 Unit 1 Teacher assessment recording sheet

Key to completion 1 = working towards 2 = working at the level 3 = working above

	David Abraham	Ikeni Mbeki	Finty Burnett	Mei-vee Liew	Josh Bergson
Creating Students are					
realising the dramatic potential of the visual and written text	2	2	2	2	3
using sound and visual images to present their own interpretations and personal responses	2	3	1	2	2
experimenting with objects, physical imagery, gesture and space	2	2	1	2	2
Performing Students are					
identifying how cultural connections can be translated in different forms, sustaining a role in a group performance,	2	2	1	2	2
using gesture and facial expression to communicate specific meaning	2	3	1	3	1
communicating the mood and atmosphere of the visual and written text	3	2	2	2	1
using the space in original ways to communicate intended meaning with awareness of audience	3	2	1	2	2
Responding Students are					
able to read the symbols/visual images	2	2	2	2	2
making connections between the three art forms	1	1	1	2	1
recognising and using a range of theatre terms, connecting these with drama in and out of school	3	2	1	3	2

Words in italics refer to the unplanned learning that took place as a result of the drama.

Unit evaluation

Unit title   **Term**

EXAMPLES/EVIDENCE OF LEARNING

(range of levels achieved)

WHICH ACTIVITIES WORKED BEST AND WHY?

EFFECTIVENESS OF RESOURCES

Summary   1   2   3   4   (1 low = negative, 4 high = positive)

Issues arising

TECHNIQUES USED

Key stage	Year

(1 low = negative, 4 high = positive)

- How effectively were planned learning
  objectives achieved by students

created drama?	1	2	3	4
performed drama?	1	2	3	4
responded to drama?	1	2	3	4

WHAT UNPLANNED LEARNING TOOK PLACE?

- as students created drama

- as students performed drama

- as students responded to drama

ANALYSIS OF GROUP'S RESPONSES TO UNIT

Summary   1   2   3   4   (1 low = negative, 4 high = positive)

Individual comments/feedback made by students

MAIN POINTS TO CONSIDER FOR PLANNING NEXT UNIT

- Particular focus on outcomes from any assessment

④ Reporting progress

Every school will have its own system for reporting on its students' progress. In England it is a legal requirement for schools to provide parents and guardians with a written report on each student's progress in National Curriculum and other subjects at least once a year. Some reporting systems make elaborate use of tick charts and graphs; others have a practice of giving one letter grade for Attainment, another for Effort and a general, but often rather meaningless, comment such as 'Helen has worked well this year and can express herself effectively.'

Neither of these approaches really helps the students, or those responsible for them, to understand what the work was about and what was learned through it. With the rapidly improving provision for technology, many schools are evolving reporting systems that provide some details of work undertaken and its rationale, in order to give a context for the comments made on each individual student. On page 59 there is an example of one such reporting slip, which usefully provides the student with the opportunity to add their own self-evaluation. The example relates to the unit of work outlined in chapter 3.7 (page 196).

⑤ Level descriptors

The levels presented below provide a more detailed description than that offered on the progression chart (pages 38–41) of what might reasonably be expected at different stages of a student's progression in drama. Once again, the descriptors given here follow progression through from Level One in order to provide an overall context for planning and assist with baseline assessment.

Level 1
Students work with others participating in whole-class and small-group dramas. They explore different ideas as they respond to the stimulus material. They suggest how to present ideas in drama and make use of simple props and other resources. They practise their ideas for acting out stories and use language, space, sound and movement to communicate meaning. They use simple drama terms when talking about drama in which they have taken part or that they have seen. They recognise key moments in the drama and talk about why they chose to use a particular voice or movement in interpreting a character. They talk about dramas (including television) that they have seen, and make connections with situations in their own lives.

Progress report from drama

Student's Name: _____

Year/Group: _____

Work undertaken this term:

The group have been working on the tragedy *Antigone,* as a way of learning about Greek theatre. The unit has involved learning about the conditions and conventions of Greek theatre, working with extracts from a Greek play and experimenting with ways of heightening dramatic tension.

Student's comment on what they came to know, understand and be able to do:

Self-assessment grade:　　　1　　　2　　　3　　　4

(**1** indicates very little progress, **4** indicates excellent progress)

Teacher's comment on student's contribution to and development through the work:

Teacher's assessment grade:　　　1　　　2　　　3　　　4

(**1** indicates very little progress, **4** indicates excellent progress)

Teacher's signature: _____

Date: _____

Level 2

Students respond to and interpret a variety of stimulus material including scripts of plays. They can work in small groups independently of the teacher, contributing ideas for the focus of their drama and performing plays so that the narrative is clear. They make use of dialogue in the text and improvise their own. They select and use a variety of simple but effective props and resources in performances and use language that is appropriate to their role. They respond to the drama they have seen, or in which they have taken part, with imaginative ideas and they can talk about how dramatic moments have been shown and atmosphere achieved. They can reflect on their own work, saying what they wanted to achieve and how it might be improved. They recognise that there are different types of drama and make connections between them.

Level 3

Students work co-operatively with others in researching the context to inform the drama. They try different ways of exploring the characters and narrative, responding effectively to the techniques used by the teacher. They record ideas for devised drama. They experiment with their voices, gesture, facial expressions and other skills to communicate meaning to others and they can participate in a performance, maintaining their role throughout the scene. They reflect on the issues or themes and comment sensitively on how intended effects have been achieved. They recognise different genres in drama such as soap, documentary and pantomime.

Level 4

Students work supportively with others, experimenting with ideas in creating drama. They devise simple scripts through improvisation and understand the use of stage directions and drama conventions. They experiment with language, sound, gesture and space and sustain individual roles in a drama performance. Their work shows understanding of the playwright's intentions. They communicate character through the use of words, movement and gesture and they communicate tension through timing, silence and the use of language. Students use a basic dramatic vocabulary when talking or writing about drama and are familiar with a small range of drama techniques. They suggest ways that their own and others' work could be improved, commenting on how intended effects have been achieved. They recognise particular forms of drama and different traditions of theatre from different times and places.

Level 5

Pupils devise and structure drama that shows an imaginative response to the stimulus material. They consistently work co-operatively and sensitively with others in a group in creating drama and exploring issues, themes, stories and ideas. They use and write plays showing the conventions of script writing and experiment with spoken/signed language, sound, gesture and space to create intended meaning. They work sensitively and supportively with others in a range of class presentations and participate in short extracts from plays including a play by Shakespeare. They show awareness of audience, using the space in original ways to communicate the intended meaning. They perform drama that demonstrates understanding of stimulus material used. They use a drama vocabulary when talking about performances seen in and out of school class. They reflect on their own and each other's drama work, providing constructive responses and ideas for improving it. They consider different ways that the same content can be portrayed and make connections between their drama and that of a wider dramatic culture, including television and film. They are adept at recording their ideas and responses.

Level 6

Pupils experiment with original and different ways that feelings and responses can be presented in drama. They challenge the ideas of others sensitively, contributing appropriate ideas and extending those of others. They make an effective contribution to the writing of an imaginative short script as part of a group. They work in a variety of small groups showing understanding of how dramatic signs and symbols can be used to communicate meaning. They contribute to the performance of a unified piece of work, showing commitment to 'role' or character. They apply different ideas to communicate atmosphere in devised or scripted drama performances. They communicate the intentions of the playwright through the effective use, for instance, of timing, space and language. They talk about the ways in which the drama successfully or otherwise engages the feelings of those watching. During the devising process, they reflect on their work and use responses to develop it further and consider whether the effects used are pertinent for the content of the drama. They explain the characteristics of different types of drama.

Level 7

Students collaborate, modifying, adapting and recording ideas as a result of reflection, research, experiment or rehearsal. They participate in the organisation and direction of drama for a specific purpose and audience. They experiment in group work with different forms and styles, shaping some into scripts. They refine their acting or technical contribution through the rehearsal process, working responsibly and sensitively with others. They maintain roles/responsibilities in a short independently devised piece for another class and participate effectively in a full-length play showing clear and imaginative interpretations of character and situations and using a range of technical and other resources to effectively enhance their performances. They perform drama which demonstrates understanding of the relationship between form and content. They analyse how plots and characters are portrayed in different dramas and analyse how effects were achieved using appropriate terminology identify. They consider how a drama about a particular theme or issue could be adapted for a different audience. They talk about preferences in drama making connections with different forms and cultural traditions.

Level 8
Students research the psychology and context of the characters and experiment with how these can be realised in performance. They solve problems in the devising process by offering solutions that demonstrate awareness of the skills of the group. They explore and use a range of forms, styles and genres in shaping and recording their ideas for devised work independently. They make increasing use of different techniques, skills, concepts and conventions when devising or interpreting plays. They show insight into characters' motivation and narrative of different plays through the effective use of spoken and signed language, words, gesture and movement. They use a range of techniques, skills and conventions and apply dramatic concepts to communicate meaning in appropriate ways, sometimes with appreciable insight. They work with others effectively and with increasing independence, performing plays for different purposes and audiences. They perform drama which shows understanding of the way form can be used in original ways and which fully engages the audience. They use criteria (agreed by the group and in line with requirements) to evaluate their contribution to a group performance, including the whole rehearsal process. When regularly evaluating professional and amateur productions, they use the language of theatre criticism. They discuss and critically evaluate whether the interpretation of play in performances was appropriate for the content presented.

Exceptional performance
Students demonstrate in working notebook thoroughness of research, development of ideas and appropriateness of decisions taken. They are flexible enough to work in a variety of groups, showing sensitivity, commitment and initiative in achieving targets. They interpret, shape and structure drama in consistently imaginative and effective ways,

organising the drama effectively, being selective and demonstrating a high level of understanding and purpose in the use of dramatic form. They participate effectively as part of an ensemble in a variety of plays produced independently, being willing to take a lead when appropriate. They reproduce the performance with good control and an ability to think on their feet when needed. They communicate narrative and character motivation to an audience so that the audience is engaged and inspired through the performance. They use the expressive potential of the elements of drama, in communicating the meaning of a wide range of texts. They perform drama which demonstrates to the audience their insights and originality in interpretation. They write about productions as a whole, using the language of a theatre critic, showing recognition and appreciation of the different forms, genres, styles and cultural traditions that they see. They analyse and critically evaluate their own work. They regularly talk about a range of theatre, making connections with known theatre artists and showing knowledge that supports what they say.

6 Drama 14–16

If students have been assessed and monitored throughout Key Stage 3, baselining will not be necessary at the start of Key Stage 4. However, if this has not been done, then teachers should use a similar range of assessments to identify where students are at the beginning of their GCSE course, and subsequently set targets for each student.

As well as providing teachers, parents and students with specific information about attainment, achievement and targets in drama, there is another value to establishing a baseline and clear procedures for monitoring and evaluating students' progress. Experienced teachers often claim to know instinctively that a student has made progress, though they are not always clear about how they know. Given an increasing expectation for teachers to be able to identify exactly how individual students have progressed, it is no longer tenable for teachers to simply state that students are 'more confident as performers' without having recorded evidence to support their professional judgement. The use of teachers' evidence is an important part of the assessment procedure at GCSE and Standard Grade. Teachers working with classes at this level need to consider how and what they teach in the light of existing records of students' prior attainment at Key Stage 3.

There has been considerable variation in the way different examining boards have expressed their aims and identified assessment objectives in drama. Similarly, the schemes of assessment offered by the various boards have demonstrated different values regarding what constitutes drama and how it should be assessed. However, accreditation procedures formalised by government agencies, such as the Qualifications and Curriculum Authority in England, have now gone some way towards standardising what is assessed and how it is assessed in GCSE Drama examinations.

The demands of examination syllabuses should not necessarily constitute the ultimate destination of any scheme of work in drama, or compromise the central tenet of a department's policy. Schools nevertheless wisely tend to take the details of the most up to date examination syllabuses into account when devising a curriculum for progression. Despite obvious differences in procedures and the weighting of assessment, a scrutiny of the schemes of assessment of different GCSE syllabuses in England, Wales and Northern Ireland, and the Scottish Standard Grade examination, shows that they all seek to register what students know, understand and can do in terms of creating, performing and responding to drama.

3
Progression in practice

Introduction

Sections One and Two of this book argued that, in the absence of any prescribed curriculum for drama, schools have the opportunity to decide both what the content of the drama curriculum might be and how students might be taught. Within their planning, schools need to address a number of factors. There are statutory obligations to be met and examination syllabuses will make their own demands. Beyond this, local circumstances such as the perceived needs of the students themselves, the time and resources available for drama, and the capacity of the teachers will all need to be considered when mapping out a curriculum for progression.

Coverage

This section is divided into nine chapters. Each chapter focuses on a specific area of study that one might expect to be covered as a part of the secondary school curriculum in drama. Each chapter describes how individual activities and structured practical explorations of different stimulus material may be used to give students a practical knowledge and understanding of that area of study. The various aspects of the art form explored in this section are far from complete and the strategies suggested are certainly not definitive. The purpose of these nine chapters is to illustrate how drama teachers may design a series of units of work by utilising a broad range of techniques and resources. Progression in drama is achieved by linking units together so that they address overall learning objectives in a coherent and logical way.

The practical ideas described and commented on in each chapter here should be regarded as being flexible. So while, for the purpose of organising this book, one particular strategy may be suggested as a way of engaging with a poem, the same technique could just as well be employed to stimulate a creative investigation of a picture, short story or play in drama. If a strategy for teaching and learning serves a purpose, use it!

In addition to suggesting a range of individual activities and resources, each chapter includes a detailed structure designed to help students progress in specific skills and areas of knowledge in a coherent way. At the end of each chapter, a specimen unit plan is included to show how the focal area of the chapter might be addressed with a particular year group. The unit plans specify the intended learning outcomes, outline the main activities undertaken and pose questions to check that the students have progressed in the ability to create, perform and respond to drama. Once again, it is not the intention to suggest that the only logical place where such work should be tackled is with one particular year group. The point is that progression involves breadth as well as depth.

Sequence

The spiral nature of the drama curriculum is reflected in the sequence of these practical chapters. So, for example:

- Chapter 3.1, *Starting out in secondary drama*, suggests ways of introducing some of the basic ingredients of the drama form to younger students. For example, they are shown how objects, lighting and sound effects help create and communicate meaning. A short fable is used as the stimulus for an activity in baseline assessment.

- Techniques for helping students devise and structure dramatic narratives as they move through Key Stage 3 and on to Key Stage 4 are returned to in chapter 3.6, *Telling tales*.

- In chapter 3.9, *Dramatisation*, a more critical eye is cast upon the whole business of communicating through drama. Here again a story is taken as a starting point, but this time it is a real life story. Students explore how objects, lighting and sound can be selected and presented in a way that reflects an overall production concept that would deliberately 'position' an audience in relation to the documentary material. Within the chapter, however, there are activities that suggest how some aspects of documentary material can be effectively employed in the lower secondary years.

Exploring how drama communicates through words and visual texts is as pertinent in Year 11 as it is in Year 7. Similarly, the metaphors of a simple fable may have as much potential for exploration at A level as for 11-year-olds. Many drama activities may thus justifiably be used throughout the secondary curriculum, but it is more likely that the teacher will choose different resources and adopt a different teaching approach to suit different age and ability groups.

3.1

Starting out in secondary drama

Students entering secondary school are likely to have varied experiences of drama. The practical ideas explained in this chapter demonstrate one way of introducing or reiterating some of the basic principles of working in drama. Starting out in secondary drama requires the students to:

- establish good social relationships
- learn what ingredients are used in communicating through the art form of drama
- understand that effective drama comes about by adhering to constraints.

Drama is always about something. By exploring content in drama students acquire considerable depth of understanding. What makes drama different from other art forms is its particular use of different elements of form. As a foundation to their work in secondary drama, students need to learn what these elements are and to gain an insight into what they involve in practice.

❶ Introduction

When students arrive for their first drama lesson in secondary school the teacher is unlikely to be sure of their prior experience and level of attainment in the subject. The National Literacy Strategy and National Curriculum Orders for English are designed to furnish students of this age with a good deal of knowledge and experience of creating, performing and responding to drama. However, it is likely that students will leave primary schools with vastly different backgrounds in the subject. A few may well have considerable experience of performing to a high standard at primary school and in youth theatre. Some may be seasoned theatre-goers. Some may have experienced drama in its cross-curricular mode but be less explicitly aware of the nature of their encounters with the art form. Others, notwithstanding the National Literacy Strategy and National Curriculum, will have had little or no experience of practical drama. Either way, it is currently unlikely that the drama teacher will be passed any specific information on what new entrants have done or achieved in drama to date.

Establishing a baseline

A priority for the secondary school drama teacher is to establish as fully as possible some kind of baseline for each student and this has been addressed in Chapter 2.2. This will allow individuals to demonstrate something of what they know, understand and can do while the whole group learns something new. More information can be gathered in Chapter 3.1 which incorporates a range of the fundamental ingredients of drama: gesture, movement, use of space, light, speech and other sounds in order to convey a sense of scene and character. Through this approach, the teacher can ensure that the whole group understand the 'clay' they will be working with in the drama course and continue to acquire a subject-specific register of terms. Many teachers display key terms around the working space or on a 'word wall'. Exposing students to words such as 'melodrama', 'commedia dell'arte' or 'naturalism', to the names of practitioners such as Shakespeare, Brecht, Churchill, Boal, and to rehearsal techniques such as hot-seating, thought tracking, forum theatre (pages 227, 82 and 145–7 respectively) and the like helps them to appreciate that drama has its own body of knowledge and that the drama undertaken in school is a part of something much bigger. Research suggests that displaying subject-specific language and references in this way, and frequently drawing students' attention to the terms in lessons, makes a positive contribution to their written and oral reflections on the work.

Establishing relationships

Another consideration with any new group is to establish a sound working relationship. As discussed in Section One, drama can make a substantial contribution to students' personal and social development. Along with colleagues in other departments, the drama teacher will have a responsibility to induct new entrants into the ethos, expectations and working practices of the school. A genuinely productive relationship will make it clear what students can expect in return for their contracting into the system.

The activities described in this chapter are particularly suitable for groups who are unused to working with each other and have varying degrees of background knowledge and experience. While this may seem to imply Year 7 groups (or first years of secondary schools) especially, the activities may serve as a useful starting point for groups of all ages that have not worked together or with the teacher before. What is vitally important in any case is that the reasons for undertaking the activities are clear to the students. It is also extremely important to build in a little time for reflection on the nature and outcomes of each activity.

Progression in drama is concerned with students increasingly taking control over the content, shape and direction of their own work. It would be counter to this ethos to have new groups, whatever their age, leave their first few drama lessons thinking that the subject involved the teacher holding up hoops through which they simply had to jump.

② Making use of games

It is understandable, to a degree, why there has sometimes been a little confusion between games and drama. Both, for example:

- contain elements of play
- contain elements of tension
- involve an active engagement
- tend to require participation by more than one person.

Some of the overall aims of drama in education pertain to many games also in that they can:

- develop a sense of trust by being non-threatening
- promote group co-operation
- help young people understand the need for rules and codes of behaviour
- help develop physical and mental dexterity
- promote intellectual and emotional flexibility
- be used to inject energy into a lethargic group or to calm down an over-excited one
- help young people learn how to manipulate space and time.

None of these outcomes relates specifically to drama, however, and playing games *ad infinitum* will not result in students progressing in the subject. However, games can serve as useful warm-ups and as ways of introducing certain key aspects of the art form, and some games can be developed into more structured and fulfilling dramas. Games and warm-ups are only really useful when they are linked to the main area of drama work to come. Teachers therefore need to be able to select games that suit a particular purpose: making this purpose clear to the students will help their learning (and also help dispel the often unproductive notion that drama is not really work but is just 'a bit of a laugh').

The term 'warm-up' could be taken to encompass all sorts of things. The point is that when people are 'warming up', they are presumably warming up in order to tackle something else. Simply running around or stretching might be the sort of physical warm-up that is required in order to loosen up the body and generate a sense of energy. Singing or undertaking some voice activities might be necessary in order to prepare for a public performance. There are many books full of ideas for these kinds of warm-ups and most actors, directors and drama teachers tend to have a stock of their own favourites. A few of these, focused on helping the group get to know and work with each other, are described in the following pages. Other games and warm-ups, being attached to an exploration of different aspects of drama, are described in the chapters that follow.

 ## Names across the circle

1 The members of the group stand in a circle and one by one, each individual in turn says their name in a loud, clear voice (this in itself may be related to the need, in drama, to be able to communicate clearly).
2 The teacher crosses the circle towards a student, saying that student's name.
3 That student then crosses the circle, saying someone else's name as they do so.
4 The aim is to get this swapping of places going as quickly as possible. The teacher may decide to ask two, three or even more people to start crossing the circle at the same time: the effect is to have a mêlée of students getting used to using each other's names.

Asking students to identify what purpose this activity has for drama can prompt reflection and an understanding of some of the basic aspects for drama. For example, the dynamics of this game may be related to the need to listen out for a cue and to think quickly and respond positively, as well as to know who you are working with.

By invitation only!

In this variation of the previous game, no one is allowed to move across the circle until they are invited. So, for example, the teacher says the name of a student, but may not move across the circle until that student says, emphatically, 'Yes!' Once invited, the teacher starts to move across the circle and the student calls someone else's name. They must not move until they hear a '*Yes!*' from the person they have named. Think it's easy? Try it!

Physical fun

- Groups are asked to support each other physically while only using a given number of points of contact with the ground. For example, can a group of five hang together by having only two feet and three hands touching the floor?
- Groups of 3–5 students are given words with the same number of letters as numbered in the group, and are asked to find a way of using their bodies to make the shapes of the letters in such a way that the word can be read by an audience.
- Groups are invited to represent some kind of mechanical device such as a lawnmower, a cuckoo clock or a food-mixer by joining their bodies together and using appropriate movements.

This sort of 'fun' activity can be justifiably linked to physical theatre and terms such as 'personification' explained. Making reference to established theatre companies which have developed this way of working rightly places these activities on a higher plane.

Gatwick airport

- The class place their chairs in a circle facing outwards. One person stands within the circle, on the opposite side to an empty chair, while everyone else sits down.
- As the student who is standing starts to move around the circle towards the empty chair, those already sitting move round in order to keep the empty space as far away as possible from the standing player; if that player changes direction, so do the others.
- An extension of this game can be worked on as a mime scheme reminiscent of, say, Mr Bean or Jacques Tati. Students can take the part of certain stereotypes that might be found in an airport and work on what those stereotypes' reactions would be to the problem of finding a seat.
- Those sitting can find interesting reasons and attitudes for moving seats; the students can experiment with different speeds, to see how comedy and pathos can be created from this simple situation.

Pass the pen

The members of the group sit in a circle. A simple object is passed around. Taking account of the size and shape of the object, each student suggests something else it might be and physically demonstrates this. So, for example, a pen might be used as a toothbrush, a stiletto heel, a telescope, a dart, a lamp-post in Lilliput and so on.

The game needs to move quickly. In reflection, the students should identify the way that drama draws on imagination in word and action and requires accepting things being what they are not. There is an opportunity here to introduce the term 'suspension of disbelief'.

 ## Juicy fruit

Not a game for the overly sensitive, this involves passing a piece of imaginary chewing gum around a circle. After miming a few chews, each player finds a revolting way of passing the gum on by, for example, putting it into their ear, sticking it on the sole of their shoe, wrapping it around their head etc. In order to make the game move faster it is best to split large classes into two or even three playing circles.

As with 'Pass the pen' the game relies on accepting the fiction. The impact and believability of the mime is extended if players use their faces to express their disgust.

What's in the box?

This is a simple mime activity that involves placing an empty box in the middle of the group circle. A student volunteers to take something from the box. They make it clear what has been taken through actions alone (a snake? a big juicy hot-dog?). As soon as one of the other students recognises the mimed object, they enter the circle and find some way of relieving the first student of the object, for example:

'Ah! Sidney! So that's where you are! Now, be a good python and let go of this lady's neck.'

'Excuse me! That's my lunch you're eating! You know that you are meant to be on a diet so give it back now.'

In reflection, the point needs to be drawn out that drama relies not only on suspending disbelief but also on careful signalling (in this case through mimed action), participants watching each other closely and picking up and developing ideas.

❸ Trust activities

There are a number of physical activities that are sometimes held up as effective ways of promoting trust between students unused to working with each other. Certainly, when introduced carefully and handled firmly, some of these activities can help pairs or small groups of students to work closely together and learn how to rely on elements of each other's physicality. In some circumstances, for example in the rehearsal of particular theatrical effects or in units of work on physical theatre, students will need to develop a sense of timing and the physical capacity to perform safety and effectively. However, asking students to take it in turns rocking each other or catching each other as they fall into waiting arms is not a guarantee that they will end up trusting each other. In fact, the number of experienced teachers that can recount incidents of skulls cracking on studio floors suggests that there are often very good reasons for students not to trust their physical well-being to classmates, even though they might be more than happy to trust them in other ways. The question is, why risk tears and injury when the actual learning outcomes are unclear to all concerned? Unless the teacher is wholly clear on the purpose of activities which rely on students physically handling each other, and on how to introduce and manage them safely, they are best left out of any introductory drama programme.

❹ Open tasks for baseline assessment

The purpose and principles of baseline assessment were set out in chapter 2.2 (see pages 45–48). It was suggested there that new groups might be given a choice of different stimuli with which to work, or be asked to create a dramatic response to a common stimulus. The crucial thing is to keep the task open-ended in order to reveal who in the group contributes what and to demonstrate the depth and breadth of everyone's existing knowledge, understanding and skill in creating and performing drama.

The Old Man and his Grandson

This is an ideal story for use as a stimulus for baseline assessment. It can be used with a wide range of students as the language is not demanding and the narrative is short. It has great dramatic potential in that it has a metaphorical and allegorical dimension that can provide the basis for dramatic exploration. On the other hand, it could be interpreted and represented simply, but nevertheless powerfully, through enactment. The challenge of the task for the students is to see if they can get to the real essence of the text, using any elements of drama form, techniques and skills they wish.

1 The teacher reads the story below to the whole class.

2 The class is divided into groups of five or six and given copies of the story.

3 The groups are given a maximum of ten minutes to make a piece of drama from the story which communicates to the others what the performing group think is really important and interesting in it.

4 The only other constraint is that their drama must last no longer than three minutes.

As the students are sharing ideas and experimenting with ways of realising them, the teacher has the chance of observing them and identifying whether they are collaborating with and supporting each other to develop the piece creatively. The teacher can also see who it is that suggests a particular theatrical device or who connects the themes of the story to wider aspects of the human condition. Further information about the students' ability to perform can be gained as each group presents its piece. The responses the students make about their own and others' presentations provide further insight into the level of understanding and knowledge in the class.

EXTRACT

There was once a very old man, almost blind and deaf, whose knees and hands trembled. At meal times he could hardly hold his spoon, and often dropped soup on the tablecloth and when he'd taken a spoonful some of it spilled out of his mouth.

His son and his son's wife thought it was disgusting and eventually told him to sit in the corner behind the stove. They gave him his food in an earthenware bowl and never gave him enough. He sat and looked sadly at the table, and he spilled tears into his soup.

One day his old hands trembled so much he dropped his bowl and it smashed to the floor. His son's wife shouted at him and he turned to the corner and sighed.

She bought him a crude wooden bowl for a few copper coins and he had to eat all his meals from it. As they were sitting there one day, the little four-year-old grandson was playing on the floor with some bits of wood.

'What are you doing?' his father asked.

'I'm making a trough,' the child replied, 'for father and mother to drink out of when I'm big.'

Husband and wife stared at each other for a while and then burst into tears. Then they asked the old grandfather back to the table and he ate with them from then on, and even when he spilled a few drops, nobody said anything.

The Old Man and his Grandson;
World of Fairy Tales by Michael Foreman

Introducing improvisations

The term 'improvisation' encompasses a vast range of activities in drama. Role-play can be seen as a form of improvisation, which simply means a spontaneous reaction to a new situation. As an element of performance, improvisation goes back at least as far as *commedia dell'arte*, where the performers would present comic improvisations called *lazzi* from a simple starting point. Stanislavski made extensive use of improvisation as a rehearsal technique and many of the strategies now associated with drama in education have their roots in his work. The term 'prepared improvisation' seems something of a contradiction, but relates to the more recent practice of playwrights working directly with actors to generate, test and shape ideas while devising new work.

The chair

1 Each student takes a chair and uses it as something other than a chair – a shopping trolley, a lawnmower, a diver's helmet. Every time the teacher claps their hands the students must change the use.

2 Still working on their own with a chair, the students imagine that it is a particular type of chair; they demonstrate the sort of chair through their actions and what they say to other, imagined, characters (for example, the pilot's seat of an airliner, a dentist's chair, a roller-coaster car).

3 This solo work is developed in pairs. A starts off an improvisation by making it clear to B what sort of chair is involved:

'So, what's it to be today, Mr Smith? Just the usual number 4 cut?'

B must then respond appropriately, accepting the idea of location and character offered. The improvisation does not need to run for more than a few seconds. What the teacher is looking for is the students' ability to:

- think of new ideas quickly

- signal location and character through word and action

- accept and develop the fiction.

4 By way of reflection, it is useful to share a few examples of this sort of work with the whole group and discuss what was being communicated and how.

Introductory work such as this can be used as part of a baseline assessment because it tells the teacher what new students understand and can do, while helping those students progress in their knowledge and skills.

---

5 Introducing elements of form

Looking at the way very slight changes in conditions can radically alter meanings is a fascinating basis for creative drama work. Using a little technology will add to the enjoyment and learning potential of this sort of work. In the first instance the teacher may decide to 'lead from the front' by way of demonstrating how some of the different elements of the drama form may work. The aim must be to move on swiftly so that responsibility for creating, performing and responding to carefully constructed dramatic images soon passes to the students themselves. Although having a well-equipped specialist drama studio is ideal, this sort of activity can just as easily be set up in a hall or classroom, using a powerful torch to suggest lighting angles and creating shadows where necessary. The 'performance space' may simply be an area on the hall floor or at the front of the classroom: all that is really necessary is that the class can see what is in the space.

Playing with images

The permutations of what can be suggested by placing one or two characters in a space with a simple prop, some simple lighting and a few different sound effects is infinite. If no stage lighting is available considerable effect can be achieved just by using a strong torch – even very young students will probably be familiar with how sticking a torch beneath their chin can make a face look pretty scary.

The candle

1 The students sit facing a defined performance space on which stands a candlestick with an unlit candle. (Ideally the candlestick itself will be of a particular kind, perhaps a large ornate gothic sort, or the sort a Victorian child might use to light the way to bed. The activity is easier and more productive if the object has a strong resonance of time and place.) They talk for a few minutes about what they see and what they are reminded of.

2 The lights are lowered and the candle lit (appropriate safety precautions having been taken). The group discuss the effect this has.

3 A student is asked to kneel in between the audience and the lit candle. What is the effect? What is the effect if the student kneels behind the candle looking over its flame directly at the audience? Or looking into the flame? Or looking heavenwards? Or striking a melodramatic pose by looking into the darkness of the wings and cowering away?

4 The other students are invited to suggest other positions in which to place the character and the candle, and to talk about the different effects of these changes.

5 From this starting point other factors can gradually be added, depending on the available resources. For example:

- Light the character and the candlestick with a tightly focused spotlight above.
- Light the image using a floor flood so that the light is coming from below the character's face.
- See what happens when the same position is taken by a boy, then a girl. What happens to the image when, for example, a girl with short dark hair is replaced by a girl with long blond hair?
- Add a second character and play around with the spatial relationship. For example, both kneeling and looking at each other through the flame; one standing looking down at the other who peers into the flame; both with their backs to each other and the candle, which has just been snuffed out so that the smoke is still rising between them.
- Try to use a light to create different sorts of shadows. How does this change the mood and tone of the image?
- Add different sound effects to the image: a departing steam train, medieval plainsong, somebody crying and so on. What difference do such sound effects make?

Through reflecting on these sorts of images young students can come to see how lighting, sound, positioning and even a performer's physical qualities (such as length and colour of hair, or gender) suggest some sort of narrative. From this basis students can be asked to work in pairs or small groups to create simple dramatic narratives for themselves. Far from oppressing or limiting the work, setting very tight constraints leads to highly imaginative and carefully crafted pieces.

● Working with constraints

From the sort of teacher-led introduction suggested above, students may be challenged to create their own dramas within tight constraints. For students new to drama, perhaps unused to working with restrictions, framing this sort of work as a kind of game in itself will help them begin to understand how meanings are created and communicated in drama, and will provide a good focus for reflection on the outcomes. More experienced students will be reminded of the need to be precise and economical in their work.

While students work to realise their brief, the teacher has an ideal opportunity to teach each group in turn how to use the lighting and sound equipment available to achieve what they need for the activity.

1 A few well chosen props are laid out on one table, clearly labelled sound tapes on another and perhaps a few pieces of costume on another. Three or four different light sources are set up and shown to the class so that the students are clear which one does what (for example torchlight, candlelight, a household table lamp and so on, as well as stage lighting).

2 The students are set a 'brief' to work with. For example:

- 'Devise a scene which tells a clear story. It must involve two characters and one prop. One of the characters must say "Oh dear, you shouldn't have done that!" and that is the only line that will be spoken.'

- 'Devise a drama with the title "There's something horrible down there!" You can use one sound effect, one light source and one prop but no speech.'

- 'Tell a story in three still images. The images may be lit in the same or different ways. The same prop will be an important part of each image. You may use two lines in whatever order and wherever you like: "What are you going to do now?" and "They asked for it!"'

3 Having experimented with briefs set by the teacher, the students are given the task of setting briefs for each other by drawing ideas from a menu of ideas. What sort of 'recipe' would they be able to concoct from the following table, for example?

PROP	COSTUME	LIGHTING	SOUND	DIALOGUE
gun	feather boa	overhead spot	maniacal laughter	'What on earth . . .?'
telephone	bowler hat	floor flood	aeroplane taking off	'So, what have you got to say for yourself now?'
cuddly toy animal	wellington boots	twinned fresnels (standard cover)	Opening theme music of BBC news report	'Go home.'
teapot	plastic mackintosh	domestic light (e.g. table lamp, torch)	church bells	'It's lovely! Not at all what I expected.'
walking stick	dark glasses	choice of colour filters	lavatory flush	'I won't be a minute.'

Students can be helped to design simple briefs by providing a template based on the example below, with gaps in place of the italicised words and phrases.

Design-a-Drama Ltd
Briefing Sheet

Make a drama involving *three* characters. It will have *two* scenes.

You must use a *cuddly toy animal* as a prop and a *bowler hat* as part of a costume.

Your line of dialogue is '*It's lovely! Not at all what I expected*'.

Instructions on sound effects:
You can use the maniacal laughter wherever you want.

Instructions on lighting:
Ordinary lighting for one scene but torchlight for the other.

Other instructions:
The three characters do not have to be in both scenes.

⑥ Structuring a unit of work on creating meaning through signs for Years 7 and 10

At the end of this chapter are two examples of units of work which focus on the use of the way visual and aural signs such as lighting, costume, gesture, positioning in space, sound effects and speech are used to communicate meaning in drama.

● Year 7

One of the proposed units is for a Year 7 group (pages 84–5). It shows how some of the fundamental techniques, skills and strategies involved in making and performing drama can be introduced and seeks to help young students start to articulate the decisions they take in this process.

▸ Introducing fundamental techniques, skills and strategies

1 The teacher leads a discussion on different types of signs and symbols – road signs, company logos, religious symbols, facial expression, gestures, greetings of different cultures, signature tunes, sign language and so on. Connections are made between them.

2 Students work in pairs or in groups, using gesture and signs (but no words) to communicate moods, instructions and messages. They reflect on how meaning can be created through a symbol or sign without the use of vocal language.

3 The class look at a set scene in a defined space, for example a chair placed on its side. They look at the scene and identify what it communicates to them and why. Connections can be made here with the way symbols are used in art, music and literature.

4 One of the students is placed next to the chair, facing away from the audience. The other students make suggestions for altering the image to make it more interesting from a dramatic point of view and discuss how their suggestions work.

5 They work in pairs to suggest a line of script that could fit such a scene, explaining why they chose it. These are shared with the class.

6 Working in groups of three, students are given an object – a broken cup, a half-completed letter, a handbag with a bus ticket, a medal, a photograph, worry beads. Each group creates a still image which includes both the object, used as a symbol, and themselves.

7 Examples of scenes are shared and those observing suggest a line that they think might fit each one. They discuss whether it matters if the audience has interpreted the scenes differently from the meaning intended by its creators.

8 Students work in pairs, to create still images that depict a concept (such as death, success, loss, freedom, captivity, loneliness). They are given words written on individual cards so that each group only sees the concept on which they are to work. They may only use their bodies, and facial expressions and gestures that represent their term. The students are asked to think about what will make their performance dramatically interesting.

9 Sample pairs present their scenes. The audience discuss what concept the scene appears to illustrate.

10 The teacher introduces and uses thought tracking (remembering that some may have seen it used in primary school), to develop further insights into the scenes. Questions such as 'How did this happen?' or 'Why are you frightened?' are used to prompt reflective responses. Having modelled the use of thought tracking, students can be invited to thought-track individuals performing subsequent scenes.

11 Students reflect on the scenes, considering what worked well and why, and the purpose and value of the technique of thought tracking.

12 In groups, students select any one of the scenes or images explored so far, and develop it into a two-minute performance which has strong dramatic meaning. They work under the following constraints:

- they may use one prop or piece of furniture, or one sound, but these must be used symbolically
- they must work within a limited space (for example, three square metres)
- they may not use words
- they have five minutes in which to prepare their scene or image.

13 Samples of the scenes or images are shared. The audience evaluate whether the targets set for the work have been achieved, and why they consider it to be the case (or why they do not).

Year 10

The second sample unit is designed for a Year 10 group (page 86). It draws on the same sort of stimuli and activities but illustrates progression in practice, in that the tasks set demand adhering to different constraints. Students working at this level would be expected to make more informed decisions and to be able to employ a greater range of subject-specific language such as *mise-en-scène* when evaluating their own and each other's work. For example, it would be appropriate at this level for students to know that a study of the sign systems used to communicate in drama is called semiotics, and be able to articulate how different dramatic effects are created by manipulating visual and aural signs.

Unit planning sheet for drama: Year 7

Unit title Creating meaning through signs   **Time scale** 2 × 50 minutes

AIMS

- to introduce semiotics
- to enable students to recognise and use dramatic potential
- to extend understanding of drama skills, concepts and techniques.

SUGGESTED ACTIVITIES

- discussion plus individual/paired activities using signing, signals and symbols
- whole-class observation of simple 'set scene' created by teacher (e.g. chair on side with student with back to audience)
- focused questioning to extract interpretations from class
- small adaptations of scene resulting from individual suggestions
- still image work in groups responding to stimulus props
- responses and interpretations shared and discussed
- words given to pairs to present physical image
- thought tracking introduced, used and discussed
- one of images taken by each group to develop into scene with specific constraints on time, props, sound and space – targets set
- sample scenes shared – responses – evaluation using targets set and focusing on what makes effective drama.

EVIDENCE OF LEARNING (CREATING, PERFORMING, RESPONDING)

Creating Are students:
- demonstrating understanding of how to use signs to create meaning?
- using thought tracking to develop and interpret images?
- working with others in creating a simple dramatic narrative within limited constraints?

Performing Are students:
- communicating character through facial expression, gesture and movement?
- using the space and simple technical resources to create meaning?

Responding Are students:
- interpreting images and other signs with imagination and insight?

INTENDED LEARNING OUTCOMES

By the end of the unit the students should know and understand:
- how meaning can be created through signs and symbols
- how the technique of thought tracking can be used to develop and interpret images.

They should be able to:
- communicate character through facial expression, gesture and movement
- use the space and simple technical resources to create meaning
- work with others to create a simple dramatic narrative within limited constraints
- interpret images and other signs.

RESOURCES

- studio lighting
- cassette playback machine
- stimulus props suggesting character/situation – broken cup, half-completed letter, handbag with bus ticket, medal, photograph, worry beads
- words written on individual cards for paired work – death, success, loss, freedom, captivity, loneliness.

COMMENTS/EVALUATION POINTS

- Levels 3–6

Unit planning sheet for drama: Year 10

Unit title Semiotics   **Time scale** 4 × 50 minutes or 3 hrs 20 mins

AIMS

- to extend and apply understanding of semiotics
- to prepare students for their improvisations for GCSE examination work.

SUGGESTED ACTIVITIES

- connections with work at Key Stage 3 (e.g. Year 7) and introduction of terms
- paired and group images of signals, symbols and signs used in society/daily life – samples presented and responses made
- simple 'set' shared using object and spot light – responses and discussion
- small group activities using images and tableaux – 2 characters, 2 lighting sets, 1 sound effect, 1 prop
- as above but introduce 1 line of script
- performances and responses
- groups give each other constraints in which to work – activity – response – reflection
- sharing tales using objects – group activities – personal histories/tales
- tales dramatised (groups to respond to selected objects) using any selected form
- reflection on interpretations and connections with original stories – evaluation and link to semiotics
- defining the space/focus on genre and story – presentations and responses
- opening and closing lines and images – each group performs to different group.

EVIDENCE OF LEARNING (CREATING, PERFORMING, RESPONDING)

Creating Are students:

- showing understanding of the terms 'semiotics', *'mise-en-scene'* and 'symbol' as they create and write about their scenes?
- able to work within specific constraints themselves to facilitate meaning and devise original drama?
- able to apply different but appropriate constraints to others?

Performing Are students:

- communicating specific meaning through the manipulation of space, objects, voice and sound?
- applying symbols to extend meaning?

Responding Are students:

- showing understanding of semiotics as they respond to their own and each other's work?
- demonstrating understanding of the skills, techniques and conventions used when creating and performing work?

By the end of the unit the students should know and understand:

- the terms 'semiotics' and 'mise-en-scène'
- the use of semiotics to communicate through theatre.

They should be able to:

- manipulate the semiotics of theatre to communicate a specific meaning
- apply symbols in their drama to extend meaning
- set specific constraints for themselves to facilitate meaning and devise original drama
- set appropriate constraints for others to work within.

RESOURCES

- props such as gun, telephone, cuddly animal, teapot, walking stick
- items of costume such as feather boa, bowler hat, wellington boots, plastic mac, dark glasses
- sources for lighting such as overhead spot, floor flood, twinned fresnels, table lamp, torch, plus small range of colour filters
- sound effects – maniacal laughter, aeroplane taking off, opening theme music of BBC news, church bells, lavatory flush and blank tape for students to create and record own sound effect
- single lines of script such as 'So what have you got to say for yourself now?' or 'I won't be a minute'.

COMMENTS/EVALUATION POINTS

Levels 4–8

3.2
Sharpening the dramatic eyesight

Drama is a polysemic art form. That is, it communicates by employing a number of different types of signs. Some of these are auditory, others are visual. The activities and resources introduced in this chapter concern working primarily on the visual dimension of drama. In doing so students will:

- understand that visual texts can carry meaning
- learn how to examine and develop the dramatic potential of visual stimuli
- become progressively able to select and employ visual imagery in their own drama.

Educating the eyesight in terms of teaching students how to interpret what they see can also contribute to the development of verbal literacy and help students structure their drama work more effectively.

1 Introduction

Actors communicate with audiences through an array of visual signals. Their facial expressions, gestures and movements all help build a picture of the character they are playing. But the actor is not alone in this enterprise. The design team's work on costume and make-up will also play a part in creating the character, while set and lighting will help establish a sense of time, place and atmosphere. The ideas in this unit aim to help develop students' understanding of visual imagery and become more selective in their own use of visual signs.

Visual images

Students are usually remarkably good at reading visual images for meaning. Most of them get plenty of practice at it through their engagement with film and television. A focused study of the way visual images communicate usefully links the subject of drama to art and media studies as we try to train our pupils to train their pupils!

Tapping into young people's existing knowledge and experience of visual texts is not a bad way to start. In fact, attending to the development of visual literacy can make a considerable contribution to students' progress with verbal literacy. 'Reading' pictures is just as complicated a thought process as reading words. Margaret Meek (1988), in her important booklet *How Texts Teach What Readers Learn*, offers a persuasive case for the part that illustrations play in learning to read. Her observations about how students are drawn to comics, yet how it is virtually impossible to read a comic to someone out loud, are of particular interest in the discussion about drama's contribution to the development of literacy. As in a performed play, a number of different signs are communicating the narrative and sub-text in a comic. In one frame we may be given what characters are saying (*dialogue*), what they are thinking (*soliloquy, direct address*), a visual representation of the scene (*mise-en-scène*) and often some sort of narrative/contextual guidance in the form of a caption (*stage direction*). Much of the humour arises out of the way these signs are juxtaposed and appear to contradict each other (a form of *dramatic irony*).

● Images as stimuli

Using well composed paintings and photographs as stimuli for drama introduces students to the way space, and the positioning of characters in that space, generate and convey meaning. This is called *proxemics*.

Starting with visual images can also serve as an introduction to somatics with older students. By working somatically, that is, from physical exteriors inwards, rather than from the conscious outwards, students become able to engage their emotional responses more directly and this can result in powerful creative work. This technique was used and developed by Stanislavski in his later work and the dynamics generated in such work has proved an effective way of motivating students to write.

As with most of the other ideas in this book, the activities outlined below could be used in isolation in order to introduce students to a particular skill, but are likely to be of greater value when they are tied into a more coherent developmental process.

❷ Exercising the eyes

A number of games have tremendous potential for illustrating how some of the elements of drama work can make a considerable contribution to the enhancement of performing skills. Rather than leaving this learning to chance, it is helpful if teachers choose games carefully and make the purpose of playing them explicit to the students. It is especially useful to encourage the students to reflect on the dynamics of a game and try to make links to what they know about the art form of drama.

Dracula

1 The teacher (Dracula), stands in the middle of the circle and starts to walk slowly and threateningly towards a student (A). The student must make and hold eye contact with a second student (B) standing opposite.

2 B must then say A's name aloud before Dracula gets to them. B then becomes Dracula's victim, and Dracula starts to approach them slowly and threateningly.

3 If Dracula reaches a victim before they have made eye contact with someone who says their name, then that student becomes Dracula.

It is important that no one talks in this game other than when saying someone's name: communication must be through eye contact alone. The way this occurs should be the focus of some reflection on the dynamics and effect of the game.

 Angels, devils and peasants

1 The class is broken down into three groups. Each group is asked to construct an image of angels, devils or peasants (or whatever suits the drama they happen to be working on).

2 Each group then teaches their image to the other two.

3 When the class know how to make all three images, each group secretly decides which of the three they will show. The teacher counts to three and every group simultaneously shows their chosen image. Are they all the same? If not, they must try again. The aim is to get the three groups choosing and showing the same image, thereby demonstrating that they are in perfect harmony with each other and can now start on the real work.

This is a variation of the popular children's game 'Paper, scissors or stone?' It demands that the students look very carefully at each other's images and be able to react to them quickly and accurately.

 The window dresser

1 The group work in pairs, imagining that they are on different sides of a plate glass window. One student (A) is given a message by the teacher which they must convey to their partner (B) through action alone. Messages might include:

• You are wearing my shoes.

• Would you like to make a date with me?

- Go home! Your house is on fire!
- Where can I catch the bus to the zoo?
- Help! There is a lion coming down the street!

2 When B has understood the message they are given a message to communicate to A.

This activity demands clear and economical signing by use of gesture, expression and mime – frantic arm-waving and distorted mouthing of words looks pretty funny for a moment or two but ultimately fails to communicate effectively.

Rodin and Co.

1 One student adopts a curious position on the floor. The rest of the students are invited to put a title to this 'statue'.

2 The first student to do so goes and joins the statue, thus changing the impact of the image. What is an appropriate new title?

3 Again, a student suggests something and joins the statue, which will again change its dynamics or mood. What is the title now?

4 As a variation, groups might be asked to re-sculpt images so that by making very small but significant changes to the positions and gestures of those in the statue, the image can be changed to one that is, for example, comical, frightening or sad.

- One extension task would be to ask students to use tableaux to represent various well known locations – Berlin, London, Paris, New York. They may show either the people in the place or, better still, the place itself.
- Further interesting work can arise from asking groups to consider abstract concepts visually: one way to start is to ask them to show, in small groups, emotions such as love, hate or fear.
- Groups can be encouraged to move away from naturalistic depictions by finding ways of showing ambiguous concepts such as 'electricity', 'freedom', 'time' or, with more experienced groups, dramatic concepts such as 'tension' or 'irony'.

In these activities students are encouraged to work in an abstract way rather than through the sort of simple miming and gesturing generated in 'The Window Dresser'. The work helps students to appreciate how meaning may be conveyed through physical and visual images.

The sound maze

This can be an interesting extension of 'Rodin and Co.', which starts to link visual images to their aural counterpart.

1 The students are asked to use their bodies to make a maze representing a given location – ideas that work particularly well are *'the jungle'*, *'the undersea world'*, *'the haunted house'* and so on – anywhere which implies easily identifiable sounds.

2 All the students must be physically linked together, and must make the appropriate sounds. Encourage them to use as wide a variety of shapes as they can, creating arches, obstacles and tunnels.

3 One, or perhaps two, students are fed into the maze with their eyes closed; their task is simply to explore the different routes through the bodies.

4 The aim of those making the maze is to give those exploring it a really interesting sensual experience that generates a vivid mental picture of the location.

Soundscapes can be inspired by, or used to add an aural dimension to, a given visual stimulus such as *The Harpies in the Wood* by Gustave Doré (opposite). Try using this picture with a whole class. While most of the group find a way of representing the harpies, two students walk through them as though they are the couple in the background. The picture raises many questions: who is this couple? Where have they come from and where are they going?

Many of Doré's engravings of London street scenes are similarly very evocative of character and situation.

'Harpies in the wood' by Gustave Doré

▶ The blindfold tour

Clearly establishing a sense of place is a powerful prerequisite for many dramas, whether they are driven by role-play or scripts. This activity illustrates to students how they can successfully build up a distinct mental picture of a location which can then be drawn on to give a sense of dimension and context to a performance. In the activity the students work in pairs.

1　A is taking a blind person, B, on a tour of a fictitious location by gently guiding them around with one hand on their shoulder. The tour may be of Hamlet's castle at Elsinore, a haunted house or the ruins of a devastated town – whatever suits the drama they are to work on.

2　B's eyes must be kept tightly shut throughout the activity.

3　A starts the activity by describing where they are going; B tries to establish as much detail as possible:

> A　We are walking down a street. It seems deserted . . .
>
> B　Are there any signs of human life here?
>
> A　Yes. There is an empty pram just to your right. Underneath it is a discarded shoe.
>
> B　What about the buildings in this street? Are they houses or offices?
>
> A　They are houses. Some are boarded up. Others seem to be burned out.

- A similar device may be used to build a mental image of a character. One student may, for example, imagine that they are a police artist taking details and helping a partner recall exactly what somebody looked like, what they were wearing and how they moved and spoke.

❸ Creating visual narratives

Freezing a moment in a drama or working towards capturing an idea in a visual image demands a careful selection of what is most appropriate and effective. Interpreting still images provides opportunities for assessing how critically and imaginatively students are responding to what they are seeing. Simply creating still images for their own sake does not necessarily challenge students or lead them on to seeing the visual elements of drama in context. However, it is not too difficult to move swiftly on from the single still image into creating and reading new dramatic narratives.

Cartoons and photo-stories

One way of getting students to appreciate how visual narratives work is to take a comic book story or a photo-story from a teenage magazine, blank out all the writing and cut the individual frames out.

1 Students work in pairs or small groups to re-assemble the story by reading the visual clues alone.

2 To develop from this point, take just a few frames from a teenage photo-story in which the speech balloons have been blanked out. Groups are asked to adopt the poses of the characters in the frames and speculate what the dialogue might be.

3 The sequence of still images is animated with the speech balloons and thought bubbles being voiced.

4 Share some examples of the work and encourage the students to reflect on the way groups used different elements of the visual text to construct a verbal narrative.

The aim of this activity should not be to see which groups come closest to matching the original, but to encourage the students to formulate a rational explanation for why they have constructed the narrative in the way they have. Therefore, when groups have finished re-assembling the frames, ask them to link with another group and compare the results, explaining to each other the decisions they made.

3-frame stories

This is an extremely useful and flexible strategy that can be introduced to new students, developed through Key Stage 3 and employed very effectively as a part of the devising process at GCSE and A level.

1 Small groups are asked to show a tableau that fits a given title, for example, 'The Accident'.

2 A second image is made which illustrates the scene immediately before the accident and a third tableau shows what the next significant scene was after the accident.

3 The students are then given two tasks:

a) Find a way of moving quickly and effectively from one tableau to the next in chronological sequence.

b) Add a defined number of speech balloons and thought bubbles to each scene (it is best to keep the number quite small).

4 This activity can be extended by setting the students the task of making a simple storyboard for a photo-story of the three tableaux. Depending on the age and ability of the group the number of frames can be varied, although ten frames will be more than enough to illustrate how visual narratives can be structured.

5 From this concrete beginning, students can be asked to realise their stories through movement and voice, or to use cameras to shoot their sequences. Speech balloons and thought bubbles can be pasted on the developed photographs and the stories displayed on the classroom wall.

The purpose of this kind of activity is to introduce students to the skills involved in making simple linear narratives and using dialogue economically. There is a wonderful opportunity here to use information communication technology (ICT) in the context of drama. By capturing the photo-stories in a digital camera the images can be enhanced and edited electronically and speech balloons and so on added through the use of a computer.

❹ Canvas to characters

By focusing on the characters shown in pictures, attention can be drawn to sub-text and irony in the juxtaposition of what is, perhaps, being said aloud or thought and what is happening physically.

The Merry Wives of Windsor by Henry Fuseli

1 In pairs or small groups, the students take a close look at *The Merry Wives of Windsor* by Henry Fuseli (page 97) and share their initial responses to it.

2 Ask the class to formulate some questions about the picture – not answers, just questions, for example:
  • Who are these people?
  • What is their relationship?
  • What appears to be going on?
  • What is the tone and mood of the picture?

3 Developing the 3-frame story device, small groups create two brief scenes, one illustrating why this chap is struggling with a laundry basket and the second showing what they think happens next.

4 The task is made more challenging by insisting that when the three frames are put together it must be absolutely clear to an audience who these people are and what their relationship is. Fun can be had by adding speech balloons and thought bubbles to the visual images.

It would be appropriate to expect older students to construct and perform the emerging narrative in a way that matches the period and style of the painting. The work thus becomes an introduction to genre. What sort of mannerisms and voices, for example, would seem to be appropriate for these particular characters? What visual clues are the students identifying in order to arrive at such conclusions?

'The Merry Wives of Windsor' by Henry Fuseli

- **Further ideas for character work**

There is an endless supply of character pictures in newspapers and colour supplements. Finding ones which have real potential for drama is not that easy, although looking for them makes for an interesting and useful research task for GCSE students, who need to be able to spot the dramatic potential of a range of resources. Some pictures just seem very evocative and seem to have a special enigmatic quality. Students may well find that an Edward Hopper painting has more impact than something taken from *Hello!* magazine.

'Are we planning a new deal for youth?' by Bill Brandt, 1943

Section 3 ● Progression in practice

Old photographs, such as the one opposite can have a magical value, particularly if they are loose. The group can be asked to imagine what memories might be attached to the picture, where the photo might be found and who might own it. By activating the students' own ability to question and speculate, a plethora of scenes and stories can be developed from a simple resource.

▶ Photos in the news

1 Working in small groups, students select a character from a collection of actual photographs and briefly discuss:
   * who the person might be
   * what other people might think of them
   * what thoughts or spoken words might be implied by the picture.
2 The group are given the information that the picture has been shown on nationwide news. Why? They devise and present the news report.

⑤ Drawing out the dialogue

▶ The Return of the Hunters by *Pieter Bruegel*

1 Project an overhead transparency of the picture (page 100) on a screen, or hand out hard copies to pairs of students.
2 Get each of the students to assume the position of someone or something in the picture.
3 In their pairs, they must now generate four lines of dialogue which will, when set with the visual image, make it absolutely clear to an audience who or what they are.
4 An alternative is to use the four lines of dialogue as the basis for a longer spontaneous improvisation.

This activity can be used to introduce the idea of personification; many students will choose, for example, to be the birds or dogs – good! If they do this they will be demonstrating their ability to move away from televisual naturalism and begin to see the dramatic, and often comical, possibilities of working in the abstract and absurd. Encourage the whole class to look for such possibilities and allow them to improvise dialogue more freely in order to see how new insights and perhaps humour may be extrapolated from taking an unexpected perspective on a stimulus.

'The Return of the Hunters' by Pieter Bruegel

⑥ Structuring a unit of work around a visual stimulus

Drama is as much a visual art form as it is a verbal one. Progression in drama therefore implies that as students move through a drama course they will become more sophisticated in their ability to respond to the visual elements of the art form. This will involve:

* spotting the dramatic potential of a visual stimulus
* 'reading' visual images for narrative
* identifying the symbolic value of visual images.

In their own work on creating and performing drama, students should become progressively better able to craft visual images which communicate meanings. This involves:

* positioning bodies and objects in a space significantly
* using light and colour to suggest or highlight meaning
* using gesture and physical expression with accuracy
* drawing on cultural context in order to give the image greater resonance (for example, making an ironic statement by positioning characters in such a way that an audience is reminded of a famous painting).

'Freeze-framing' a piece of improvised drama or a rehearsal of a scene to inspect in close detail how characters' positioning and gesturing add to the meaning helps students focus on new aspects of their work by making the implicit explicit. Similarly, setting the task of crafting a still image in order to convey a specific message can focus attention on the symbolic value attached to space and gesture. However, while 'living pictures' (or *tableaux vivants*' to give them their original theatrical name), were at one time a popular form of entertainment (see page 159), it is more usual now to use the still image as a means of achieving insights which will move the participants and audience on to something else.

The unit described here seeks to demonstrate how pictures tell stories and how drama is made more effective when its visual aspect is handled with care.

The Rime of the Ancient Mariner by Samuel Taylor Coleridge, illustrated by Gustave Doré

1 Warm-up activities for this work could include: 'Dracula' (page 90; adapted to suit the context of the poem) and 'Angels, zombies and mariners' (adapted from 'Angels, devils and peasants', page 90).

2 The teacher projects some of Doré's engravings on an overhead or video projector. While the class are looking at these it is helpful to tell them the basic story of the Ancient Mariner. It may be that this unit can be paralleled to a study of the poem in English.

3 The students are encouraged to consider the responses the scene suggests to the senses, for example, a door handle covered in barnacles, slimy seaweed clinging to a rope, the eerie lapping of water against creaking boards.

4 They then work in pairs; one closes their eyes while their partner carefully leads them on a tour of an imaginary deserted ship.

5 The pairs return to the circle and share what they have seen, heard, felt and smelt.

6 The class brainstorm words which suit the mood and atmosphere of the images shown on the projector and which they brought back from the drama activity.

7 The whole class work on creating a soundscape to fit one of the images, for example the one which accompanies the lines:

> They groaned, they stirred, they all uprose,
> Nor spake, nor moved their eyes:
> It had been strange, even in a dream
> To have seen those dead men rise.

The helmsman steered, the ship moved on;
Yet never a breeze up-blew!
The mariners all 'gan work the ropes,
Where they were wont to do:
They raised their limbs like lifeless tools –
We were a ghastly crew.

8   The class add movement to the soundscape. Using studio lighting and videoing the effect can serve as a very helpful focus for reflective discussion on this activity.

9   The students work in groups. Each group is given a different engraving to which to add sound and movement. The idea of a 'movement system' may usefully be introduced here so that each group's sequence can be replayed over and over in a machine-like way. This can be achieved by asking the students to choose just three key positions or physical attitudes based on the stimulus, then to find a simple way of moving from one to the other. After making the third image they move back to the first.

10 Each group experiments with ways of using a plain white sheet to capture an element of their resource image, for example suggesting the albatross, the 'Life in Death' character or the movement of waves, sails or clouds.

11 Short extracts of the poem are handed out to each group. The students can use these to accompany their visual images or as the basis of their own short dialogue sequences.

12 Working in the same groups, students discuss how symbols and imagery capture the essence of what artists, writers and directors want to communicate. A representative from each group provides feedback on their discussion.

Rather than seeing and discussing each group's piece in turn, it is more effective to run the scenes in sequence. Again using studio lighting and videoing the outcome will add an extra dimension and encourage the students to regard the work as a piece of theatre rather than a time-filling activity.

---

13 Further progression may be made by introducing the class to Michael Bogdanov's play version of the poem (pages 106–9). In groups the students rehearse a chosen (or given) scene focusing on the visual imagery.

The spectre-woman and her Death-mate on the skeleton ship, from 'The Rime of the Ancient Mariner' illustrated by Gustave Doré

The bodies of the ship's crew rose up and worked the ropes, from 'The Rime of the Ancient Mariner' illustrated by Gustave Doré

A spirit plagued them 'nine fathom deep', from 'The Rime of the Ancient Mariner' illustrated by Gustave Doré

A strange sound is heard.

SAILOR 3	A little speck,
ANCIENT MARINER	And then it seemed
SAILOR 5	A mist;
SAILOR 4	It moves, it moves,
ANCIENT MARINER	And took at last A certain shape
YOUNG MARINER	I wist.
SAILOR 1	A speck,
SAILOR 2	A mist,
SAILOR 3	A shape
YOUNG MARINER	I wist! And still it neared and neared: As if it dodged a water-sprite, It plunged and tacked and veered, With throats unslaked, with black lips baked, We could not laugh or wail; Through utter drought all dumb we stood! I bit my arm, I sucked the blood And cried A sail! A sail!
ANCIENT MARINER	With throats unslaked, with black lips baked, Agape they heard me call:
YOUNG MARINER	Gramercy! they for joy did grin, And all at once their breath drew in, As they were drinking all.
SAILOR 4	See! See! She tacks no more! Hither to work us weal;
SAILOR 5	Without a breeze, without a tide, She steadies with upright keel!

ANCIENT MARINER	The western wave was all a-flame.
	The day was well nigh done!
	Almost upon the western wave
	Rested the broad bright Sun;
YOUNG MARINER	When that strange shape drove suddenly
	Betwixt us and the Sun.

Back light. Shadow of strange rib-shape boat is seen on the sail.

ANCIENT MARINER	And straight the Sun was flecked with bars,
SAILOR 3	Heaven's Mother send us grace!
ANCIENT MARINER	As if through a dungeon-grate he peered
	With broad and burning face.
YOUNG MARINER	Alas!
ANCIENT MARINER	Thought I, and my heart beat loud
YOUNG MARINER	How fast she nears and nears!
SAILOR 2	Are those her sails that glance in the Sun
	Like restless gossameres?
SAILOR 5	Are those her ribs through which the Sun
	Doth peer, as through a grate?
SAILOR 4	And is that Woman all her crew?
SAILOR 3	Is that Death?
SAILOR 2	And are there two?
SAILOR 1	Is Death that Woman's mate?

From back slowly comes the Death boat. It is a skeletal boat with a ribbed mast with scraps of tattered sail. DEATH *is a skull in black and the* WOMAN *is in white.*

SAILOR 4	Her lips are red,
SAILOR 3	Her looks are free,
SAILOR 1	Her locks are yellow as gold:

SAILOR 2	Her skin is as white as leprosy,
YOUNG MARINER	The nightmare Life-in-Death is she, Who thicks man's blood with cold.
ANCIENT MARINER	The naked hulk alongside came, And the twain were casting dice;

DEATH *throws dice six times, pointing to a* MARINER *after each throw, save the sixth. The shaking of the dice is like a death-rattle.*

WOMAN	The game is done! I've won, I've won!
ANCIENT MARINER	And then she whistles thrice.

Three strange whistling sounds which pain the MARINER'S *ears.*

ANCIENT MARINER	The Sun's rim dips; the stars rush out: At one stride comes the dark; With far-heard whisper, o'er the sea, Off shot the spectre-bark.

The boat slides off in a burst of blinding white light.

We listened and looked sideways up!
Fear at my heart, as at a cup,
My life-blood seemed to sip!
The stars were dim, and thick the night.
The steerman's face by his lamp gleamed white;
From the sails the dew did drip –
Till clomb above the eastern bar
The hornéd Moon, with one bright star
Within the nether tip.

One after one, by the star-dogged Moon,
Too quick for groan or sigh,
Each turned his face with a ghastly pang,
And cursed me with his eye.

Four times fifty living men,
And I heard nor sign nor groan,
With heavy thump, a lifeless lump,
They dropped down one by one.

DEATH removes souls symbolically. An effect must be found for the souls to fly up.

> The souls did from their bodies fly –
> They fled to bliss or woe!
> And every soul it passed me by,
> Like the whizz of my cross bow!

Break back to present, dancing, music etc. A repeat of the ghostly celebration. Up stage centre where boat was seen, WEDDING-GUEST appears.

WEDDING GUEST   I fear thee, ancient Mariner!
I fear thy skinny hand!
And thou art long, and lank, and brown,
As is the ribbed sea-sand.

I fear thee and thy glittering eye,
And thy skinny hand, so brown –

ANCIENT MARINER   Fear not, fear not, thou Wedding-Guest!
This body dropt not down.

YOUNG MARINER   Alone, alone.

ANCIENT MARINER   All, all alone,
Alone on a wide wide sea!
And never a saint took pity on
My soul in agony

The many men, so beautiful!
And they all dead did lie:
And a thousand thousand slimy things
Lived on; and so did I.

The Ancient Mariner by Michael Bogdanov

Unit planning sheet for drama

Unit title 'The Rime of the Ancient Mariner'   **Time scale** 4 × 50 minutes or 3 hrs 20 mins

AIMS

- to identify, explore and realise the dramatic potential of a visual stimulus
- to consider how images can be translated through different art forms

SUGGESTED ACTIVITIES

- introductory practical activities such as 'Dracula', ('Albatross'), and group work images of angels, zombies and mariners – focus on gesture and facial expression
- 'The Rime of the Ancient Mariner' read and studied in English lessons in parallel with drama
- class recap on 'story'
- paired activity – 'blindfold' tour of ship, focusing on atmosphere – use of senses
- images of Gustave Doré's illustrations of 'The Rime of the Ancient Mariner' shared through OHT or as copies – discussion in pairs on mood and atmosphere – feedback including focus on why these have dramatic potential
- introductory taught work on creating sound collage/soundscapes
- students in groups to create soundscape using movement and sound that reflects selected engraving
- sample group soundscapes shared.
- responses and evaluation to identify whether mood/atmosphere of engraving is communicated
- extract of two verses of poem shared
- whole-class discussion on which lines of text portray strongest visual images and why
- small-group improvisation using thoughts in heads of mariners
- movement system – individual then group activity using written text as stimulus; create 3 images that are repeated – experiment and rehearsal
- teacher demonstration using sheet to capture element within text – wind/waves etc.
- group discussion on key words that are visualised in image and discussion on key colour of mood
- discussion recap on earlier Y7 work on using symbols – link of symbols and imagery
- group activity using sheet, movement, sound to create one aspect/element that represents poem – rehearsal
- work of all groups performed with chosen studio lighting and key words identified – related to evaluation

EVIDENCE OF LEARNING (CREATING, PERFORMING, RESPONDING)

Creating Are students:
- realising the dramatic potential of the visual and written texts?
- using sound and visual images to present their own interpretation and personal responses?

Performing Are students:
- identifying how cultural connections can be translated in different forms?
- using gesture and facial expression to communicate specific meaning?
- communicating the mood and atmosphere of the visual and written text?

Responding Are students:
- able to read the symbols/visual images?
- making connections between the three art forms?

By the end of the unit the students should know and understand:
- what gives a visual stimulus dramatic potential
- how visual effects can be used as symbols
- how cultural connections can be translated in different forms.

They should be able to:
- read visual images for narrative
- use gesture and physical expression with insight and imagination
- use sound and visual images to present feelings and responses in drama
- communicate the mood and atmosphere of the text.

RESOURCES

- 'The Rime of the Ancient Mariner' by Samuel Taylor Coleridge
- selection of pictures of engravings from Gustave Doré's engravings illustrating 'The Rime of the Ancient Mariner' by Michael Bogdanov
- studio lighting (if studio space available), selection of gels
- 7 white sheets
- video camera, tape and recorder

COMMENTS/EVALUATION POINTS

Levels 3–6

- ensure planning and timing for unit relates to English planned for Year 8
- video recording to be made of final presentations if support staff or post-16 media student available
- extension activity using extracts from Bogdanov's play – focus on visual imagery

Chapter 3.2 ● Sharpening the dramatic eyesight   111

3.3
Working with the voice

The activities and ideas offered in this chapter draw attention to the way in which vocal sounds communicate meaning and develop the students' skills in using their own voices effectively. As they progress in drama, students should:

- understand how meaning is modified by tone, pitch, volume, pace, resonance and timbre
- be able to use their voice to communicate character, mood and sub-text
- be able to realise the dramatic potential of a range of written texts.

Playing with the sounds of words helps students appreciate how written texts are mediated in performance. In this chapter a number of poems are suggested as offering opportunities to develop students' use of voice and further their understanding of texts.

❶ Introduction

The focus of this chapter is on the aural dimension of drama. Regarding drama simply as a sub-section of literature places an undue emphasis on the written word, yet in performance it is the sounds of words that communicate meaning to an audience. What has sometimes been overlooked in the study of dramatic literature is how students can be helped to understand the written word by actually speaking aloud. The practical ideas in this chapter can, of course, be used in the context of English to enhance students' understanding of literature, but more pertinent to the intention of this book is to consider how the sound and rhythm of the voice contribute meaning to the actual choice of words being presented to an audience.

Drama and poetry

Arts philosopher Suzanne Langer once described drama as 'an enacted poem'. By this, she did not mean that drama just involved taking a poem and acting it out: rather, she was describing the way good drama uses verbal and visual language economically in order to attain a symbolic value. The allusion also reminds us of the way drama, like poetry, communicates through metaphor and allegory. In poetry, as in drama, meaning is encapsulated in the relationship between content (what is being said?) and form (how is it being said?).

Without appropriate teacher intervention and left to their ow
devices, students will all too often tend to create drama which
vaguely naturalistic. This is hardly surprising, given that it is t
predominant form of drama they experience on television. By
poems as a stimulus in the drama lesson, students can come to
appreciate the power of economical and rhythmical language. The
relationship between drama and poetry is two-way in that drama
methods may be used to give students an insight into both the
content and form of the poem, or the poem may be used as a stimulus
for creating and performing drama:

Drama methods used
to explore ...   →   Poems   →   ... used to stimulate
drama

The same is true of short stories and other resources, of course. A
number of drama methods can be used to explore the narrative
content of poems and stories and some of these are outlined in
chapter 3.6 (*Telling tales*). Narrative poems such as Gibson's 'Flannen
Isle', Alfred Noyes' 'The Highwayman' or the anonymous 'The Ballad
of Charlotte Dymond' have inherent dramatic qualities in the stories
they tell and make excellent resources for drama work at Key Stage 3.

Other poems can be especially useful for developing and
communicating character: try John Foster's 'Four o'clock Friday' or
Charles Causley's 'Riley' with Years 7 and 8 students. Roger McGough's
'Nooligan' or 'Bestlooking Girl' work well in Year 9 while McGough's
collection of character profiles entitled 'Unlucky for Some' can inspire
tremendously sensitive work and be an economical and effective way
of illustrating sub-text with GCSE groups.

Exploring form and content

Exploring the content of poems and the characters they suggest may
involve using a range of standard drama strategies such as:

- *role on the wall* (page 227) to extend an understanding of the
  characters and their implied relationship with each other
- *hot-seating* to explore the motivation of the characters
- *role-play and improvisation* to explore the events depicted in the
  poem
- *forum theatre* (page 145) to 're-write' the poem in terms of finding a
  more satisfactory outcome for the characters.

A class might also usefully explore how the poet has conveyed the
content through a particular use of form. Practical voice activities can
help students gain a better understanding of:

- alliteration, assonance and dissonance
- rhythm and rhyme
- mood and tone
- diction (that is, the actual choice of words).

Applying a wider range of performance strategies to the poem can make tangible some of the concepts that are often so hard to understand through literary criticism. This is because drama involves physicalising content and form. In so doing, it appeals to the whole gamut of students' learning styles. In addition to serving as a device for supporting the teaching of literature, poems are an invaluable resource for the drama teacher keen to help students develop drama-specific skills. Working with poems provides a focus on:

- effective use of the voice
- selecting visual imagery which complements or productively contradicts what is being said in an ironic way
- economy of imagery.

❷ Warming up the voice

As with other games and warm-ups, most actors, directors, drama teachers and workshop leaders will have a stock of their own favourite ways of preparing the voice. The following are just a few examples.

▶ Exercising lips and tongue

Simply exercising the tongue and lips by rapidly repeating the sounds of consonants and hanging on to the long vowel sounds is very helpful. Ask the students to try sandwiching the different sounds together and paying particular attention to exactly what is involved physically:

```
t t t t t t t t t t t t t t t t t t t t t t t t
o . . . . . . . . . . . . . . . . . . . . . . . . . . . . . . . . .
d d d d d d d d d d d d d d d d d d
u . . . . . . . . . . . . . . . . . . . . . . . . . . . . . . . . .
mmmmmmmmmmmmmmmmmm
ahhhhhhhhhh . . . . . . . . . . . . . . . . .
```

The purpose of this sort of activity is not to move into the realms of elocution in order that the students all learn to 'speak nacely', but it is worth stressing that for an audience to understand what characters in a drama say, they must hear the sounds of vowels and consonants clearly.

Tongue-twisters

As a whole group, recite 'tongue-twisters'. Choose one with a strong rhythm. Keep going through it, varying the volume and pace and perhaps also using a range of stereotypical voices – a priest, a very rich person, a policeman and so on. For example:

> She's the girl that makes the thing
> That drills the hole
> That holds the spring
> That pulls the rod
> That turns the knob
> That works the thingumebob.

Try this one, using a metronome to set the rhythm and pace:

> To sit in solemn silence in a dull, dark dock
> In a pestilential prison, with a life-long lock
> Awaiting the sensation of a short, sharp shock,
> From a cheap and chippy chopper on a big black block!

Or reshape well known tongue-twisters or skipping rhymes into manageable forms which can be sung or rapped as rounds:

> Peter Piper picked
> A peck of pickled peppers
> Where is the peck of peppers
> Peter Piper picked?

Rounds

It is very useful to have a collection of short songs with different tones, which classes can sing in rounds. Once the students feel confident with the words and the tune and can sing the round in four parts, ask them to walk around the space, weaving in and out of each other. This activity develops the ability to concentrate on one's own performance and not be put off by the fact that other people are doing something different. Examples of suitable rounds are:

> My poor bird
> Wing thy flight
> Far across the meadow
> On this dark night.

> I sat next to the Duchess at tea
> It was all that I feared it would be
> Her rumblings abdominal
> Were simply abominable
> And everybody thought it was me!

Groups can have a lot of fun developing their own a cappella rhythms. Standing in a circle, one person starts a vocal rhythm and one by one others join in. The problem with this activity is that sometimes the harmony is so good it's almost impossible to stop!

❸ Finding meaning in rhythm

Simply playing with sounds and rhythms in the way suggested above might be a lot of fun, but unless it is taken further students' understanding of its purpose and relevance to drama is unlikely to develop. Working on a poem which has a particularly strong rhythm can illustrate how meaning is conveyed not only through the semantic meanings of words, but also through the sounds that emerge when they are put in certain sequences. The last line of the much used 'A Case of Murder' by Vernon Scannell is a splendid example of the sounds capturing both visual image and movement:

> There'll not be a corner for the boy to hide
> When the cupboard swells and all sides split
> And the huge black cat pads out of it.

W. H. Auden's poem 'Night Mail' similarly combines words to reflect image and action:

> This is the Night Mail crossing the Border,
> Bringing the cheque and the postal order,
>
> Letters for the rich, letters for the poor,
> The shop at the corner, the girl next door.

▶ Choral work

A poem such as 'Night Mail' can be used as an introduction to choral work:

1 The class are divided into groups, some of which are given different sections of the poem to rehearse. They can choose to have some lines spoken by an individual or by pairs of voices, while others are spoken by the whole group: each group's decision should be governed by what seems to its members to best convey the meaning of the line.

2 Other groups, perhaps just two, are set the task of devising *a cappella* rhythms to capture the sound of a steam train.

3 After a short amount of rehearsal time, the teacher 'conducts' a whole-class rendition of the poem by gesturing when different groups should start their verse. The *a cappella* groups can keep their rhythm going the whole time to underscore the reading and be brought up in volume between verses.

This activity may sound a little bizarre but it is an enjoyable way of discovering how important it is to attend to the rhythm of lines in performance.

④ Sounds to scenes

● Making sense of sounds

Simply attending to the sounds of words and the way whole lines run together can help students make sense of them far more quickly than trying to give lengthy explanations of their semantic meaning. For example, ask a class to say aloud any words they can think of that start with the letters SN. Ask them to move around the room saying their chosen words to each other with as much feeling as they can. Encourage them to watch as well as listen and be attentive to what they themselves are doing as they say SNEER, SNOT, SNITCH, SNIVEL. Do they notice how many words there are starting with SN that are to do with the nose? And what have SNAKE, SNUGGLE and SNOG got in common? An awareness of what happens to one's face when emoting these words demonstrates the relationship between the speaker's physicality and the meaning of the words.

Working with words in this way is tremendously helpful when introducing Shakespeare to students. Many a fine play has been killed stone dead by a teacher intent on interrupting a reading after virtually every word to explain what it all means. Better by far just to read longer sections aloud, emphasising the actual sounds being made and then discuss in general terms what seems to be the nub of the piece. For example, consider this extract from *Hamlet*:

1   Sleeping within my orchard,
    My custom always of the afternoon,
    Upon my secure hour thy uncle stole
    With juice of cursed hebona in a vial,
5   And in the porches of my ears did pour
    The leperous distilment; whose effect
    Hold such an enmity with blood of man

That swift as quicksilver it courses through
The natural gates and alleys of the body,
10   And with sudden vigour it doth posset
And curd, like eager droppings into milk,
The thin and wholesome blood. So did it mine.

Reading this passage aloud and simply listening to the sounds of the words and noting where the pauses are reveals a lot about what is happening. Notice the ponderous rhythm of the first two lines compared to the sense of creeping step by step in line 3. More impressive still is the way the effect of the poison is described in one long breath – you simply have to read it quickly or die from lack of oxygen! Phrases such as 'swift as quicksilver' slip off the tongue whereas 'posset and curd, like eager droppings' seems to send the whole face into a paroxysm; the line neither sounds nor looks very nice. (After working on this speech a 10-year-old boy answered the vague question 'What's going on here?' with the immortal line, 'Well, I don't know what cursed hebona is but it does horrible things to you and it does them very fast.' What more do you need to know?)

▶ **The caravan**

One way of getting students to trust their own ability to make sense out of sound is to work on poems such as 'Karawane' by the Dadaist poet Hugo Ball (page 119). At first they will see only nonsense but by speaking the imaginary language aloud and being guided by the typography, sense will emerge.

1   The poem is handed out and read aloud by the teacher in as neutral a voice as possible. The students suggest how the different typefaces may suggest tone and volume. They should also consider how the punctuation and sounds of words might suggest mood.

2   The class work in groups of five or six. The students are encouraged to read the poem aloud several times over, commenting on the others' delivery. It is very important that they do not add to or change the lines, but concentrate on trying to read the words phonetically.

3   The next step is to contextualise the piece. The clue here is in the title, so ask the students to suggest situations connected with a desert caravan. For example, riding in the heat of the day; loading up the camels in the morning after a night in the open, saddle-sore and sitting around a camp fire. Having discussed the context, each group considers the different sorts of characters suggested by the lines and 'casts' the text accordingly.

4 The students rehearse the scene. The lines must be spoken in the order in which they are printed. The situation being conveyed must be absolutely clear, as must the relationships between the different characters.

This lesson gives students valuable insights into the relationship between the sounds of words and their potential meanings. Moreover, it demonstrates how, in drama, the printed words must be interpreted into action and how such interpretation can never be finite. In a different vein, this same poem can be used as an introduction to, and illustration of, 'grum-a-lot', the improvised language of commedia dell'arte.

If each group has chosen a different context it may be worth seeing all the scenes, in order to illustrate and discuss how completely new meanings were ascribed to the same starting point. However, it should be remembered that watching more or less the same scene six times over can be tedious and is not an effective use of limited time.

KARAWANE
jolifanto bambla ô falli bambla
grossiga m'pfa habla horem
égiga goramen
higo bloiko russula huju
hollaka hollala
anlogo bung
blago bung
blago bung
bosso fataka
ü üü ü
schampa wulla wussa ólobo
hej tatta gôrem
eschige zunbada
wulubu ssubudu uluw ssubudu
tumba ba- umf
kusagauma
ba - umf

'*Karawane*' by Hugo Ball

Sound effects

The text below was originally presented as a monologue with a pre-recorded background soundtrack. A lot of fun can be had by playing with the text as a whole class or in small groups. In essence, the work is simply an activity in animating a story through a variety of aural devices. The students need to identify every possible opportunity for providing their own background noises while one person (possibly the teacher in the first instance) reads the text. By focusing on effective use of tone, volume, pitch and pace of voice as they rehearse the piece, students can reflect further on how meaning is dependent on content and form. Techniques such as the line story (see page 182) can also be employed to develop the text into a very entertaining piece of theatre.

EXTRACT

Toby Farnham, crouched over the wheel of his TR 2, was not enjoying the ride. Visibility was down to a few yards as the fog arched its back against the windscreen like a fat grey weasel. Outside a distant church clock chimed midnight but the only sound he could hear was the steady hum of his finely tuned engine and the incessant swish of the windscreen wipers. He'd never make London at this rate.

'What a damned fool I've been,' he muttered to himself, 'I should have left hours earlier.'

In an attempt to dispel his gloom, Toby switched on the car radio. His mind drifted back to the weekend he'd just spent. Houseparty at the Hursts'. Boring old lot, except for Jilly, she'd brightened it up no end. He whistled, almost contentedly. Suddenly, and without warning, the car spluttered to a halt. He cursed softly to himself.

'Running out of petrol at this time of night! In filthy weather and in the middle of nowhere! What foul luck!'

He switched off the ignition, the windscreen wipers and the radio. Rather than sit all night imprisoned in his car he decided to brave the elements for a while in the hope of finding a garage, even a farmhouse. Anything. He took a deep breath and got out.

The fog leapt upon him, its paws on his shoulders, clinging to him, pushing its cold tongue into his nose and ears. He stumbled on blindly.

'What a pea-souper!'

The only sounds he could hear were his own muffled footsteps and the occasional hoot of a distant owl. He was just on the point of giving up and resigning himself to a lonely night in the car when straight ahead he could dimly make out the blurred outline of a building. Too big for a farm house. Manor house more likely, even some sort of a church. No lights on anywhere.

He groped along the outside looking for an entrance. He found it. A heavy wooden door slightly ajar. Putting his left shoulder to it, he pushed and pushed. It creaked slowly open.

He was in just in time when the door clanged shut behind him. Strangely, there was no handle on the inside. It was pitch black and wherever he was, he was locked in. He cursed softly to himself.

Unable to see anything in the eerie blackness he shuffled forward like a blindfolded two year old wearing his father's shoes. His left elbow brushed against something cold and hard. And then he heard it. The laughter, cruel, bloodcurdling. He turned around and as he did collided with what seemed like a column. A werewolf howled. He turned and ran. Footsteps echoed after him. Thunder rumbled all around. The wind roared. He crashed into a wall. There could be no escape. In his mind's eye, he saw the thing coming towards him. Half man, half beast, half pissed. Panic stricken, he dug his fingernails into the wall. A headless rider on a ghostly horse galloped into view followed by a horde of Indians hotly pursued by the 14th Cavalry, the 7.55 to St Pancras . . .

Hands over his ears he screamed, 'Stop, stop, stoppppp!'

And that was how they found him next morning, dead, in the sound effects department of Broadcasting House . . .

'FX' by Roger McGough

5 Voice characterisation

Poems such as the one below offer younger students the opportunity to play with their voices and bodies to convey character and situation. It is important that teachers read new texts like this aloud to a class. Students need to become familiar with the content of the poem or story without being distracted or worried by words they are unable to read fluently for themselves: the object is to provide a text for drama rather than test of literacy. The learning outcomes in this instance are to do with the effective use of voice to convey character. Teachers need, of course, to be proficient at reading aloud themselves in order to hold the students' attention.

▶ Reading aloud with character

1 Michael Rosen's poem (below) is read aloud to the class and then the students read it through for themselves.

2 In pairs, and taking alternate lines, the students read the poem aloud. Some students will automatically start to put some character into their voices and this should be encouraged. If there is time, it can be useful to invite a few pairs to share with the rest of the group the way they read a short section of the poem.

3 In groups of four, one student reads all the narrative lines and the others chorus the lines of direct speech, developing appropriate voices to capture the whining and the boredom of the children.

4 Finally, the students use the poem as a script for a presentation; they may set out chairs like a car and add any sounds and actions they think appropriate, but they must not change or add any lines to the poem.

5 Some students may put too much action and noise into their work with the result that the presentation will be cluttered and chaotic. Draw attention to this and go on to explore possible ways of editing movement and sounds in order to keep the focus more tightly on the original text.

It is rarely a productive use of time to have every single group showing work of this nature. In fact, repeating the same thing over and over becomes tedious for students and teachers alike. In terms of advancing learning it is more useful to watch just one or two groups and invite the rest of the class to comment on how the work compares and contrasts to the way they tackled the task in their group.

EXTRACT

The car trip

1   Mum says:
    'Right, you two,
    this is a very long car journey.
    I want you two to be good.
5   I'm driving and I can't drive properly
    If you two are going mad in the back.
    Do you understand?'

    So we say,
    'OK Mum, OK. Don't worry,'
10 and off we go.

    And we start The Moaning:
    Can I have a drink?
    I want some crisps.
    Can I open my window?

---

15 He's got my book.
    Get off me.
    Ow, that's my ear!

    And Mum tries to be exciting:
    'Look out the window
20 there's a lamp-post.'

    And we go on with The Moaning:
    Can I have a sweet?
    He's sitting on me.
    Are we nearly there?
25 Don't scratch.
    You never tell him off.
    Now he's biting his nails.
    I want a drink. I want a drink.

    And Mum tries to be exciting again:
30 'Look out the window
    there's a tree.'

    And we go on:
    My hands are sticky,
    He's playing with the doorhandle now.
35 I feel sick.
    Your nose is all runny.
    Don't pull my hair.
    He's punching me, Mum,
    that's really dangerous, you know,
40 Mum, he's spitting.

    And Mum says:
    'Right I'm stopping the car.
    I AM STOPPING THE CAR.'

    She stops the car.

45 'Now, if you two don't stop it
    I'm going to put you out the car
    and leave you by the side of the road.'

    He started it.
    I didn't. He started it.

50 'I don't care who started it
    I can't drive properly
    If you two go mad in the back.
    Do you understand?'

    And we say:
55 OK. Mum, OK, don't worry.

    Can I have a drink?

Michael Rosen

6 Ensemble performance

The learning outcomes of ensemble performance concern organising space and considering the needs of an audience in performance.

Playing games

The poem on pages 126–8 is used in conjunction with the painting by Bruegel the Elder (page 125) to create something of an instant performance involving the whole class. Further learning is achieved by reflecting on the combination of words and visual image to convey atmosphere and character. The learning outcomes of ensemble performance concern organising space and considering the needs of an audience in performance.

1 The class look carefully at the picture either on a hard copy or projected through a colour overhead transparency or data projector. They are asked to offer words and phrases which relate to the picture. (This sort of brainstorm can be organised in such a way that their individual first responses become an interesting sound collage in its own right.)

2 Each student assumes the position of a character in the picture (it does not matter if the same figure is chosen by two or more students). The whole class then freezes in their chosen positions.

3 On a given signal, the picture is spontaneously brought to life through movement and sound for about 30 seconds.

4 The students reflect on what was achieved in terms of atmosphere. Some students may have suggestions to make about the depiction that could be used to develop the activity further.

5 Each student is given a verse from the poem about the painting by William Carlos Williams. There are 22 verses, so either some students should be given two to read or some verses will have to be read by more than one voice.

6 The class stand in a circle and rehearse the reading. Each student must make sure they know who speaks before them as they will need to listen out for their cue.

7 The scene is set in motion once more, but with only muted sound; one by one the players freeze and read aloud their verse but then continue to add a quiet background soundscape. By the end of the poem the students should be standing in a tableau akin to the painting; the soundscape fades out.

8 In reflecting on the scene they have created, the students consider this activity as a piece of theatre in its own right and discuss what would be conveyed to an audience through the enactment.

This sort of work is obviously highly orientated towards honing performance skills. Encouraging students to research into the potential of other poems for this kind of treatment, working on them and considering ways of juxtaposing different poems can lead to highly entertaining and often quite moving collages. (It is worth remembering that Andrew Lloyd Webber's Cats *is an example of this sort of work.)*

Videoing work such as this provides a powerful focus for reflective discussion and elicits comments and suggestions which can be used to polish the scene further. It is also useful to remind the students of the words and phrases they started with, and consider the extent to which these were communicated through the use of sound and space.

'*Children's games*' by Pieter Bruegel

Children's Games

i

1   This is a schoolyard
     crowded with
     children

2   of all ages near a village
     on a small stream
     meandering by

3   where some boys
     are swimming
     bare-ass

4   or climbing a tree in leaf
     everything
     is motion

5   elder women are looking
     after the small
     fry

6   a play wedding a
     christening
     nearby one leans

7   hollering
     into
     an empty hogshead

ii

8   Little girls
     whirling their skirts about
     until they stand out flat

9   tops pinwheels
     to run in the wind with
     or a toy in 3 tiers to spin

10   with a piece
      of twine to make it go
      blindman's-buff follow the

11   leader stilts
      high and low tipcat jacks
      bowls hanging by the knees

12   standing on your head
      run the gauntlet
      a dozen on their backs

13   feet together kicking
      through which a boy must pass
      roll the hoop or a

14   construction
      made of bricks
      some mason has abandoned

            iii
15   The desperate toys
      of children
      their

16   imagination equilibrium
      and rocks
      which are to be

17   found
      everywhere
      and games to drag

18   the other down
      blindfold
      to make use of

19   a swinging
      weight
      with which

20 at random
    to bash in the
    heads about

21 them
    Brueghel saw it all
    and with his grim

22 humour faithfully
    recorded
    it

William Carlos Williams

❼ Structuring a unit of work around a poem

Artists, like athletes, employ activities to sharpen their ability to manipulate elements of form. This is why actors undertake voice training. The concern of the drama teacher, however, is not simply to produce actors but also to foster students' wider understanding. Using a poem, or a number of different poems, as the basis of a whole unit of work may provide opportunities for creating, performing and responding to drama. Such a unit can make a substantial contribution to the students' understanding of poetic form and imagery. Interpreting poems through drama can give students new insights into their meaning.

In the work outlined below, two contrasting approaches are made to the same poem, 'Charlotte O'Neil's Song' (page 131). The first and more detailed of the two focuses on exploring the form of the poem. The second considers ways of exploring the content and using the poem as a stimulus for creative extension work.

1   The teacher facilitates a whole-class discussion on the use of the voice, encouraging students to make connections with other work that they have done on this. They are encouraged to make connections with professional performances that they have seen where the voice has been used very effectively.

2   Working individually, students are asked to create some physical images that reflect mood or emotion – fear, joy, despair, excitement. These are done quite quickly and a few are shown, so that the other students can link words to the images.

3   The poem is read aloud and the students given time to read a copy of it for themselves.

4   Working alone or in pairs, students underline any words that they find particularly powerful or interesting (they do not have to know why – maybe they are just attracted to the sound of the words or the mental images they conjure up).

5   The teacher reads the poem through again. This time students echo the words that they have underlined. The group discusses those words that a number of people echoed – what is it about them that had such a wide appeal? If some students were alone in picking out some words they should be encouraged to say what they personally liked about the word(s) as this may give the whole class new insights.

6   Students work in pairs on the first ten lines of the poem. They each take a line in turn, and pretend that they are having a conversation in a certain tone, for example, speaking the lines as if they are:

   - a rap
   - a commercial jingle on radio
   - the message in a cheap birthday card
   - a children's skipping rhyme.

7   Discuss the effect of treating the lines like this. It may have generated laughter – why? The activity illustrates the link between content and form in that it shows that for some words and phrases certain tones of voice are simply not appropriate. What happens to the meaning of the lines when they are 'performed' in this way?

8   The students discuss what an appropriate tone, pitch and pace for a reading of this poem would be. They stand in a circle and each one is given a single line of the poem to remember. They will need a minute or two to practise the line aloud and commit it to memory.

9 The students shut their eyes and, as a group, recite the poem using the pace, pitch, tone and volume they think are appropriate. After going through the whole poem they discuss the effectiveness of speaking the lines and hearing the poem in this way.

10 Working in small groups, the students choose a short sequence of lines for themselves. They then work on an 'appropriate' vocal presentation of the lines, drawing on what they have learned about rhythm, rhyme, choice of vocabulary and tone.

11 The students identify what the strongest visual images were in their chosen section. They may select between one and four. How can these visual images be added to the way they are reading the lines in order to develop the presentation? The project here is to create a visual poem that complements the verbal one.

12 The class share and discuss examples of their work.

A detailed exploration of the form of a poem clearly links work in drama to the project of the English classroom. This kind of practical approach to the way words work can really help students understand literature. However, far from simply putting drama time at the service of another curricular subject, the work has important implications for creating, performing and responding to drama as a subject in its own right.

EXTRACT

From Passengers, Nineteenth-century ship's records

Clara Roskryge, 16, Domestic servant, Cornwall, *Indian Empire* 1864.
Charlotte O'Neil, 17, General servant, Origin unknown. *Isabel Hercus* 1871.
Ann James, 33, Laundress, Abergavenny, *Light Brigade* 1868.
Harriet Attiwell, 20, Domestic servant, Leicestershire, *Cameo* 1859.
Eliza Lambert, 14, Domestic servant, Surrey, *Mystery* 1858.

Charlotte O'Neil's Song

1   You rang your bell and I answered.
    I polished your parquet floor.
    I scraped out your grate
    and I washed your plate
5   and I scrubbed till my hands were raw.

    You lay on a silken pillow.
    I lay on an attic cot.
    That's the way it should be, you said.
    That's the poor girl's lot.
10   You dined at eight
    and slept till late.
    I emptied your chamber pot.
    The rich man earns his castle, you said.
    The poor deserve the gate.

15   But I'll never say 'sir'
    or 'thank you ma'am'
    and I'll never curtsey more.
    You can bake your bread
    and make your bed
20   and answer your own front door.

    I've cleaned your plate
    and I've cleaned your house
    and I've cleaned the clothes you wore.
    But now you're on your own, my dear.
25   I won't be there any more.
    And I'll eat when I please
    and I'll sleep when I please

    and you can open your own front door.

Fiona Farrell

1 In groups, the students go through the poem and pick out any images that occur to them that could be dramatically effective. They jot these down in terms of a 'brief' for a scene:

  - Charlotte O'Neil clearly exhausted by polishing the floor. 'Madam' walks straight in, busily chatting to 'Sir'. They cross the wet floor without noticing Charlotte.

  - 'Madam' is lying in bed while Charlotte clears away her breakfast things. She is lecturing Charlotte on her ideas about the natural order of things.

  Students may improvise their own ideas and it can be useful to pass the briefs on to another group for its comments.

2 Students suggest questions they would like to have answered about Charlotte's life. Why would she have taken such a job? What was her life like before? Later in the poem it is implied that she has left Madam. Why? Where is she now? In groups they improvise short scenes that give possible answers to these questions. Although they can only be speculation, the key question to ask when reviewing them is whether or not they fit the tone and sense of the poem.

3 The poem focuses on two characters. We hear Charlotte's voice, but not Madam's. In pairs, students devise and perform two monologues, one for each character, and experiment with inter-cutting these to create dramatic effect through their contrasting content and tone.

4 Small groups devise a dream sequence in which Charlotte's memories of working in the house come to life and swirl together. The scene should draw on what is actually said in the poem.

5 Students find a variety of objects either explicitly mentioned or suggested in the poem. The objects are placed in the middle of a circle. Each member of the group makes up a line and action that might go with one of the objects and that would fit the content and tone of the poem as well as adding a new insight into why certain memories have stayed with the narrator. The line may be spoken in the voice of the poet or one of the characters implied by the poem. The students take turns to enter the circle and either strike a pose with a chosen object or position themselves in a spatial relationship to it and speak their line.

The poem 'Charlotte O'Neil's Song' suggests a strong character with a story to tell. It is thus ideal for exploring and extending through creative drama work. Students need to be reminded, however, that what is conjured up through their drama is dependent on their interpretation and imagination. For example, they may create a character for Charlotte O'Neil and depict her as a black woman working below stairs in a grand house between the wars. While such a representation may have considerable dramatic potential, it cannot be substantiated by the poem. Nevertheless, some creative drama work can certainly give new insights into how the poem is working by drawing on the relationship between its form and content.

Unit Planning Sheet for Drama

Unit title Working with the voice   **Time scale** 5 × 50 minutes or 4 hrs 10 mins

AIMS

- to enable students to understand more about their voices and to develop skills in using them
- to consider how the writer's intentions can be interpreted in devised drama.

SUGGESTED ACTIVITIES

- whole-class discussion on use of voice – what is a 'good voice' and why? Connections with previous work and any drama activities where the voice has been particularly important. Connections with school dramas, professional theatre, TV and films where voices have been used very effectively, and how they were used
- warm-up activities and games for the voice
- physicalisation of words that reflect mood or emotion (connection with work on signs and symbols – Y7) – fear, joy, despair, excitement etc. in groups – quick responses, presentations and feedback
- introduction and readings of poem 'Charlotte O'Neil's Song' by Fiona Farrell (whole-class activities)
- paired preparation focusing on words that conjure up images or are powerful – shared and discussed
- paired work on first ten lines of poem – pairs to present lines with particular tone and audience in mind
- discussion on effects created and need for connection between form and content – further work on rhythms and rhymes – rap, commercial jingles etc. leading to discussion and experiment of how voice should be used for this poem (tone, pitch, pace, volume)
- small group (5/6) select short extract from poem to prepare and perform vocal presentation, and to present visual image(s) that is/are appropriate to their extract (max. of 4)
- work performed by groups and reflection made on why key words were selected and how they work as images (connect with physical images) – feedback given focusing on effectiveness of work – what it was and how it was achieved plus ideas for improvement
- group work focusing on creation of scenes that are based on specific writing and images within the text and/or other scenes drawn from ideas that are speculative, but must fit the tone and sense of the poem. During preparation, sample groups share pieces and use feedback to inform development of work
- small groups devise dream sequence of Charlotte's memories (again must connect clearly with poem)
- whole-class activity using objects explicitly identified in poem as stimulus for one line and action (again must connect clearly with poem)
- final performances and evaluation on whole unit

EVIDENCE OF LEARNING (CREATING, PERFORMING, RESPONDING)

Creating Are students:
- demonstrating how meaning is modified by tone, pitch, volume and pace as they develop the work?
- able to use selected drama techniques effectively when exploring the sub-text of the poem?
- experimenting with different ways that words can be used to create moods and images?

Performing Are students:
- demonstrating an ability to write and speak or sign so as to convey specific imagery and mood?
- communicating convincing character through using spoken or signed words effectively?
- using their voices/signing effectively to communicate their own interpretation of the poem and its mood and imagery?

Responding Are students:
- articulating understanding of the writer's intentions as they reflect on their own and each other's work?
- using the feedback they are given to develop and improve their work?

Key Stage 3 **Year** 8

INTENDED LEARNING OUTCOMES

By the end of the unit the students should know and understand:
- how meaning is modified by such qualities as tone, pitch, volume and pace of voice
- how words can be written and spoken to convey specific imagery and mood
- how some drama techniques can be used to explore the sub-text of a piece of writing.

They should be able to:
- experiment with different ways that words can be used to create moods and images
- communicate the intentions of the writer through their dramatic interpretation of the poem
- communicate convincing character through the effective use of spoken or signed words.

RESOURCES

- variety of voice exercises
- metronome for voice exercises
- copies (one per pupil) 'Charlotte O'Neil's Song' by Fiona Farrell
- selection of objects mentioned in poem – plate, silk pillow, scrubbing brush, duster, chamber pot

COMMENTS/EVALUATION POINTS

- Levels 4–7
- link with English work for Y8 (prior to poetry unit being introduced in English)
- optional activities which can be developed as part of the unit, if time is available and group would gain from further practical work on this unit

3.4
Discourse in drama

Young children are often characterised by their propensity for asking questions, and it is probably as questioning infants that we learn most rapidly. Questioning is a key skill in learning. In order to progress in drama, students must be enabled to question, discuss and speculate. In this way they will be better able to:

- generate and explore the dramatic potential of new ideas and stimuli
- review the development and effectiveness of their own drama work
- make connections between their personal responses to drama and the wider cultural context in which it is received.

This chapter reviews ways of heightening students' abilities to question in order to progressively deepen their capacity to create, perform and respond to drama.

❶ Introduction

Drama that raises questions is more engaging than drama that is closed in its meaning: considering why Chekhov's three sisters did not go to Moscow is more stimulating than a documentary about what happened when they got there. The quality of students' work in creating, performing and responding to drama is enhanced when teachers develop a better understanding of their own questions and encourage their students to formulate questions for themselves. Arguing against a mechanistic 'back to basics' model of education based on teachers simply transferring their knowledge into students' heads, educationalist Neil Postman (1975) claimed that 'in the development of intelligence, nothing can be more "basic" than learning how to ask questions'.

❷ Developing students' questioning skills

The activities below are simply enjoyable ways of drawing students' attention to the different ways in which questions are asked, and why.

The yes/no game

1 Working in pairs, one student asks a series of quick-fire questions that their partner must answer verbally, without using the words 'Yes or 'No' and without making non-committal sounds. For example:

    A What's your name?

    B Charlotte.

    A What did you have for breakfast?

    B Cereal.

    A And you said your name is Charlotte?

    B I did [*not* Yes].

The aim of the activity is for the questioner to catch their partner out by slipping in questions that would normally require a simple yes/no answer. It is an amusing activity but demands players listen carefully and think quickly.

Who am I?

1 In pairs, one student (A) thinks of a famous person.

2 Their partner (B) must discover who they are by asking a series of questions which lead them to answer the question by a process of elimination.

3 (A) may only answer 'Yes' or 'No' and so the questions must be formulated accordingly.

- A variation of this game is for the teacher to stick the name of a different famous (real or fictitious) character on the back of each member of the class. The students then mill around the room trying to find out who they are; they may only ask each new contact one question.

- The game can also be adapted to suit a particular play, genre or historical period being studied.

● **Questioning to build belief**

A central idea in a good deal of drama is that we '*suspend our disbelief*', that is, we choose to immerse ourselves in the fiction even though we know that it is a fiction. By recognising the students' ability to see something clearly in the mind's eye and appealing to that, the drama teacher can quickly help a class feel and exhibit some degree of commitment to the fictional situation and characters being developed. Here again, questioning can help enhance students' understanding of and ability to manipulate the art form of drama.

Sometimes a series of quick-fire questions may be used to establish a sense of place as the foundation on which a role-play may be built. For example, a drama structure which requires the students to adopt the role of people who might be involved in a police investigation could start with the teacher trying to help the students visualise the scene in the police station by asking a series of short closed questions:

- What colour are the walls?
- Is there anything on the walls?
- What do the posters show?
- Is there a clock? What does it look like?
- What's the floor like?
- Who brought you here?
- Have you been waiting long?

The last two questions move away from establishing a sense of location and on to creating the basis of a character. Developing a character may be facilitated through asking a new series of questions. For example, having been told that they are professionals who sometimes help the police, the students may build a basic character profile for themselves as the teacher asks:

- How long have you been doing your job?
- Is this the first time you have been to this police station?
- What was your last case about?
- What were you doing when the phone rang to ask you here today?

A parallel strategy which very effectively creates a sense of location is 'The blindfold tour' described on page 94.

It is always important, at some point, to make the nature and purpose of these sorts of questions clear to the students themselves so that, when devising their own drama, they are able to use the device for themselves.

- **Hot-seating**

Hot-seating (page 227) is a well known, flexible and enormously useful device which is used extensively by teachers in many subjects. Unfortunately, it can be used quite indiscriminately and all too often its dramatic and educative potential is lost. At its simplest, it can be used to find out obvious details about a character such as their age, job, favourite hobbies and so on. What is more interesting and productive is when the technique is used to create a character from a minimal starting point and questions are formulated which expose actual character traits.

For example, a group might be working on a drama about a runaway girl. Four students take on the roles of the girl's father, mother, sister and boyfriend. These students are given no time to prepare their characters but are immediately exposed to questions from their classmates. The task of the questioners is not to catch the characters out (for example, asking the mother how old the father is and then asking the father how old he is to see if the answers agree), but rather to discover contradictions. Asking the father, for example, if the girl was happy at home may produce a positive answer but when the sister is asked the same question the answer may be negative. It is within these contradictions that a genuine sense of character and a great deal of dramatic potential may develop.

In a similar vein, directing questions to a character from a stated perspective can be revealing: would Hamlet give the same answer to Claudius as he would to Horatio when asked why he was so sad?

❸ Creating drama through questioning

In the structure outlined below the students' ability to formulate questions in order to move the drama forward is extended.

▶ Kaspar Hauser

The dynamics of the unit, built on the 'true' story of the enigmatic Kaspar Hauser, is related to the popular genre of the detective thriller.

1 The class are asked to imagine an archetypal German town of some 200 years ago; the blindfold tour technique (page 94) can be used to build a mental picture of what it would be like there on a busy market day.

2 The teacher directs a series of short, sharp questions to the group or individuals, in order to develop the sense of place and character further.

3 The class improvise the scene in the market-place: some begin to sell things, others to buy; some mime juggling, others pick pockets.

4 The teacher adopts the role of Kaspar Hauser by moving silently into the middle of the space and standing with a bewildered expression, holding an envelope in their hand addressed to 'The Captain of the 4th Squadron, 6th Cavalry Regiment'.

5 Gradually, 'the townsfolk' will begin to be interested in why the teacher is standing like this. In answer to any questions the teacher simply answers 'Don't know' and acts as if they are confused and frightened.

6 After some moments, just long enough to intrigue the class, the teacher drops this role and narrates the story to the class:

26 May 1826 was Whit Monday and the cobbled streets of Nuremberg were alive with people enjoying the annual public holiday. Standing in the square was a young man, perhaps 16 or 17 years old. He was dressed in clothes that had once been of fine quality but were now in tatters. When he moved he did so with stiff, bow legs. His toes stuck out from the ill-fitting boots which had been reinforced with horseshoes and nails. Eventually, it was the local cobbler who approached the staring and bewildered boy. He had very little speech but presented the cobbler with a letter addressed to a cavalry officer stationed in the town. He was taken to the barracks where he began to exhibit strange reactions to his environment. He tried to pick up a candle by its flame and screamed in terror when it burnt him. He was nauseated by the smell of cooking and could only eat bread and drink water.

The cavalry officer could make nothing of the boy or the letter, which requested he be turned into a soldier or hanged. The boy seemed unable to answer any questions with anything other than 'Don't know', yet when given a piece of paper and a pencil he was able to write his name clearly. It was Kaspar Hauser.

7 The students work in pairs. The task is to formulate a series of questions which express their interest in the story by having a discussion which comprises nothing but questions. For example:
   - Who was he?
   - Was Kaspar Hauser his real name?
   - How could we find out?
   - How will we know whether what he says is the truth?

8 Working in groups, the students draw a simple outline figure to represent Kaspar. Inside the figure they jot down what they already know about him. Outside the figure they note down questions that they would like answered. (This is one variation of 'Role on the wall' see page 227).

9 The class discuss who would be in a meeting of Town Councillors to discuss what should be done with the boy; the teacher should help them build a mental picture of the council chamber using a series of short questions such as what would they see, hear, smell and feel in such a place.

10 The students decide who is to be a Town Councillor and who a witness. In pairs, they question each other in order to get a basic sense of their character.

11 The scene shifts to the council chamber.

It is helpful for the teacher to take on the role of the mayor and formally lead the class into the council chamber. Setting up the scene with appropriate pomp and ritual helps to set the tone and build belief. Some teachers feel perfectly comfortable with this kind of role-play. Others take the opportunity to relate the activity directly to theatre presentation by asking the students to imagine that they are in a scene from a play. The suggestion has purpose in that it draws attention to the way performers make decisions in order to gain a particular response from an audience.

Adopting the role of the mayor also allows the teacher to chair the meeting and decide when to bring it to an end, which should be when the teacher feels that the class have raised a sufficient number of questions which now need to be explored in new ways. At that point the witnesses should be hot-seated in an attempt to get to the bottom of the mystery of who Kaspar is.

12 A number of chosen characters are hot-seated. This may be done individually, as if they are giving evidence to the Council, or groups (in role as Councillors) visit four or five other students in role as witnesses, to interview them.

There is no straightforward ending to this drama because no one ever found out for certain who Kaspar Hauser was or where he had come from. One way of tying up this drama project would be to ask students to suggest speculative questions, for example:
* *Was Kaspar Hauser a fraud working alone?*
* *Was he the illegitimate son of a nobleman who needed to be rid of the boy yet wanted to cover his tracks?*
* *Was Kaspar part of a conspiracy? Or part of an elaborate confidence trick?*

13 Having opted for their favoured explanation, small groups prepare their case as if they were lawyers either defending or prosecuting Kaspar Hauser. They then have to defend or prosecute him while the other students cross-examine them.

Exploring the story of Kaspar Hauser in this structured way offers the class a number of opportunities for learning about the way drama becomes interesting when it raises questions for an audience, and how a drama can be structured so that it does this. By way of reflective discussion, students are asked what it is about the story of Kaspar Hauser that gives it dramatic potential. If they were to make a play about the boy, where would they start the story? With his arrival in the town? With his death? (He died after being stabbed. His killer was never found. Some said he stabbed himself in order to stay in the limelight.) Then telling the whole story in flashback? What would make the 'best' sort of play in their eyes? What thoughts and feelings do they suggest it would be worthwhile conjuring up for an audience in a play about Kaspar Hauser?

➍ Questioning to deepen responses in drama

A central tenet of this book is that teachers become better able to plan lessons which move students forward if they have a clear sense of direction and regularly monitor the work in order to evaluate if they are on target. By the same reasoning it makes sense to encourage the students themselves to monitor their own work through asking specific questions, such as:

- What will make a good drama?
- Where is the best point to start to tell the story?
- What should be included and what should be left out?
- What is the real nature of our interest in the story?
- Will an audience share such an interest? If not of their own initial volition, then how shall we capture their interest?
- What do we personally want to say about the story we are telling?
- What models and sources can we draw on to help us tell our story more effectively?

Using questions to understand criteria

Questions help students evaluate their own drama work and drama they see elsewhere, as well as playing a crucial role in helping students develop their own drama work.

I know what I like

1 The teacher gives out two contrasting statements about the same film:
- It was brilliant! Loads of blood and guts. People getting blown up all over place. A fantastic car chase and some really sexy bits!
- It was awful. No story, no characterisation – just a lot of noise and gratuitous sex and violence. Men acting like kids going around bang banging each other. All the women were played as brainless bimbos and a few really tacky sex scenes!

2 The students jot down a list of the kind of ingredients which the films they personally enjoy contain, then compare their list with at least three other students and discuss the following questions:
- Might there be any reasons why they would not enjoy a film even though it had all the ingredients they mentioned?
- How would the company they were in affect their enjoyment of a film which had all the ingredients they liked in it? Would they still be happy to watch a very violent film in the company of young children? How comfortable are they watching 'the mucky bits' when in the company of adults?

Short, focused discussions such as these help students realise how criteria change according to what seems appropriate to the context. Some factors are to do with personal expectations and some are socially contingent. In questioning the appropriateness and effectiveness of any dramatic performance all these things need to be considered.

Reviewing through questioning

There are a number of basic questions that students can be taught to apply to any drama which they experience or are involved in and which will provide them with a foundation on which to build an evaluation. In the case of their own work, addressing such questions as part of the process of creating drama will help pinpoint what needs to be done to develop and polish the work. When students are preparing to watch a piece of drama, simple notes may be made on some of these things before the actual performance of the play even starts.

Title What is the play called? What expectations does this set up for you?

Author Who wrote it? Do you know anything about this writer? If so, does this raise any expectations?

Venue Where is the play being performed? Does this suggest anything about how the play might be done and what sort of audience will be present?

Director and company Are they well known? What other things have they done that you know of? Does the programme give background details?

Date When is the performance? Is this in any way significant?

Some students try to make notes during the play itself, but then they may well miss bits of the play and they certainly fail to really get into the experience it is offering. It is therefore usually more productive to encourage students to use the following checklist as soon as possible after the event, by way of forming the basis of a review.

Staging Was the play presented on a conventional stage? In the round? Amongst the audience?

Set What was the set like? What did it show?

Costume and make-up Were the characters set in some particular period? What colours were used? Were they realistic or in some way strange?

Lighting	Were lights used simply to illuminate the action or were there any special effects?
Sound	Was there any music? Were the sound effects simply functional (for example, doorbells, telephone rings) or were some of them strange in some way?
Acting	Were the actors believable in their roles? Could you hear what they were all saying and see what they were doing clearly? How well did they seem to communicate with you as an individual? Who was the star?
Narrative	What story did the play actually tell? From whose perspective? In what order did the events unfold?
Theme	What sort of issues did the play seem to delve into? Did it seem to give a particular message or focus on any one particular aspect of human existence? Did it try to affect the way you think about things?
Genre	Did the play seem similar in any way to others you know? Is it a comedy, a tragedy, a historical play, a melodrama?
Structure	Did the play follow through a story in sequence or did it seem to jump around? Did it reach a climax at the end or were there a number of moments when the tension was very high? How did the play try to grab the audience's attention?
Characterisation	Which characters did you find most interesting? Were they believable or did they have some other function which has perhaps given you a new insight into something?
Context	What do you know about when the play was written, who wrote it and under what circumstances?

None of this information by itself will make a particularly full or interesting review unless the students add their own personal comments about how these different elements actually affected their enjoyment and understanding of the play. In the context of this chapter, the important point is that students can be helped to acquire the habit of asking key questions of all they do, see and hear in drama.

❺ Structuring a unit of work around forum theatre

Forum theatre is a term which may be used to cover a wide range of activities in drama in which the audience are as actively involved in shaping and questioning the content and form of the work as the performers. The technique is explained fully in Augusto Boal's useful compendium *Games for Actors and Non-Actors*. In essence, 'forum theatre' opens up a scenario for discussion by all those engaged in the experience whether they are active participants or audience. Forum theatre techniques can be used by students as a part of their work in devising or employed as a means of testing solutions to moral dilemmas. Forum theatre is a good way of generating talk to a purpose and gives the English or drama teacher the chance to assess students' abilities in this skill against the Attainment Targets of *Speaking* and *Listening*. With older groups it can also spark discussion regarding the purpose of drama. For example, to what extent should drama be didactic and impose a viewpoint on an audience? Should it rather provoke questions for an audience and instigate a dialogue?

The purpose of the structure outlined below is to introduce students to some of the techniques of forum theatre, use them to create characters and a dramatic situation and to inspect a controversial issue through the emergent drama.

▶ Whose right is it anyway?

1. In preparation for this lesson the class are set a homework task involving collecting newspaper extracts and pamphlets on issues relating to animal rights. These are presented and discussed at the start of the lesson.

2. The students are asked to construct a mental image of a typical chemist's shop window, through a series of belief-building questions.

3. They are told that one night the chemist's shop is the target of animal rights campaigners who spray graffiti on the window.

4. Working in pairs or small groups, the students speculate what sort of slogans might have been sprayed on the window (the teacher might help by suggesting some examples). Ideas are anonymously written or drawn on sheets of card which are then displayed, and the students comment on them in terms of what the slogans suggest about their authors.

5. The teacher narrates how shortly after the attack a teenage girl was arrested for being in possession of a spray can. She admits to being responsible for some of the graffiti, but not all.

6. The class build up a sketch of this character. This can be done via a succession of quick-fire questions from the teacher, hot-seating the teacher or a student in

role or setting up the space as if it were the girl's bedroom and suggesting what sort of things would be found in it.

7 The students suggest a variety of people who would be interested in or affected by the graffiti incident. They adopt the role of any one of these and are invited to formulate a question they wish to ask the perpetrator. Again, this may be realised through hot-seating, or 'staged' as a series of characters asking the unseen teenager the question through the locked bedroom door.

The purpose of the activity is to consider how different characters might phrase the same sort of questions. This leads to a reflective discussion on what sort of tone and attitude are likely to evoke an answer and which a hostile silence.

---

8 The class work in pairs or small groups to create a piece of writing inspired by the graffiti incident. For example:
- a message written by the chemist to customers and pasted on the window next to the graffiti
- the headline and first paragraph of the local newspaper reporting the incident
- a letter in the local newspaper written in support of the sentiments behind the attack
- a letter in the same newspaper abhorring the incident.

9 These pieces are passed on to other students who use them as the script for a scene. They may not add any dialogue.

The students must make it apparent through their use of space, gesture and voice who they are and what their attitude is towards the incident. Some of these scenes are shared and the audience are invited to comment on what is learnt about the characters and their attitudes towards the incident through the way the 'script' is presented. They may also suggest how adjustments could be made in order to make these characters and their attitudes clearer.

---

10 The class split into three groups. One group will represent the teenager, one their father or mother and one the headteacher of their school. The class are told that the headteacher has called the student and their parent to a meeting. The three groups gather together to discuss and decide:
- What would be the best outcome of such a meeting from their perspective? That is, what should they try to argue for in the meeting?
- What would be the worst outcome for them? That is, what scenario must they try to avoid?

11 Each group nominates one student to play the part of the group's given character. The scene in the headteacher's office is set up, students are

reminded of the conventions of forum theatre and the meeting is improvised using a forum theatre device.

This technique is particularly effective if the groups sit close behind their 'player'. They need to listen carefully to everything that is being said. If the meeting appears to be taking them towards their 'worst case scenario' any member of the team, including the player, may call 'STOP!' At that point the teams may consult in private for a minute before the teacher re-starts the meeting. Another option is for the 'player' to be replaced by another team member.

The purpose of this kind of forum theatre is not to see who 'wins' an argument but to:
- *explore as many different sides to the argument as possible*
- *consider what sort of arguments have more weight, and why*
- *look at the most effective ways of putting an opinion forward so that it is heard and considered fairly.*

---

12 The teacher can act as a referee in this sort of debate. They may raise or lower the temperature by adding new pieces of information either to the whole class or selected groups. For example:
- the headteacher could be reminded that the chemist sits on the school's governing body and has demanded a personal apology
- the parent could be made aware that none of the other graffiti writers have so far been found, and their daughter is the only one that has owned up to being involved
- the teenager could be furnished with an apparent trump card in that the graffiti attack took place following a class discussion on the issue of animal rights. It was in this lesson that the teacher showed the class examples of animal rights propaganda and set them the task of writing punchy slogans.

13 At some point the meeting will have to finish. It may be that the meeting comes to a natural close with some sort of agreement being reached, or perhaps one or other of the parties walks out. If necessary the teacher will have to find a way of closing the meeting (for example, entering in role as the headteacher's secretary to remind them of another appointment). Once the meeting is closed the different groups reflect on:
- How successful were they in achieving their pre-determined intention?
- What helped or hindered them in this?

It is worth sharing these reflections as a whole class by way of focusing on the inter-relatedness of content and form. To what extent, for example, did the students sympathise with the arguments being made yet feel uncomfortable with the way they were being made? Did they warm to a character even though they opposed what the character was saying?

● Developing a pre-text

Inside every little pre-text for drama there are hundreds of epics scrabbling to get out. Students can 'click on to' a subject such as animal rights and use what has been created so far as the foundation for further exploration of the issue through drama.

Working in this way can be exciting and rewarding for the students and the teacher. However, because the students' responses are not always entirely predictable, the teacher must be quick to seize learning opportunities as they arise. Planning for progression can become rather tricky if this way of working is the mainstay of the teacher's classroom practice. On the other hand, it can serve as a very good measure of the students' ability to take control of the form and direction of the drama. They may, for example, be given the opportunity to select from a menu of possible scenes:

- The girl needs to pick up a prescription. The chemist's shop she attacked is the only one open. She goes in . . .
- The girl meets up with some of the others involved. They want to know what happened in the meeting with the headteacher . . .
- The teacher who brought up the issue of animal rights stops the girl in the corridor . . .

Even within these suggestions there are other possibilities. For example, what is the relationship between the girl and the teacher? Maybe the latter is inexperienced and frightened of losing their job. Perhaps the girl has a bit of a crush on the teacher and was trying to impress. Exploring different possibilities not only involves exploring the intricacies of issues but also their dramatic potential. A measure of the students' progress will be their ability to suggest their own starting points for scenes such as these. Students should also be able to reflect on:

- what new insights they would give an audience into the issue in focus
- the extent to which they were appropriate to the tone and atmosphere of the work created so far.

A practical problem teachers may face with this kind of work is that it can be much easier to initiate than to close in a satisfactory way. If the drama is allowed to fizzle out students may feel dissatisfied and be left wondering just what it is they have learned. The best solution to this is for the teacher to plan the unit with a clear idea of the learning objectives. When it is adjudged that these have been met, it is time to move on.

Unit planning sheet for drama

Unit title Forum Theatre   **Time scale** 5 × 50 minutes or 4 hrs 10 mins

AIMS

- to enable students to prepare for and use forum theatre to develop and focus drama
- to enable students to understand how this drama technique can be used to explore and present different perspectives on a topical subject.

SUGGESTED ACTIVITIES

- pre-session task to gather and read information, news cuttings etc. on issues related to animal rights
- class share and discuss materials in small groups of 5/6; combined findings shared with class
- teacher sets context for drama through using questions – focus on chemist's shop
- graffiti incident introduced – students work in pairs, speculating what sort of slogans might have been used – samples (can be drawn from research) written up and displayed
- whole-class, teacher-led discussion on type of person who might have written any one of these (addressing stereotyping where necessary)
- teacher narrates background to incident – girl's arrest and admission of role in incident
- class build up character sketch of the girl through hot-seating teacher/or creating girl's bedroom (this can be used as extension activity or used for homework – students must be selective in choice of items for room – each item must be rationalised for real purpose within a drama
- students adopt roles of people affected or interested in incident – each prepares question to ask perpetrator. Focus on tone and attitude they would use in posing the question
- one student takes on role of perpetrator and others pose their questions
- reflection and analysis on why certain questions evoke silence and others elicit different responses. Were these appropriate for the different roles? What has now been learnt about the scenario?
- group writing activities – setting background for another group to use as basis for script of scene (no dialogue, but focus on use of space, gesture, voice and attitude of central figures in the scene)
- sample scenes prepared and shared – responses to focus on new insights presented and points for development of characters etc.
- preparation for forum – three groups – the teenager, the mother or father, the headteacher (teacher identifies specific points for focus of preparation and reminds students of conventions to be used for the forum itself)
- forum takes place and conventions applied by students – teacher adds information as necessary to increase/decrease tension or complexity of issues
- out-of-role reflection on forum, focusing on specific objectives of the three central figures and analysis focusing on relationship between content and form and purpose/value of forum theatre
- discussion (plus, if time is available, preparation and performances) re other possible scenarios connected to central narrative – what has dramatic potential and why?
- individual evaluations on unit.

EVIDENCE OF LEARNING (CREATING, PERFORMING, RESPONDING)

Creating Are students:
- using their research to develop the characters and situation?

Performing Are students:
- using words, tone and physical expression that are appropriate for the context and are convincing?
- contributing to the development of the drama through contributions to the forum as actors or spectators?

Responding Are students:
- developing their interpretation of characters in response to feedback from others?
- demonstrating that they have gained new insights into the issue and characters explored through making clear connections between content and form?

INTENDED LEARNING OUTCOMES

By the end of the unit the students should know and understand:
- how different drama strategies and techniques can be used to explore a controversial issue and create drama
- the importance of further research into the issue to build potential characters and situation for the drama.

They should be able to:
- develop and portray characters that are appropriate for the context and are convincing through their choice of words, tone and physical expressions
- reflect on and analyse the insights they have gained through the forum work.

RESOURCES

- press cuttings, leaflets, articles etc. on scientific experimentation on animals
- cards (three per group) and felt pens (one per group)
- chairs or large mat for the forum circle.

COMMENTS/EVALUATION POINTS

- Levels 3–6

Students bring with them to secondary school a good deal of vernacular knowledge about genre and the difference between this concept and that of style as the terms apply to drama. The job of the drama teacher is to make this knowledge explicit so that the students can:

- recognise different genres and styles and their place in the wider cultural context of drama

- draw on a range of genres and their associated conventions when creating and performing

- reflect upon and discuss their own and other people's drama in a critical and informed way.

The practical ideas described in this chapter focus on helping students clarify the concept of genre and develop a working knowledge of the conventions associated with them.

❶ Introduction

The catch-phrase 'I'll name that tune in two' derives from a quiz game involving being able to identify a piece of music from the first few bars. Players are able to do this because they have probably heard the piece several times before in the same way that certain teenagers are able to turn on a television and instantly say '*Friends*, Series 5, the one in which Joey . . . '.

This sort of identification may be seen as the apex of a triangle. Extreme familiarity can take us straight there, but the destination can also be arrived at through a process of elimination. For example, a contestant on a music quiz may not be able to identify precisely a piece of music as the second movement of Tchaikovsky's Symphony No. 2 – they may not even know that it is Tchaikovsky – but there may be something they recognise in the music as being 'Russian', or 'nineteenth-century'.

When students turn on a television it seems to take them only a few moments to identify what sort of thing is being broadcast, even if they do not instantly recognise the programme. They will be able to see straight away, for example, that the programme is a scathing cartoon comedy: a particular genre. Both *The Simpsons* and *South Park* may be seen as examples of this genre but they have a very different style; the drawings look different, they deal with different subjects, target different issues and have a different tone. In a similar vein, aficionados of the Western will doubtless be able to speak at length about the different directorial styles of John Ford and Clint Eastwood.

In practice, genres and style often overlap. Comedy and tragedy in the Greek tradition are clearly distinguishable. Shakespeare wrote in both genres but in many of his plays he seems to mix conventions associated with both. Some would argue that *Romeo and Juliet* starts as a comedy but ends as a tragedy – a notion exploited and developed in John Madden's 1998 film *Shakespeare in Love*. Whether writing plays that are tragical, comical, historical or pastoral, Shakespeare also has a pretty distinctive style of his own, though not perhaps as distinctive as Jonson or Marlowe, who were, of course, writing for the same audiences.

In terms of progression in drama, being able to identify the different components of genre and style allows students a greater range of options when creating their own drama. It also helps them make appropriate choices in their performance work and aids their critical discussion of drama.

❷ Working with stereotypes

Another analogy through which an understanding of this concept may develop would be to see genre as a regional accent, marked by certain inflections and perhaps dialectical words. Within this framework, individuals will have their own style of speech marked by tone, pitch, resonance and timbre and perhaps reflecting other regional accents that have played a part in their personal history.

People with particular accents are often stereotyped. Their individuality is obliterated by the general characteristics they are assumed to have inherited along with the accent. Stereotypes are, unfortunately, frequently negative when used in this way. However, in drama, stereotypes may be used to great effect in that they can move an audience to the point of recognition quickly. Judicious use of stereotypes can serve to make a particular point while subverting stereotypes can offer new insights into the way we see and categorise experience.

The practical suggestions below may serve as an introduction to the nature and use of stereotypes in drama. What will always be of importance is the reflection on how and why stereotypes are used and what their actual effect is on an audience.

Mug-shots

1 Each student is given a photograph or drawing of one of the following character 'types':
   - police officer
   - teacher
   - city gent
   - hippy
   - football fan.

   Alternatively, pictures of well known stereotypes from television programmes currently in vogue with the students could be used.

2 The students decide on one action and one line that matches their picture and mill around the room showing their action and delivering their line to everyone they meet; they must also be sure to watch and listen to the other person.

3 When they meet another character they think is the same 'type' they team up and continue to go round the room, looking for more characters of their type. How quickly does the class form into five groups of characters? What was it about the actions and lines that helped them to do this?

4 In the first instance students may justifiably choose the most obvious clichéd lines: ''Ello, 'ello, 'ello. What's all this 'ere then? You're nicked, old son!' The enterprise becomes more intriguing when students are encouraged to use subtle ways of creating a 'shorthand' for their character. What sort of actions and lines do they then call on to convey a clearly recognisable character type, without necessarily making the portrayal wholly superficial?

   - This sort of game may be used in many other contexts, for example, to identify characters from different plays or periods of history.

Reflective discussion, albeit brief, should focus on the nature and resonance of the visual and aural signs employed to depict the characters quickly and clearly.

3D–TV Times

This activity again draws on students' knowledge of film and television in order to help clarify the concept of genre.

1 Small groups are given a clipping from a television guide describing a programme (or film) that clearly falls into a particular genre, for example, science fiction, thriller, romance, soap opera, situation comedy.

2　They are told that the clipping was accompanied by a still photograph which made it obvious what sort of programme it was. In the first instance the group simply make the still.

3　As an extension to the task, they could be asked to add a prescribed number of lines of dialogue to an animated depiction of the scene.

In reflecting on some examples, the class seek to identify what sort of visual signals were chosen and how they communicated the genre.

Registers

Just as some people's geographical roots may be placed by their accent, so their occupations can be recognised by their use of *register* and diction, that is, their choice of vocabulary and the manner in which they speak it. Stereotypically, the character of medical personnel could be quickly established by using an expressionless voice to say things like '*Scalpel . . . drain . . . swab . . . suture!*' Specialist use of vocabulary is often accompanied by instantly recognisable command, such as 'Stand clear!' in this case.

Students can be set the research task of collecting words and phrases associated with different occupations or given examples of lines and asked to identify them through a variation of 'Mug-shots' (page 154). An extension might involve setting groups of students the task of improvising a scene in which they must use as many examples of register as possible, including new words that simply sound as if they would fit. For example:

- the crew of the space-cruiser *Star Chaser* encounter difficulties as they enter orbital approach to Zargon 5
- 'Fingers' Malloy and his brassy moll 'Trixy' Padowski make their presence felt in Smokey Joe's speakeasy
- Professor Halsentreim discovers to his horror that the glamorous Ulrike Winkelmann is not in fact a lepidopterist, but a Nazi spy whose interest in the Peruvian Leopard-Spotted Hawk Moth has little to do with environmental protection.

It is important to place activities such as this in the context of a critical consideration of stereotypes. The students really need to have the opportunity of discussing why scenes like this may appear funny, insulting, trite or just plain daft. Rather than reinforcing stereotypes, particularly ones that are negative, attention needs to be drawn to the way in which language and visual imagery are used selectively to convey meaning.

Cut

This activity involves the whole class turning the working space into a film set in which the teacher will work in role as a stereotypically megalomaniac director. The purpose is to identify all the components of a particular genre through the deliberate use of parody (in much the same way that films such as *Airplane* commented upon formulaic disaster movies). This could involve students:

- using whatever furniture or rostra etc. are available to dress the set
- filling the set with character types
- rehearsing a movement sequence to set the scene
- introducing one simple piece of action with associated dialogue.

1 The teacher reads or hands out a specially prepared film script, for example:

> *A bar packed with the toughest guys in town. Villainous one-eyed jacks and hombres jostle in the smoke-filled saloon. Painted ladies weave among the card tables, casting sensual patterns through the whisky-heavy air.*
>
> *Sand on the floor. Spittoons by the bar rail. Jimmy, the barman, slides another red-eye down the polished top to Big Tex.*
>
> *On the gallery above, the lasciviously languorous Lilli Lacey peruses the scene. In the corner, Old Mad Joe tinkles out a tune on the smoke-stained ivories.*
>
> *Suddenly, the saloon doors crash open. Standing in the doorway against the fading sunset is Clancy Burrows, six-shooter in each hand:*
>
> BURROWS I've come to get you, Kincade!

2 The scene is rehearsed a number of times. In the first instance the students attempt to play the scene as 'straight' as possible.

3 With each successive run-through the teacher/director levers in more and more clichés and stereotypes before eventually inviting the students to comment on the ultimate effect.

Rehearsing extracts from plays or devised scenes in this way can also illustrate how stereotypes may be subverted and used and parodied for dramatic effect. John Godber's Bouncers, *for example, uses stereotyping to comment on behaviour while Tom Stoppard's* The Real Inspector Hound *satirises clichéd dramatic writing.*

- **Archetypes**

  While the term 'stereotype' is most readily applied to assumed regional or professional characteristics, 'archetype' refers to status and a sort of state of being within a society. Archetypes such as the Fool, the Innocent, the Hero, the Mother and the Trickster have been used in the mask work of theatre companies such as Trading Faces and Trestle Theatre Company. Older students may usefully research into the history and psychology of archetypes and relate them to drama as diverse as Greek comedy and tragedy, medieval mystery and morality plays and contemporary parables. The essence and dynamics of archetypes can also inform work with younger students and link in with techniques such as centring (see page 229).

❸ Starting big

The success of the activities above depends largely on encouraging the students to accentuate characters. Playing 'big' in this way can be a great deal of fun as well as drawing attention to the different types of signalling through which drama communicates to an audience. On the negative side, if this type of work is not introduced and handled carefully by the teacher, some students will feel threatened in that it requires a certain amount of controlled 'showing off'. (By the same token, some students find role-play intimidating because it can seem to demand they expose themselves.) The sort of superficial characterisation and 'ham acting' likely to arise from these activities is not directly applicable to all genres of drama and one would expect GCSE and A level candidates to be able to exercise discretion and choice in their character work. Nevertheless, working in this way usefully exposes the 'sham' of drama. The characters are patently insincere and inauthentic, but because the mechanics of such characterisation are so overt, 'starting big' can serve as the foundation on which subsequent, more subtle and sensitive work may be built. A way of counter-balancing the apparent superficiality of such work is to place it in the context of a particular historically located genre. In this way, students learn something about different performance styles and how cultural conditions affect the nature of drama and how it is interpreted.

- **Melodrama**

  The term 'melodrama' is now often used in a pejorative way. It conjures up images of a grandiose, declamatory acting style and a simple morality in which virtuous country maidens are, eventually, rescued from the villainous rotten apples of an otherwise noble and just gentry. Such notions arise from the way in which theatre in the early nineteenth century aimed to capture the attention of the expanding working-class populations of industrial towns. This largely illiterate audience, it was assumed, wanted short, action-packed dramas in which the moral message was clear and comforting and the emotional impact served as an antidote to their otherwise depressingly dreary everyday life. An inflated performance style was also needed in the context of theatres that were dimly lit and lacked any electronic amplification to cut through an atmosphere heavy with tobacco smoke and fumes from the gaslight.

The antecedents of the characters and narratives common to Victorian melodrama reach back to Roman tragedy and are certainly identifiable in Shakespeare, Jacobean revenge dramas, pantomime and the gothic novel. Contemporary film and television are full of melodrama. Having discussed its constituent elements, it can be an interesting activity to collect examples from the students' own list of favourite films. Notable ones from the 1990s would include *Ghost, Titanic, Good Will Hunting, Speed* and *Independence Day.* The enduring appeal of musicals such as *The Phantom of the Opera* and *Miss Saigon* is testimony to the pulling power of a simple story told in a spectacular way, the Disney corporation has cashed in on the cosy morality of melodrama and animated films such as *The Lion King* and *Beauty and the Beast* have been transformed into successful stage shows.

Stock characters from melodrama such as the Hero, Heroine (and her friend the Lovable Rogue), Villain (and his half-witted Henchman), Aged Parent and Mysterious Gypsy or Oriental type, can all be introduced fairly easily by, for example:

- displaying drawings and photographs of examples
- creating tableaux
- exploring ways of walking and speaking archetypal lines
- watching clips from silent movies such as D. W. Griffiths' *Broken Blossoms.*

Silent movies are also good resources for observing and adopting the emphatic acting style. While acting in this manner today may simply seem comical, setting students the task of creating a short, silent scene to a carefully drawn brief can be a real challenge and demand an economical yet highly charged use of gesture.

Ideas for such scenes may be drawn from the narratives of extant melodramas. The teacher may choose to read through an example of such a play with a class, or to focus on an extract in order to provide an insight into the way conventions are used to heighten emotional impact.

Synopses such as the ones below can be given to small groups who are then challenged to:

- re-tell the entire story in no more than six still images with narrative links
- create a trailer or *tableau vivant* (freeze-frame) for a production of one of the plays: it must capture the excitement and emotional impact without giving too much away
- write or improvise a scene which would fit into one of the synopses using as many as possible of the lines given on page 160. They all come from genuine melodramas. (One of the reasons why few Victorian melodramas are performed today is because the quality of writing was often very poor. In part, this was due to writers having to work under tremendous pressure to deliver a constant supply of new plays. Characters, storylines and indeed the dialogue itself were re-cycled over and over again.)

LUKE THE LABOURER – A MORAL TALE!	BLACK-EYED SUSAN – THE SIN OF LUST AND ITS CONSEQUENCES EXPOSED!	THE BELLS – A MAN HAUNTED BY HIS DARK PAST!	MURDER IN THE RED BARN – THE SLAUGHTER OF INNOCENCE PUNISHED!
Too lazy to work, Luke harbours a grudge against his employer, Farmer Wakefield, and gets Mike the Gypsy to help him kidnap the farmer's son. He then helps the local evil squire to abduct the farmer's beautiful daughter but their plan is thwarted when the heroic son returns. In the final struggle, Luke is killed.	A host of villains tries to woo the faithful Susan away from her sailor husband, William. Even William's captain seeks to win her, with the result that William wounds him in a sword fight. Repenting his wickedness, the treacherous captain reveals that he has already released William from the navy. This allows William to escape from being hanged for striking an officer.	Matthias robs and kills a rich traveller but is then haunted by the sound of the traveller's sleigh bells. He hopes that by marrying his daughter to the Chief of Police he will escape justice, but his crime is discovered when he is hypnotised. On awaking, he dies in terror at what he has re-lived in his trance.	Sweet young maid Maria Marten is seduced by the playboy William Corder, who then murders their baby and lures Maria to the Red Barn, where he kills and buries her. Her mother's strange dream shows where the body lies. Corder is hunted down by an intrepid police detective. On the night before his hanging he atones for his sin to the ghost of Maria, which appears in his cell.

Lines from melodramas

'He was brave. He was open-handed. He had the heart of a lion and the legs of a fox.'

'Say your prayers – if you ever knew any – for your time is come.'

'Zoe, you are suffering – your lips are white – your cheeks are flushed.'

'Curse their old families – they cut me – a bilious, conceited, thin lot of dried-up aristocracy. I hate 'em.'

'Dead! Dead! And never called me mother!'

'Oh, how I lapped up her words like a thirsty bloodhound! I'll have her if it costs me my life!'

'My home, my home! I must see you no more. Those little flowers can live, but I can not.'

'We'll retire to a snug little cottage of our own, get plenty of sheep and then how happy we shall be dandling a chubby babe on our knee!

④ In the manner of . . .

An indication of the degree to which a student has assimilated the ingredients of any given genre or style is their ability to appropriate it to work of their own. As Key Stage 2 students are expected to be able to 'write new scenes or characters into a story, in the manner of the writer' it may be a reasonable expectation and a useful activity to help students at Key Stages 3 and 4 approximate different styles of dramatic writing.

New angles on old tales

1   In small groups, students remind themselves of the chronological sequence of a well known story.

2   The group re-tells the story by applying the register and diction associated with a contrasting genre or style. For example:
   - 'Hansel and Gretel' re-told as an item on *Crimewatch*
   - 'The Princess and the Frog' as a story from *The X-Files*
   - 'Jack and the Beanstalk' as the comic ramblings of a merry drunk.

This type of activity is a useful way of exemplifying perspective. A development would be to animate the tales 'in the manner of . . . ' using the 'Line story' technique (page 182)

Going in the wrong direction

The dynamics of part of a script and the components of a given genre may be exposed by deliberately mismatching them. Short extracts from plays can be handed out to groups along with a stage direction guiding them towards the way the script should be played. For example, this extract from *Waiting for Godot* by Samuel Beckett, could be played to a variety of briefs:

- The end of the affair

  A and B are lovers. Their love has gone cold.

- Stalag 13

  Wing Commander Dicky Carruthers tries to keep up Ginger Campbell's morale.

- The Bill

  WPC Eileen Hanks does her best to keep an old rogue out of further trouble.

EXTRACT

A (*hurt, coldly*) May one enquire where His Highness spent the night?

B In a ditch.

A (*admiringly*) A ditch! Where?

B (*without gesture*) Over there.

A And they didn't beat you?

B Beat me? Certainly they beat me.

A The same lot as usual?

B The same? I don't know.

A When I think of it . . . all these years . . . but for me . . . where would you be . . . ? (*Decisively*) You'd be nothing more than a little heap of bones at the present minute, no doubt about it.

B And what of it?

A (*gloomily*) It's too much for one man. (*Pause. Cheerfully.*) On the other hand what's the good of losing heart now, that's what I say.

Waiting for Godot by Samuel Beckett

Find the tree in the forest

This is a straightforward but valuable and flexible activity of particular use to older students. The work involves small groups reading a number of short extracts and considering which genres they might fall into. Four examples of suitable extracts are given on pages 163–6; each has a strong dramatic identity of its own, making it easier for students to approximate the style of language and presentation.

1 Students read through a script extract and decide what sort of genre they think they are dealing with. They jot down for later discussion why they think this.

2 The group then select 4–6 lines of dialogue from their extract and write these out on a slip of paper.

3 The slips are passed to a different group who are given no other information about the lines or the context from which they come.

4 Each group now tries to hide the lines in an improvised scene of their own by assimilating the style of language and using any other clues regarding context and genre they can find.

5 The scenes are shared. The challenge for the audience (excluding the group who chose the lines, of course) is to try and identify what lines came from the original script.

6 The group who passed the lines on are invited to comment on how well the performers hid the lines.

7 Reflective discussion focuses on the challenges of the activity, the way in which some lines lend themselves to flexibility in the way they may be performed whereas others strongly suggest a very particular genre or style.

The National Health or Nurse Norton's Affair by Peter Nichols

BOYD *comes up front steps in light, white clothing – cap, boots, trousers, short-sleeved shirt. He takes own pulse rate. Goes down on his hands and does a few press-ups. Holds up one hand to check its steadiness.* SISTER McPHEE *comes into the area, wearing white theatre gown.*

SISTER	Mr. Boyd.
BOYD	Ah, Sister – they're ready?
SISTER	Ready and waiting, sir.
BOYD	(*he begins to wash his hands*) And – Neil? –
SISTER	There's been no change.
BOYD	And – the donor? –
SISTER	Staff Nurse Norton is ready.

(*BOYD stops washing his hands.*)

BOYD	Aye, she's ready. Ready to give a kidney to save my son's life.
SISTER	Aye. Because she loves him. Because her life wouldna be worth living without him.

(*He goes on washing. She looks at him.*)

I know how she feels.

(*Boyd stops again, looks at her. With his elbow he operates a nail-brush dispenser, taking the brush with his other hand and using it to continue washing.*)

BOYD	Mary – I wish I knew what to say to comfort ye. I tried – God knows I tried – to make him leave the girl.
SISTER	No!
BOYD	Aye, the girl who's about to risk her life that he may live.
SISTER	No.
BOYD	Aye. And whose fault is it his disease is so far advanced? Mine.
SISTER	No.
BOYD	Aye!
SISTER	You mustn't ever think that, even for a moment.
BOYD	Why not? It's the truth, woman.

Loot by Joe Orton

> HAL *stares at the coffin as* DENNIS *screws the lid down.*

HAL Has anybody ever hidden money in a coffin?

> DENNIS *looks up. Pause.*

DENNIS Not when it was in use.

HAL Why not?

DENNIS It's never crossed anybody's mind.

HAL It's crossed mine.

> *He takes the screwdriver from* DENNIS, *and begins to unscrew the coffin lid.*

> It's the comics I read. Sure of it.

DENNIS *(wiping his forehead with the back of his hand)* Think of your mum. Your lovely old mum. She gave you birth.

HAL I should thank anybody for that?

DENNIS Cared for you. Washed your nappies. You'd be some kind of monster.

> HAL *takes the lid off the coffin.*

HAL Think what's at stake.

> *He goes to the wardrobe and unlocks it.*

> Money.

> *He brings out the money.* DENNIS *picks up a bundle of notes, looks into the coffin.*

DENNIS Won't she rot it? The body juices? I can't believe it's possible.

HAL She's embalmed. Good for centuries.

> DENNIS *puts a bundle of notes into the coffin. Pause. He looks at* HAL.

DENNIS There's no room.

> HAL *lifts the corpse's arm.*

HAL *(pause, frowns)* Remove the corpse. Plenty of room then.

DENNIS Seems a shame really. The embalmers have done a lovely job.

No Orchids for Miss Blandish by Robert David MacDonald

> (*Sirens heard approaching*)

MA   Garbage. All our lives. We live in garbage cans, and up above, the high-roll assholes and the cops are there, sitting on the lids.

LOUDHAILER Grisson. Come on out Grisson. Come out with your hands in the air.

MA   Gimme a drink, Doc.

DOC   Sure, Ma. Better pour it yourself. Don't want to waste it.

MA   End of the road, Doc.

DOC   (*Breaks down in tears*) It looked so good, didn't it?

LOUDHAILER Come on out in there. This is the last time. Come on out or we come in.

DOC   It's going altogether too fast.

MA   You'd better go.

DOC   Come with me.

MA   I'm staying here. So long, Doc.

DOC   Come with me, Ma.

MA   Not without Slim.

DOC   He was mine too, Ma.

MA   Sure he was. Go out slow, with your hands in the air. Those guys out there sound fit to pop.

DOC   It's been a real privilege, Ma'am.

> (*Exits.* MA *shoots him in the back*)

MA   Sentimental old fool. Come on then, you ignorant yellow armies. Come and get me.

> (*She goes to the door. A rattle of gunfire. She staggers back in, the front of her dress drenched in blood. As she lurches against the radio, it switches to raucous, garish jazz.*)

The Widowing of Mrs Holroyd by D. H. Lawrence

MRS HOLROYD	Hark!

(There is a quick sound of footsteps. BLACKMORE comes into the light of the doorway.)

BLACKMORE	They're bringing him in.
MRS HOLROYD	*(quickly putting her hand over her breast)* What is it?
BLACKMORE	You can't tell anything's the matter with him – it's not marked him at all.
MRS HOLROYD	Oh, what a blessing! And is it much?
BLACKMORE	Well –
MRS HOLROYD	What is it?
BLACKMORE	It's the worst.
GRANDMOTHER	Who is it? – What does he say?

(MRS HOLROYD sinks on the nearest chair with a horrified expression. BLACKMORE pulls himself together and enters the room. He is very pale.)

BLACKMORE	I came to tell you they're bringing him home.
GRANDMOTHER	And you said it wasn't very bad, did you?
BLACKMORE	No – I said it was – as bad as it could be.
MRS HOLROYD	*(rising and crossing to her MOTHER-IN-LAW, flings her arms round her; in a high voice)* Oh, mother, what shall we do? What shall we do?

5 Structuring a unit of work around a genre

Commedia dell'arte

Literally meaning the 'comedy of art', this genre has influenced a good deal of the drama that young people are possibly most familiar with. The comic routines of pantomime, Punch and Judy, circus clowns and any number of popular entertainers and performers have their roots in the characters and *lazzi* of *commedia*. Rowan Atkinson's accident-prone and alarmingly innocent Mr Bean is a direct descendant of the original Zanni, as was Jacques Tati's Monsieur Hulot before him. Basil Fawlty, Manuel and Polly may similarly be regarded as latter day versions of Brighella, Zanni and Columbina. If the names of some of the *commedia* characters initially sound strange, thinking of modern equivalents can help students tune in to the stereotypes: for Zanni read 'zany'; Brighella is linked to 'brigand', that is, someone who looks for a fight; and a good modern example of Il Capitano is Captain Mainwaring of *Dad's Army*.

As with melodrama, these characters must be played big but within clearly defined parameters. The performance style of *commedia* is highly visual, relying more on the physical than the verbal. There are obvious opportunities to teach students how to make and use masks as part of a unit on *commedia* if time and resources allow.

Improvisation is an important element, but far from being shapeless and free-ranging, improvisation in *commedia* demands economy and teamwork. A *commedia* troupe knows exactly what an audience expects and how they are likely to respond; they use that knowledge to surprise and delight. For younger students, working to constraints such as these provides goals to aim for and the means to achieve them.

Another notable gain in exploring *commedia* is that it places students' own classroom-based improvisations into a context of drama that embraces the traditions of different ages and national cultures. Such a study signals to students how other times and places have influenced what we may otherwise mistakenly assume to be original and culturally specific.

The characters of *commedia* may be introduced using the same sort of techniques as described for melodrama (page 157). Showing a clip from a video of *Fawlty Towers* could instigate a discussion on the nature of the comedy and the sort of comment it is making about people like Basil Fawlty:

- What sort of things do people find funny? Can we explain why?
- In comedies like *Fawlty Towers*, what are the audience led to expect will happen? How is this done?
- What actually happens? How?
- Are the characters and events believable? Even if they are not, what is there about them that reminds us of people and situations we know?

The table on page 169 outlines some of the main characters of *commedia* and their traits. Students can usefully try to match these character sketches to characters from television comedies, films and so on. Greater insight into both the performance style and purpose of *commedia* can be gained by considering the way audiences are likely to react to certain characters.

▶ *Commedia* in action

1 Working on their own, the students try to pose themselves as the teacher describes some of these characters. Many professional actors work from the feet up in order to assume such character types. From the still pose, the teacher can talk the students through the different walks and set moves. For example:
   - Brighella's switch from lumbering, grumbling landlord to dagger-wielding, evil smiling cut-purse
   - Pantalone's twitchy-fingered lecherous lurching walk, to the way he falls on his back and waves his arms and legs helplessly in the air when he realises he has been robbed
   - Il Capitano's more gradual change from strutting, swaggering peacock to apologetically smiling, backward-stepping shrinking coward.

   A good approach to adopting these big, externalised characteristics is to find an appropriate 'centre' for them (page 229). Pantalone, for example, may be governed by his overly padded cod-piece, Brighella by his hips which give him a stout, rolling gait.

2 Having established the key physical characteristics, the students need to try and put more rhythm into the different walks. This can be encouraged by playing suitable background music. An ideal piece is Perez Prado's *Guaglione*, which was used for a successful Guinness advert – itself a fine example of *commedia* movement [*Mundo Latino*, Sony TV2 CD 31-480699-10].

3 In pairs, the students practise some simple stage fighting routines, for example, being spun around by the hair, pulled by the nose, picked up by the ears or sent flying with a left hook. In groups of three, they put a sequence of such effects together to make a comic fight.

NAME	DESCRIPTION	CHARACTERISTICS
Pantalone	Aged, avaricious, amorous – in other words, a tight-fisted dirty old man.	He tries to disguise his old age by wearing clothes that are too tight. He pulls lecherous faces at all the women and tries to grab them with clutching fingers. He walks with bow legs and always has a money pouch bouncing about his genitals.
Il Dottore	A pompous pedant – a real bore who doesn't know half of what he pretends to know.	Most of the time he talks gibberish but makes it sound important and meaningful. He has a pot belly – no doubt because he only ever talks about work and never does any.
Il Capitano	Pretends he's very brave and dashing but obviously isn't. Always trying to plot to fill his perpetually empty wallet.	Always boasting of his great victories and gallantry, he struts around with nose in the air and his chest thrust out – until there's a sniff of danger when he is likely to tip-toe away in an exaggerated manner.
Arlecchino	A Zanni. He is completely stupid yet has the cunning of a 7-year-old.	Extremely agile and acrobatic, he speaks like a parrot. He is the master of disguises and cannot help but mimic everyone and everything he sees and hears.
Brighella	Usually an inn- or shop-keeper. He can be pretty ferocious and while frequently cheating others out of money he never seems to be a victim himself.	Stocky and rather heavy footed, others are likely to mistake him for being a bit slow in every sense. In fact, he can be cat-like in his movements and very cunning. He stands with knees slightly bent, shoulders relaxed but elbows slightly raised as if about to draw two six-shooters – in fact, what he can draw with lightning speed is a dagger.
Pulchinella	The model for Mr Punch, he is empty headed and violent and has no morals.	He moves around like a demented hunchbacked cockerel, pecking with his crooked nose. He squawks rather than speaks.
Columbina	A serving girl – pretty, intelligent, skilful in dance and talk.	A happy-go-lucky character, Columbina likes to joke and join in with schemes. She has a charming and witty interest in sex!
Pierrot	A type of Zanni. He is always sad and silent, being full of unrequited love.	His movements are slow but flowing as if he is always in a dream. He sighs a great deal but can suddenly execute acrobatic twists and turns.
Isabella	The object of love and lust. She is beautiful and pure.	Full of poise and class, Isabella drifts in and out, always moving with ease and control.
Zanni	There are in fact a variety of Zanni but they are always low status, servant types who can talk directly to the audience.	A comic Zanni has nervous, urgent movements – his body shows exactly what he is thinking and feeling. He is boisterous, always on the look-out for mischief and fun. He takes small steps, raising his knees high as he does so.

A number of simple rules and tricks need to be used when introducing stage fighting:

- *No one actually gets hit or hurt. As far as possible the 'victim' (A) is the one who does all the work. For example, in the 'hair pull' the aggressor (B) only needs to place a clenched fist on A's head. A clings to B's wrist. B tries to pull away from this but A clings on. As A shakes their head it appears that B is doing the shaking. The same principle is used for nose and ear pulling.*
- *Audiences look for the reaction more than the action. So, a quick slap or punch by B doesn't need to connect – what is important is that A reacts as if it has done.*
- *Timing is crucial. A must know precisely when B is going to strike but neither must show the audience they are bracing. Only practice will get the timing right.*
- *Positioning hides the cheat. The performers must be aware of what the audience cannot see and use that space to hide the slaps, kicks and punches from them.*
- *When practising stage fighting routines it is very important to pay close attention to health and safety guidelines. Students should wear baggy clothing and remove all jewellery including watches. Practise routines slowly and build up the speed very gradually.*

4 At the heart of *commedia* is the semi-improvised comedy routine or *lazzi*. Students work on their own or in pairs to develop a routine based on a selection of examples such as these:

Arlecchino is bothered by a fly. He eventually manages to catch it. He studies it, pulls off its wings then devours it as if it were a tasty piece of roast chicken.	Il Dottore convinces Pantalone that his bad breath is due to rotten teeth. Using oversized or ridiculous tools, he tries to extract them in mime.
Pulchinella is trying to eat a plate of macaroni but he is constantly distracted by spotting beautiful women passing by (or in the audience).	As Il Capitano practises how he will serenade Isabella, Columbina contrives to throw the contents of a chamber-pot over him.

Lazzi may be described as 'semi-improvised' because the responsibility of making the sequence work for the audience lay with the performers who had the leeway to extemporise and develop visual gags so long as they had the audience's attention. Behind the routine, however, lay a number of set moves and devices and a complete understanding on the part of each performer as to how their fellow performer worked. There are published collections of lazzi dating back to 1611. Some of the routines are for solo performers, others are for pairs and work in the same way that more modern comedy duos use the funny man/straight man relationship.

5   The next step is to give the characters a voice. *Commedia* characters tend to throw very rude insults at each other a great deal. One way of crafting an effective insult is to work in groups to draw up a 'pick 'n' mix put-down chart'. Individuals select one idea from each column:

BODY PART OR FUNCTION	ADJECTIVE	ANIMAL
puke	snivelling	toad
dribble	sniffing	three-toed sloth
arm pit	licking	ship rat
bum	shuffling	dog flea

6   Having crafted a suitably disgusting line to say, the students decide which character they wish to speak the line. Only experiment will allow them to find a voice which matches the stance and movement but this can be effected by simple milling around and shouting, mumbling, whispering, spitting the insults at every other person in the room.

7   *Commedia* dialogue is characterised by short lines that tend to bounce off each other (stichomythia). As with the movement, dialogue needs to have a distinct rhythmical pattern to it. In pairs, students work on short sequences in which each character appears to be speaking their own monologue without listening to the other. The tirades are nevertheless intercut to produce a fast and furious argument:

HE	Go away!
SHE	Disappear!
HE	. . . from my eyes.
SHE	. . . from my sight.
HE	Fury with a heavenly face!
SHE	Demon with a mask of love!

HE	How I curse . . .
SHE	How I detest . . .
HE	. . . the day I set eyes on you.
SHE	. . . the moment that I adored you.
HE	How can you dare . . .
SHE	Do you have the audacity . . .
HE	. . . even to look at me?
SHE	. . . to remain in my presence?
HE	I could never have imagined . . .
SHE	I could never have been persuaded . . .
HE	. . . that heaven could become such a hell!
SHE	. . . that Cupid could become such a Devil!

8 Finally, the class work in groups of three or four to realise a longer scenario involving physical and vocal characterisation, dialogue and *lazzi*. For example:

1	2	3
Brighella is polishing glasses in his bar. Il Capitano struts in followed by his servant, Zanni. He proclaims his love for the inn-keeper's daughter. Brighella is appalled. Il Capitano and Brighella argue. Il Capitano becomes more cowardly as Brighella gets nastier. As this scene develops, Zanni tells the audience the truth about Brighella's greed and Il Capitano's cowardice.	Il Capitano tells Zanni to send a ring and message of love to Brighella's daughter but Brighella overhears this and stops Zanni. He gets Zanni drunk and steals the ring. Zanni must confess the loss of the ring to Il Capitano, who is angry and punishes him.	Il Capitano sends Zanni on a mission to tell Brighella's daughter, Columbina, that he loves her. Zanni is told not to tell anyone about his mission. Columbina overhears this and is delighted. Zanni goes into a bar and tells the barman all about his task, not realising that he is telling Brighella! Brighella gets Zanni drunk to stop him meeting with Columbina. Columbina discovers what has happened and berates her father for interfering.

9 After working to a scenario provided by the teacher, students devise their own, involving other characters. Groups can work to a commission: for example, Group A tell Group B they need a scenario involving Il Dottore, Pantalone and Zanni. Group B must provide Group A with a situation involving these three characters, and Group A then develop it into a *lazzi*.

Unit planning sheet for drama

Unit title *Commedia dell'arte* **Time scale** 5 × 50 minutes or 4 hrs 10 mins

AIMS

- to extend students' knowledge of dramatic genre
- to enable them to apply their knowledge in performance.

SUGGESTED ACTIVITIES

- introduction to the genre through discussion and questioning – pantomime, Punch and Judy, circus clowns, and contemporary performers such as Rowan Atkinson, followed by showing paintings and photos of stock characters in melodrama
- identifying and applying specific physical characteristics of archetypes – incorporate these into warm-up activities (done only as refresher if this work has already been covered in mask work)
- students to create improvisations in pairs or small groups based on specific scenarios where two or three archetypes might meet
- sample scenes shared brief responses on effectiveness of types and how physical behaviours fitted types
- extract of *Fawlty Towers* shown followed by discussion on the genre and how and why it works plus how it connects with students, own scenes on archetypes
- identify the character – students try to match main characters from archetypes studied and from *commedia* list with characters from television and film
- individual work – students select one of stock *commedia* characters and research further using Internet and library to prepare for next activities – they bring props if they wish
- introduce *lazzi* – students to focus on two stock *commedia* characters – use of set movements – gaits, stances and mannerisms
- whole group perform movement of characters to *Guaglione* – sample work shown and responses given on what made these effective plus how they might be developed further
- challenging the stereotypes – role reversal etc.
- comic stage fighting – connect with stage fighting done in Y8 – now using stock *commedia* characters
- students to work in pairs or individually creating own original physical *lazzi* based on specific scripted scenarios
- using the voice – paired work selecting and matching insults to stock characters and applying appropriate voice
- further possible work on *stichomythia* – sample given and students create own
- students work in groups on scenario provided by teacher focusing on each area – physical, vocal dialogue and *lazzi*
- group work devising original scenario for performance utilising all taught aspects of *commedia* work
- performances and feedback focusing on appropriateness of scenarios to characters identifying and analysing how effects were achieved – how they were intended and whether they were successful .

EVIDENCE OF LEARNING (CREATING, PERFORMING, RESPONDING)

Creating Are students:
- developing and adapting ideas as a result of research and feedback?

Performing Are students:
- showing understanding of how archetypes can be physicalised?
- effectively performing some of the stock characters from *commedia* in an original brief scenario?

Responding Are students:
- articulating characteristics of *commedia dell'arte* are and making connections with it and with other drama?
- providing feedback on performance using specific criteria?

By the end of the unit the students should know and understand:
• the characteristics of *commedia dell'arte*
• the connections between the genre of *commedia* and other comic dramas
• how to physicalise archetypes.

They should be able to:
• research for further information on *commedia dell'arte*
• perform some of the stock characters from *commedia* in a short original scenario
• provide feedback on performance using specific criteria.

RESOURCES

• computer with access to Internet
• paintings and pictures of scenes and characters from *commedia*
• music of Perez Prado's *Guaglione*
• sample props for *commedia* stock characters
• extract from *Fawlty Towers*
• sheet describing stock characters from *commedia*
• sample scenarios for archetypes
• sample scenarios for lazzi/comic routines (some for physical work only)
• insult activity word list.

COMMENTS/EVALUATION POINTS

Levels 5–7

This chapter focuses on creating, developing, structuring and ultimately communicating narratives. As students progress in drama they should become increasingly adept at exploring stories and presenting stories in engaging ways. This involves learning how to:

- generate ideas for stories
- identify the dramatic potential of stories
- use a range of drama skills and techniques to communicate them to an audience.

Telling tales in drama requires sensitivity. Students need to develop a sense of stewardship and understand how the use of form affects an audience's interpretation of the content of a story. Through the process of dramatising stories, students gain new insights into characters and events and learn to appreciate that their interpretation of texts is not necessarily exactly the same as anyone else's.

1 Introduction

The difference between story and plot was famously summarised by E. M. Forster:

> The king died and the queen died. That's story. The king died and then the queen died of grief. That's plot.

To define drama as the business of telling a story through dialogue is a gross and unhelpful simplification. The plain fact is that not all drama is concerned with telling stories, and dialogue is just one of the many mediums which may be employed to communicate to a drama's audience. However, it would be foolish to deny the strong connections that exist between drama and the art of telling stories. Many of these connections are embedded in drama's historical roots in oral traditions which make stories and storytelling worth exploring for that reason alone. Other connections are more practical and immediate. Students at Key Stages 3 and 4 are expected to be able to speak in a range of contexts and for different purposes. Being able to tell a story in a way that holds the attention of the listener is a skill that has considerable use beyond the bounds of the drama or English classrooms.

Helping students understand the relationship between story (that is, the events being related) and plot (that is, the cause and effect of those events) is an important aspect of progressing in the ability to create and relate tales in an appropriate way. By changing the order or manner in which events are revealed, a drama comes to acquire new meanings. Similarly, the term 'narrative' needs to be considered. Sometimes this term is used synonymously with story. The device of the narrator, that is, the one who tells the story, is something of a hallmark in some lower school drama and can be used as a sophisticated device in 'story theatre'. But the term 'narrative' can also be used to refer to that which is being explored and communicated in a broader sense.

The practical work described in this chapter serves a number of purposes. On the one hand the activities aim to help students progress as dramatic storytellers, giving them practice and guidance in the art of making up stories and relating them in interesting ways. The second purpose is to further the students' understanding of how, in drama, the content and form of stories are related and how the meanings received by an audience are dependent on this relationship.

❷ Stories from scratch

The games and activities outlined here encourage students to see themselves as being latent creators of stories. To progress in this aspect of drama, students need to trust in their own ability to generate new ideas, be able to relate the spoken word to action and develop a sense of the dramatically viable.

▶ The story circle

In this activity, the group aims to make up a simple story as a collective activity. Students might just add a word at a time but this tends to generate incoherent stories. A more effective and productive method is to allow each participant to say a little more but insist they finish in the middle of a sentence:

A It was a dark and stormy night. The thunder was crashing and when the lightning flashed the grim outline of the castle could be seen high on the mountain. Down in the village below . . .

B . . . Hans the undertaker was finishing off another coffin and chuckling wickedly to himself. Suddenly, there was a tap on . . .

C . . . the door. He went to open it and there stood . . .

Going around the circle sequentially can put tremendous pressure on students. As the story moves closer and closer towards them, some students begin to panic about what to say and stop listening to the tale, which makes it even harder for them to add to it. It is better, therefore, to introduce a way of making the story jump across the circle, for example by throwing a ball from one storyteller to the next or passing an object round the circle very quickly until the teacher says 'Stop'. If students cannot instantly think of something to add they may throw the ball or pass on the item until the teacher calls 'Stop' again.

 ## Fortunately/unfortunately

This game can be played as a whole group or in pairs. The simple constraint is that the story shifts from positive to negative as each player takes a turn:

A   Once upon a time there was a man who was unfortunately dying of thirst in a desert.

B   Fortunately, he suddenly saw a café.

C   Unfortunately, he didn't have any money on him.

D   Fortunately, he discovered that on that particular day they were giving drinks away.

E   Unfortunately, they had no glasses.

F   But, fortunately, they had plenty of buckets.

 ## And then . . .

As a variation to 'Fortunately/unfortunately', the students get into pairs. One starts a story but finishes half way through a sentence by saying 'And then . . .' The other student picks the story up, adds a little then stops with another 'And then . . .' Having tried the technique out, progression, of sorts, is achieved by asking the students to simultaneously act out everything that has been said, no matter how bizarre.

3 Stewarding a story

A powerful story is one that, for some reason, resonates with an audience. If members of an audience see elements of their own lives, beliefs and feelings reflected in the tale told, it will inevitably have a greater impact on them. This is not to suggest that the most powerful stories are about ordinary people and events: a story may well be moving and memorable because it appeals to our fascination with the fantastic, and sometimes fantasy provides remarkably clear insights into reality because of its use of metaphor.

A measure of students' progression in drama will be their increasing ability to create and tell stories in a variety of ways and have just such an effect on an audience. Setting out to achieve an effect on an audience means appreciating that the magic and medicine of stories needs to be handled sensitively. In creating their own dramas, students will draw on their own experiences, beliefs and feelings. Given this, the need for sensitive and mutual respect for each other's stories is paramount. One is reminded of W. B. Yeats:

I have spread my dreams under your feet;
Tread softly because you tread on my dreams.

The structured activity described below makes this requirement clear to students. It also instigates discussion on what criteria are used when considering the dramatic potential of a story. It explores how quite ordinary objects can hold, or in drama be given, tremendous symbolic value. The objects could be picked from a collection supplied by the teacher such as those used in the 'baseline' activity described on page 46 – for example, a red rose, a white feather, a torn photograph, an airline ticket, a key, a dry-cleaning receipt. Alternatively, each student can be asked to bring a small but personally significant object to the lesson. This latter course tends to create richer drama because of the personal values involved. In fairness to the students, though, they should be warned that they will be asked to tell the rest of their group why they have chosen to bring in that particular object; this will safeguard against them feeling that they are being exposed against their will.

The activity can be adjusted to provide a neat demonstration of the concepts of narrative. Change the positioning of the objects in relation to each other and the narrative changes. For example, setting out the following objects in a straight line might suggest a straightforward narrative:

- a ticket to a disco
- a photograph of boy and girl in a disco
- a gold ring
- a passport
- a baby's dummy.

Some very different narratives might be suggested when the objects are placed in a different order. The effect of placing objects together in different ways can, of course, also be pointed out to younger students who share a fascination with the way things relate to each other. The point is to see how new stories are suggested by making new connections.

Symbolic objects

1 The students work in groups of four or five to position a number of objects on a sheet of white card.

2 They should play with a variety of groupings: sometimes, placing objects together in a certain way will be comical, at other times quite the reverse.

3 The students then take it in turns to tell the rest of their group the story of why their chosen object is special to them. If the objects were selected from a pool provided by the teacher, the students will need to make up a story (which they should do as a group).

4 Each group decides which story has the most potential for development through drama. This inevitably involves them in considering what sort of criteria they are using.

5 One member of the group takes the chosen story, along with the object, to another group. This 'steward' must not be the student whose story it is, and it is very important that they do not reveal whose story they are telling – to do so would be to compromise the trust placed in them by the owner of the object. The best way to ensure anonymity of the owner is for the steward to pretend that it is their own story, speaking the narrative in the first person. This imperative constraint should be reflected on at the end of the activity.

6 When the group has heard the story they decide on the specific moment that the object appeared to have taken on a special value and try to show this in a tableau.

7 The next task is to find a way of showing, through whatever dramatic devices they choose, what led up to this moment and to do so in a way that illustrates why it is so dramatic. This process will involve the group selecting, editing and interpreting the story they have heard.

The aim of this activity is to make it clear to an audience why a particular object is of such importance to its owner. It is important to emphasise to the class that the stories they are handling are true and belong to someone in the room – they must therefore be treated sensitively and truthfully. When the resultant work is shared with the rest of the class, the owners of the original story can be given the option of revealing themselves. They might then comment on how well the stewards retained the sense and integrity of their story and what it was like to see their own story dramatised. Students should also be allowed to remain anonymous or to make no comment on the interpretation and portrayal of their story.

---

8 Work such as this raises a number of points for reflection and discussion:
   • After the story was dramatised, whose story was it? The person that originally told it, or the group that made it into a play?

- How do stories change when they are mediated through the process of drama?
- To what extent did the knowledge that they were telling someone's real story affect the way they worked?
- What different criteria were used to decide which stories would be most suitable for dramatisation?

❹ Story theatre

'Story theatre' is one of those nebulous terms that crops up in drama books as a label for all sorts of presentations. What is always in focus, however, is the use of form to draw an audience's attention to the content and nuance of a given story. Students exploring enactive ways of telling stories can have their attention drawn to the links with, for example, Brecht's *Street Scene*, medieval jongleurs and the oral traditions of Asian, African and Australasian cultures. Voice, movement and gesture are employed to make the story clearer but, generally speaking, props and set are dispensed with to allow fuller attention to be paid to the verbal thrust of the narrative. Experimenting with animating stories in this way helps students appreciate what subtle and powerful tools their voices are in conveying atmosphere, mood and character. Working within tight constraints to tell a story can also foster the ability to select and use gesture and facial expression with clarity and economy.

▶ Eyewitness

This activity, which can be extended and developed over a number of drama lessons, involves groups of students giving fictionalised accounts of historical events.

1 Groups of students are set the task of thinking of a well known historical incident such as the sinking of the *Titanic*.

2 They consider who could provide interesting and contrasting eyewitness accounts of the event (for example, a cabin boy, a passenger in First Class, an ordinary seaman, a stowaway). Each member of the group takes a character.

3 Each character then starts to formulate a personal story of the event by building on a few simple stepping stones, for example, where exactly were they, what were they doing, what did they see and hear, how did they manage to survive to tell the tale?

4 The group prepare a presentation of the different accounts by cutting them together. A useful constraint is to have the characters sitting facing the audience and not relating to each other.

This activity is more interesting for the audience, and more challenging for the performers, if the actual event is not mentioned directly. In this way students' attention can be drawn to the dramatic effect of withholding information and making the audience 'work' for the meaning. For example:

A *I was down in the engine room when I realised something terrible had happened . . .*

B *Herbert and I had just got up to dance. It was such a magical evening. Then suddenly there was a huge bang . . .*

Line stories

The key constraint employed in this activity is that the performers must stand in a straight line and use direct address to tell the audience a story. The story is split up so that it bounces from one teller to another. The storytellers must never look at or relate to each other, but they can react to or act out what is being spoken. The technique takes a good deal of discipline but can be tremendously satisfying for an audience, who must never be able to predict who is going to speak next.

1 In groups, the students remind themselves of the details of a well known story.

2 Sitting in a circle, the group re-tell it, using one of the 'Story circle' techniques (page 177).

3 The group now try to tell the story by standing in a straight line facing forward. Encourage them to use their voices to create a sense of character and atmosphere. It may be useful to work with one group in order to demonstrate some of the possibilities. For example:

C So Little Red Riding Hood set off through the forest but soon saw . . . (*A starts skipping on the spot. B, D and E adopt the shapes of spooky trees*)

A . . . some beautiful flowers! Look, just over there (*she points out to the audience*).

E But they are off the path, Red Riding Hood. And didn't your mother say . . . ?

D (*adopting motherly pose and wagging her finger at the audience*) Promise me that you won't stray off the path. (*A, B, D and E all react as if the finger is wagging in front of their nose.*)

A, B, D, E (*chorus*) No, mother. I promise.

A (*pleading to audience*) But they look so beautiful and I'm sure Granny would love them . . .

4 A variation on this technique is to have one storyteller sitting in a chair. The rest of the group find ways of working around or with the chair – perhaps even to the extent of physically making a seat on which the storyteller sits.

In reflecting on these ways of dramatising stories, the class should comment on the balance between those sounds and gestures that successfully added extra dimensions to the tale and those which detracted and distracted. This will also help students to realise the importance of choosing images carefully and avoiding cluttering up presentations by doing too much.

⑤ Working with scripts

The techniques introduced above can be developed further by transferring them to scripts. It is a useful introduction into both physical and non-naturalistic theatre. Two examples are given here, both offering an opportunity for focusing on different aspects of storytelling:

Rainbow's Ending by Noel Greig

Rainbow's Ending is a fable about two greedy giants whose insatiable appetites devastate their world. In the end it is the courage of one little girl that offers some hope for the future. This multi-faceted play is accessible to students across the entire secondary age group. While the language is wholly accessible to all ages, the richness of the metaphors and infinite possibilities for staging can present exciting challenges for the more experienced groups. A short extract such as this provides students with the opportunity to play with ways of bouncing a story around a group of performers and being physically inventive in depicting characters and events.

A   There were these two giants.

B   They were huge.

C   Enormous.

D   Gi-normous.

E   Gigantic.

F   Anyway, they were very big.

G   'I'm bigger than you,' one of them boasted (and no kidding, this chap was as big as the post-office tower).

H   'Push off, titch,' said the other (who was as high as the Empire State building).

G   'Bet I can eat more than you at a go,' boasted the first.

H   'Oh yeah?'

G   'Yeah.'

H   So they decided to have an eating competition, to see who could guzzle the most in one sitting.

G   Mealtimes for giants lasted a couple of hundred years,

H   So they shook hands,

G   And agreed to come back when they'd had a good old tuck-in,

G/H   And off they went.

I   A little later in the day, a woman was sitting by the riverbank, with a fishing rod. It was a sunny day and the trout were almost queuing up to get themselves hooked.

G   A couple of miles downriver, one giant lay down and started to lap up the water.

I   'That's funny,' said the fisherwoman, 'the water's going down.'

G   'Slurp slurp,' went the giant, as he drained the river dry, 'come on little fishes, into my gob.'

I   So the fisherwoman packed up her tackle and trudged off to find another river.

H   But there wasn't one, because the other giant had drained them all dry.

J   Over the hill, a farmer was feeding his herd of cows.

G   When from out of the sky a mighty hand swooped down

K/L   And up into the clouds went the cows.

G   And, 'Very beefy, very tasty,' said the giant, as he marched off in search of the next course.

J   Leaving the farmer to mutter, 'Ruddy giants, that's the second herd they've guzzled this week.'

Rainbow's Ending by Noel Greig

Under Milk Wood by Dylan Thomas

Written as a 'play for voices', *Under Milk Wood* emphasises the voice as an instrument for conveying character and atmosphere. The opening scene printed here is particularly good to work with. Many students will no doubt be able to remember restless nights of their own and be able to draw on this. The sequence offers a lovely blend of nightmare and gentle comedy while the different voices from Captain Cat's past have highly individualized voices.

EXTRACT

FIRST VOICE	Captain Cat, the retired blind sea-captain, asleep in his bunk in the seashelled, ship-in-bottled, shipshape best cabin of Schooner House dreams of
SECOND VOICE	never such seas as any that swamped the decks of his S.S. *Kidwelly* bellying over the bedclothes and jellyfish-slippery sucking him down salt deep into the Davy dark where the fish come biting out and nibble him down to his wishbone, and the long drowned nuzzle up to him.
FIRST DROWNED	Remember me, Captain?
CAPTAIN CAT	You're Dancing Williams!
FIRST DROWNED	I lost my step in Nantucket.
SECOND DROWNED	Do you see me, Captain? the white bone talking? I'm Tom-Fred the donkeyman . . . we shared the same girl once . . . her name was Mrs Probert . . .
WOMAN'S VOICE	Rosie Probert, thirty three Duck Lane. Come on up, boys, I'm dead.
THIRD DROWNED	Hold me, Captain, I'm Jonah Jarvis, come to a bad end, very enjoyable.
FOURTH DROWNED	Alfred Pomeroy Jones, sea-lawyer, born in Mumbles, sung like a linnet, crowned you with a flagon, tattooed with mermaids, thirst like a dredger, died of blisters.
FIRST DROWNED	This skull at your earhole is
FIFTH DROWNED	Curly Bevan. Tell my auntie it was me that pawned the ormolu clock.
CAPTAIN CAT	Aye, aye, Curly.
SECOND DROWNED	Tell my missus no I never
THIRD DROWNED	I never done what she said I never.
FOURTH DROWNED	Yes they did.

Under Milk Wood by Dylan Thomas

⑥ Exploring and animating stories

Using drama techniques to animate short stories or extracts from novels has a double benefit in the same way that exploring poems through drama has. In chapter 3.3 (*Working with the voice*), a number of activities were described which could be used to help students develop the way they used their voices. Alongside the development of vocal skills, opportunities for further learning with regard to the content of the work were highlighted. In the work described below, insights into a piece of prose are stimulated by dramatising it through use of mask and movement.

When working on literary stimuli like this, it is important to encourage the students to identify both what is made explicit in the extract and what is implied. It is also important that they can identify the difference between 'what they know' and 'what they assume'. All too frequently students lose marks in essays or answers to comprehension exercises because they have taken as indisputable fact something which is actually just their interpretation. Working as a group to discuss stories helps students see that different interpretations are sometimes possible and what is said about a character or event needs to be justified and supported.

Identifying the ingredients

1 The teacher reads the story opposite aloud to the group, then distributes copies and asks them to read it for themselves.

2 After reading the extract for themselves, the group jot down what they have learnt from the story by filling in four cards headed:

Characters   Actions   Locations   Things we'd like to know

They should be encouraged to think around what is actually mentioned and include what is implicit. For example, under 'Characters' they might put: teacher, classmates, boy who had his teeth knocked out, witnesses to this, other football fans, parents and so on.

3 Students discuss the story in terms of:
- what we actually know about Barry
- what our assumptions are about him
- what other people's attitudes towards him are.

They then jot down their ideas in or around an outline representing the character (this technique is sometimes called role on the wall).

When Barry Weatherall was six, he wet his pants one morning while struggling to read to the teacher. He was a big boy for his age but he couldn't learn to read. Everybody else had read at least four books, but Barry was stuck on Little Book One.

He wasn't called Barry in those days. He was called Nigel. Nigel Robert Weatherall. After he wet his pants the teacher grabbed him and dragged him out from behind her table so everyone could see him.

'Look, children!' she had cried, crushing his wrist with bony, spiteful fingers. 'Look what this great big baby has done.' And she held him there, at arm's length, with an expression of disgust on her prim face, until everybody had a good laugh and slow, clumsy Nigel had dissolved into tears of humiliation.

A full year had been too short a time for Nigel to master reading, but he learned in a day how to win the respect of his peers. At playtime he tracked down those of his classmates who had laughed loudest and beat them up, with the result that, though the teacher referred in class to Nigel's little accident from time to time afterwards, nobody laughed. And when, a few years later, a boy at his middle school told him Nigel was a poncy name, Nigel knocked out most of his teeth as a way of demonstrating that you can't always go by names.

Nevertheless, when he was fifteen he took to calling himself Barry, and it wasn't long before everybody else learned to call him Barry too.

So now it's Barry Weatherall, King of the Hillside Kop. He has long since forgotten the embarrassing incident when he was six. The teacher died on a rubber sheet in nineteen eighty-one, and if anybody else remembers they're not dumb enough to remind him. He's forgotten the incident, but not the lesson it taught him, which is that everybody's good at something, and the secret of success is to find out what you're good at and do it with all your might. He still doesn't read too well, but a lot of people follow him on Saturday afternoons and a lot more admire him from afar. And some of them can read quite well.

Staying Up by Robert Swindells

4   The class work in three groups. One group makes a tableau of Barry's classmates showing what they think and feel about him. Another group shows his fellow football fans. The third shows different aspects of Barry himself as they perceive him to be. Is he completely hard? Or is there evidence in the story to suggest that he does mind what others think about him? These tableaux are shared and discussed.

5   Each group formulates a statement about what they think and feel about the other two groups. They are invited to speak aloud while holding their image.

Activities such as this work well when they are 'staged'. Position each group in a different corner of the working space and, if possible, use some stage lighting on them. Rather than hearing one group's presentation, discussing it and then moving on, run straight through all of the groups as if the whole sequence were a scene in a play. In this way the work feels more satisfying and comments made in reflection are enriched because the students will have seen and experienced the juxtaposition of images and lines.

Using masks to develop narrative

Plain paper bags with holes cut out for eyes and mouth can be used for this activity, as can hand-held stick and card masks decorated with felt pens. The main point is to use the mask to make the feelings obvious. Using very simple methods for this activity is a more productive use of time and resources than launching into a complex mask-making project. This would be tangential to the main learning objective of the unit, which is to explore ways of animating a story.

 ## Working with the ingredients

1   Students work in the same three groups as in 'Identifying the Ingredients' and are set the task of making simple masks for themselves.

  - the 'classmates'' masks show the faces as Barry would have seen them aged 6 – grotesquely laughing and jeering
  - the 'fans' masks show blind, unthinking aggression
  - the masks made by the 'Barry' group emphasise the different aspects of his character, so there will be a mixture of masks showing anger, fear, embarrassment, violence, tearfulness etc.

2   The groups work on rhythmical movements and gestures which suit the attitudes of their masks:

  - the 'classmates' develop a routine involving, for example, pointing and taunting an imagined Barry as he stands in front of them with wet pants

- the 'fans' create a routine showing the Saturday afternoon ritual on the terraces as they follow an imagined Barry, King of the Kop
- the 'Barry' group will need to split into two. Half work out a physical response to fit the classroom taunting scene, half devise a routine that shows Barry as King of the Kop, leading his louts.

3 The groups bring their work together to create a movement/mask presentation representing Barry Weatherall's development as a character from 6-year-old victim to terrace terrorist.

The work could be left here and reflected upon in terms of its dramatic effectiveness. By way of an alternative or extension task, though, the movement sequences could be blended with some of the storytelling techniques explained earlier in this chapter, in order to incorporate and develop the original text. Consider, for example, how the extract could be used as a piece of story theatre:

A 'Look, children!' cried the teacher
B as she crushed Nigel's wrist with her spiteful, bony fingers,
A 'Look what this great big baby has done.'
C And she held him there, at arm's length, with an expression of disgust on her prim face
D until everybody started laughing . . .
(First movement sequence starts involving classmates circling around Barry. As they point and jeer ritualistically in time to the music, the 'Barry' group closes in on itself and 'dissolves into tears of humiliation'.)

---

7 Structuring a unit of work around storytelling

'I wants to make your flesh creep', says The Fat Boy in Dickens' *Pickwick Papers*. If there is one kind of story that is likely to engage an audience it is the type that makes the flesh creep. As testimony to this, one might consider the phenomenon of the 'urban myth', that is, a tale circulated by word of mouth that purports to be true yet is always sufficiently distant from the storyteller to avoid being exposed as false by close questioning. Just as folk tales are located in a fantasy world by starting with 'Once upon a time, in a land far away . . . ', so urban myths are located in the 'real' world by openings such as 'My sister knows this bloke who . . . '. Urban myths seem to play on common anxieties and are thus generally gruesome, reflecting the worst excesses of contemporary life.

Dramatising urban myths

1 The teacher enables the class to make connections with previous storytelling work in drama and English, particularly line stories (page 182).

2 Students work in groups of seven to create a line story based on a well known short myth or tale. These are shared and responses given on skills and techniques used and how well these matched the story.

3 The teacher focuses the class on the nature and function of the urban myth by telling one. It is important to tell such a tale with conviction – urban myths always purport to be absolutely true. Choosing one that the students are already likely to know serves to expose their falsity very well (for example, the old chestnut about the escaped lunatic banging the severed head of the boyfriend on the car roof).

4 The teacher is adamant that this really happened to a friend of theirs, well, a friend of their sister's actually. When the class can contain their scepticism no longer, the teacher reveals what they are really up to and invites the students to share some of the stories they have come across that work in the same way.

5 In reflecting on this activity, students consider:

- similarities between the stories told
- the techniques used by the storyteller to try and engage an audience
- how the techniques match the content
- why such stories seem so common and popular.

6 The students gather ideas about the conditions that are connected with story telling. A simple chart such as the one below can be drawn up to categorise some of these. As the students jot down their ideas they should add as many details as possible under the general headings.

TYPICAL LOCATIONS	TYPICAL SITUATIONS	TYPICAL WEATHER
A country inn (blazing fire; quiet mysterious man sitting in corner; locals stop talking when strangers enter etc.)	People taking shelter after car has broken down in a lonely place.	Rain
		Thunder
A derelict house (litter on floor; broken windows; shutter banging; creaking hinge etc.)	Strangers stopping for directions in a village that is not on the map.	Lightning
		Howling wind
An old castle (suits of armour standing against grey stone walls; cobwebs; painting of ancestor with staring eyes etc.)	Teenagers exploring a place they have been warned to stay away from.	Swirling mysterious fog
A dusty attic (abandoned ventriloquist's dummy, leaning against old tea chest; old half-broken one-eyed dolls etc.)	People trapped by heavy snowfall etc.	

7 A fourth column could be added to the chart opposite, in which the students consider the reason 'why' people might tell such stories, for example to impress, to scare someone off, for the vicarious pleasure of scaring themselves.

In reflection on this work students' attention may usefully be drawn to literary devices such as pathetic fallacy by which human emotions are reflected in the natural world (as in the storm scene in King Lear *and any number of horror films). It is also worth addressing the way particular techniques are used in telling tales in order to generate certain responses in the audience, and identifying more clearly what these techniques are.*

The Weir by Conor McPherson

1 The class are given an extract from Conor McPherson's play *The Weir* (overleaf) together with the location and set description at the start of the play, to read through in groups. They discuss their own initial responses to Jack's story.

2 The class are told that the story is a part of a play set on one night in a bar in a remote part of Ireland. From this information alone they speculate what the stage set might look like, how lighting could add to the atmosphere and what sort of effect the writer and the actor playing Jack would want to create for the theatre audience.

3 They compare Jack's story with their own earlier work on urban myths. Do they think that Jack's tale is just the rural equivalent of an urban myth, or are there details in his story that suggest that Bridie and Maura are real characters in the area who genuinely experienced this strange incident?

4 In groups, the students pick out key events in Jack's story, jotting them down on slips of paper which they then put in chronological order. For example, they may decide that the first event is Bridie shouting down the stairs at the young children, followed by the time when the older ones were getting ready to go out and so on.

5 The students depict this chronological sequence of events in a series of still images.

6 One member of each group is nominated to play the part of Jack sitting at the bar telling his tale to the other (unseen) customers. The rest of the group find ways of linking their still images with appropriate movements. In this way, a dumb show is created as a background which could illustrate and add to the theatrical effect of Jack's story.

7 On the basis of this exploration, the students are invited to create another story that might have been told in the bar that evening, and experiment with a way of telling and illustrating it. Focus is given to the work by stressing that groups must work with the following constraints:

- the tale must be told as if the storyteller has faith in its truth
- it must be credible as, potentially, another part of Conor McPherson's play
- the group must decide what response they want from the audience and make the decisions on how to tell the story accordingly.

8 Groups perform scenes and those observing provide feedback and evaluation using criteria based on the constraints.

EXTRACT

JACK   Bridie. She was a well-known woman in the area. A widow woman. She was a bit of a character. Bit of a practical joker and that, you know? And Maura would say that when she was young, she was, Bridie was, always doing things on the older kids, hiding their . . . clothes and all this, you know? And she'd tell them old fibs about what a certain prospective boyfriend or girlfriend had said about them out on the road and this about coming courting or that. And she was always shouting from upstairs or this 'There's someone at the door.' She was always saying there's someone at the back door or there's someone coming up the path. You know. This. And there'd never be, anyone there. And people got used to her. That she liked her joke.

And Maura used to say that one Saturday evening back in about 1910 or 1911, the older ones were getting ready to go out for a dance or whatever was happening. And the mother, Bridie, came down the stairs and said, 'Did no-one get the door?'

And they were all, 'Oh here we go,' you know? But – Bridie came down and *opened* the door, and there was nobody there. And she didn't say anything. And she wasn't making a big thing out of it, you know? And Maura said, she was only young, but she knew there was something wrong. She wasn't cracking the jokes. And later on, when the others were all out, it was just her and her mother sitting at the fire. And her mother was very quiet. Normally she'd send Maura up to bed, early enough, like. But Maura said she remembered this night because Bridie didn't send her up. She wanted someone with her, you see. And in those days, Valerie, as you know, there was no electricity out here.

And there's no dark like a winter night in the country. And there was a wind like this one tonight, howling and whistling in off the sea. You hear it under the door and it's like someone singing. Singing in under the door at you. It was this type of night now. Am I setting the scene for you?

They laugh.

So there they were, sitting there, and Bridie was staring into the fire, a bit quiet. And smiling now and again at Maura. But Maura said she could see a bit of wet in her eyes. And then there was a soft knocking at the door. Someone. At the front door. And Bridie never moved. And Maura said, 'Will I get the door, Mammy?' And Bridie said, 'No, sure, it's only someone playing a joke on us, don't mind them.' So they sat there, and there was no more knocking for a while. And, em, in those days, there was no kitchen. Where the extension is, Valerie, that was the back door and only a little latch on it, you know? And that's where the next knocking was. Very soft, Maura said, and very low down the door. Not like where you'd expect a grown man or a woman to be knocking, up here, you know? And again Bridie was saying, ah, it's only someone having a joke, they'll go away. And then it was at the window. Maura couldn't see anything out in the night, and her mother wouldn't let her go over. And then it stopped. But when it was late and the fire went down, Bridie wouldn't get up to get more turf for the fire. Because it was out in the shed. So they just sat there until the others came back, well after midnight.

Well Maura said her mother never told the others, and one day when it was only the two of them there, a priest came and blessed the doors and the windows. And there was no more knocking then. And it was only years later that Maura heard from one of the older people in the area that the house had been built on what they call a fairy road. Like it wasn't a road, but it was a . . .

JIM   It was like a row of things.

JACK   Yeah, like a . . . From the fort up in Brendan's top field there, then the old well, and the abbey further down, and into the cove where the little pebbly beach is, there. And the . . . legend would be that the fairies would come down that way to bathe, you see. And Maura Nealon's house was built on what you'd call . . . that . . . road.

VALERIE   And they wanted to come through.

JACK   Well that'd be the idea. But Maura never heard the knocking again except on one time in the fifties when the weir was going up. There was a bit of a knocking then she said. And fierce load of dead birds all in the hedge and all this, but that was it. That's the story.

The Weir by Conor McPherson

Unit planning sheet for drama

Unit title Telling tales **Time scale** 5 × 50 minutes or 4 hrs 10 mins

AIMS

- to enable students to understand some of the ways that theatre practitioners use a range of skills, techniques and concepts to engage an audience
- to explore and realise in performance the dramatic potential of an original story.

SUGGESTED ACTIVITIES

- connections made with previous story telling work in drama and English and particularly line story work
- students create their own line stories
- teacher tells an urban myth, told with conviction but designed to prompt scepticism
- connections made through class discussion on other urban myths that have been heard by students – e.g. following an accident or a person who simply disappeared – common features etc. drawn together
- group activity where students focus on typical locations, situations or weather for such 'stories' and what the purpose of each is – conclusions shared with whole class
- connections with plays seen (including television) or read that these features were designed for a purpose, e.g. *The Tempest*
- group activity where students read the extracts from *The Weir* by Conor McPherson and the location and set described at the start of the play – discussion on responses to Jack's story and comparisons with their work on urban myths
- teacher poses specific questions for students to consider when reflecting on Jack's story, focusing on techniques used by playwright to engage the audience and how this matches the content
- groups decide chronological order of events of Jack's story and depict these through a series of tableaux
- groups create original way of telling the story through drama that may use the images and narration, but may use other forms suggested by the group – purpose is to apply techniques which will engage an audience
- students read first part of the play up to Jack's story (could be homework)
- students (in same or different groups) create new story that might have been told in the bar and experiment with ways of re-telling it though drama and with specific guidelines
  - it must be credible as another part of the play
  - it must be told as though the storyteller has faith in its truth
  - the group must decide the response they want from the audience and make decisions on how to tell the story accordingly.
- groups work independently, but teacher extends learning through questioning students as a group on purposes etc. of decisions re use of elements, skills and concepts
- groups perform scenes (could be for another class)
- feedback and evaluation using criteria provided and how effectively these were achieved.

EVIDENCE OF LEARNING (CREATING, PERFORMING, RESPONDING)

Creating Are students:
- experimenting with form?
- interpreting, shaping and structuring their work imaginatively?

Performing Are students:
- using a range of appropriate skills, techniques and concepts to create dramatic effect?

Responding Are students:
- analysing how playwrights, directors, designers and actors apply techniques to engage an audience?
- identifying how effects were achieved and whether these were successful?

By the end of the unit the students should know and understand:
- how a playwright can use techniques to engage an audience
- how actors, directors and designers can use techniques to engage an audience (connect with previous work).

They should be able to:
- use the manipulation of form to engage an audience
- apply the techniques within a play to inform their own work.

RESOURCES

- copies of extracts from *The Weir* by Conor McPherson (one per student)
- staging/rostrum and stools to suggest a bar
- stage lighting to be available if possible
- sound – to be determined by groups.

COMMENTS/EVALUATION POINTS

- Levels 4–7

Form is of course an integral part of all drama work. However, where drama is primarily used to explore issues or pre-texts the form employed is often left implicit. In order to progress in their knowledge of how drama is created and performed, students need to deepen their understanding of:

- the different elements of drama form

- the way in which form and content work in conjunction to create and communicate meaning

- how elements of form may be manipulated to engage an audience and achieve dramatic effect.

In this chapter a number of activities, resources and structures are used to demonstrate how students can acquire an explicit understanding of the way in which elements of form are used to generate dramatic tension and irony.

1 Introduction

Whether students are role-playing, improvising, devising or rehearsing from a script they will be exploring, creating and communicating meaning through their use of voice, space, gesture and movement. As they move towards devising their own dramas at GCSE, AS and A level, students need to ask whether the content of their work is interesting, relevant, appeals to the emotions, raises questions and addresses concerns. They will need to be able to identify the dramatic potential of stimulus material and ideas. They will also need the wherewithal to shape and perform their drama in such a way that it keeps the attention of an audience. If students are to progress, therefore, the teacher must create opportunities for them to become increasingly able to use these skills consciously so that they can produce drama that has something to say and says it in a way that will captivate and intrigue.

To move students towards this goal, teachers need to take every opportunity to help them explore and understand how drama is enriched when its content and form combine to induce some kind of tension. Dramatic tension is likely to be a strand of much of the students' work in the secondary drama classroom. Many drama teachers are highly skilled in the art of creating and using dramatic tension to engage classes in role-plays and the structured exploration of given pre-texts. However, the notion of dramatic tension is also worthy of exploration in its own right.

② Exploring tension

Many games are successful because of the way they generate and are driven by a tension between the players. In sport this tension also affects the spectators (although you may be able to think of a few games or particular teams where this is a rarity!). In the context of teaching students about the dynamics of tension and its application to drama, it is useful not only to play a game but also to reflect carefully on how it was working. What exactly made it fun to play? What did the players have to do in order to get better at it?

> ### The blood potato

1 Students stand in a space of their own with their eyes closed.

2 The teacher explains the rules of the game to the waiting students in a way that builds up the tension (using a low, portentous voice, for example) and chooses one student to be 'the blood potato' by tapping them on the shoulder.

3 The aim of the chosen 'blood potato' is to 'blight' everyone else. The group start to walk carefully around the space with their eyes still tightly closed.

4 When players bump into each other they all, except the blood potato, say 'Potato'. The blood potato, of course, says 'Blood potato' and the other player must scream and drop to the floor, before moving out of the way of the other players.

This is an excellent game which is as much fun to watch as it is to play. Reflection on the way the game works on its players offers the chance to discuss the nature of tension and how the dynamics of this link to the subject of drama. Tremendous tension is generated for the audience of this game as they watch the 'blood potato' blindly missing the other players by centimetres. Similarly, the players experience tension when they hear someone next to them scream as they are 'killed'. The experience may be likened to the mixture of emotions one experiences when watching a horror film – you hate it, but also rather enjoy it.

Undercover agents

1 The group stand with their eyes closed.

2 The teacher gives two or three members of the group a slip of paper and then chooses, by a gentle tap on the shoulder, a 'secret policeman'.

3 The group open their eyes and start to move around the room silently. The students with the slips of paper are 'undercover agents' whose aim it is to secretly pass the paper on to other players. Whoever receives a slip may then pass it on to someone else.

4 The aim of the secret policeman is to observe what is going on while pretending to be an ordinary player.

5 After a few minutes the teacher calls 'Freeze'. The secret policeman must try to identify and then arrest those holding the message at that moment.

As with 'Blood potato', reflecting on the dynamics of this activity may reveal a number of fascinating insights into the nature of dramatic tension. The tension of games such as these can be utilised to give students insights into actual situations. 'Undercover agents', for example, could be used as a part of a dramatic exploration into life in a police state.

The phantom tickler

1 The class start, once again, in a space with their eyes closed.

2 The teacher taps one student (A) who must open their eyes. This student will be the 'phantom tickler'.

3 The teacher points to another student (B) who will be the phantom tickler's victim.

4 The aim of the phantom tickler is to get close behind the victim and tickle them around the waist.

5 The group open their eyes and move around the space trying not to let anyone get close behind them. The phantom tickler, of course, must pretend to be a potential victim themselves while surreptitiously moving in on their target.

A critical feature of this game is timing. If the phantom tickler strikes too quickly the whole effort seems wasted. Conversely, if the game goes on too long players become restless and bored. Reflecting on this is in itself a useful piece of learning when related to drama. Here again, the teacher may lead by example and explain the game in hushed tones, perhaps contextualising it by conjuring images of the dank, misty Victorian cobbled streets in which the original Phantom Tickler lurked . . .

③ A taxonomy of tension

In some plays the main element of interest is the tension experienced by the characters. This can be comic, tragic, or a mixture of the two: should Vladimir and Estragon keep waiting for Godot? What might they miss out on if they go and he arrives? Conversely, what will be the consequences for them if they just continue to wait and Godot never arrives? Either way, underlying the dynamics of the drama and what keeps it interesting is the question 'What's going to happen next and what will the consequences of that be?'

• Considering suspense

It is useful to ask the students to work in small groups to describe briefly moments from their own lives or scenes from television series or films that were full of suspense. The teacher then suggests three of the recognised forms of suspense to the class:

- *Sympathetic suspense*: this is when an audience identifies with a character's situation. The tension is often intensified through dramatic irony by which the audience knows something that the character does not. Students might be reminded of thrillers, which work in this way (for example, scenes in which an unsuspecting and innocent character is in a house with a killer that the audience knows to be there). Sympathetic suspense can also provide painful empathetic experiences.
- *Suspense of ignorance*: in this case the audience is held in suspense because, like the characters themselves,they do not know what is going to happen next. This sort of suspense is utilised in the whodunnit.
- *Performance suspense*: this classification applies to moments when the performer is exercising a particular, usually physical, skill and the audience is aware that things may go wrong. Most obviously, suspense of this nature is experienced in circus acts or highly stylised forms of drama such as mime.

The next obvious step is to get the class to identify dramas or performances that fit under each of these headings.

• Sympathetic suspense in action

The nature of sympathetic suspense is worth exploring further because it is the category that students are most likely to come across in drama they create and experience. A number of short improvisations can be used to investigate ways in which sympathetic suspense can be induced.

The present

1 Students work in pairs, A and B, on the following sequence of spontaneous improvisations.

2 It is A's birthday. B gives A a present. A opens it and is delighted.

3 A is on the telephone to an unseen friend, jokily expressing the hope that they do not receive a particular present for their birthday. B arrives with that very present. A tries to show delight to B but must signal their disappointment to the audience.

4 The students try the same scene as in 3, but this time starting with B on the telephone to an unseen friend describing how difficult it has been to save for and find the present.

5 Students are then asked to suggest other examples of situations in which this kind of tension might occur.

6 Working in pairs or small groups, students jot down an idea for a scene which is driven by sympathetic suspense. These briefs are swapped around and realised by other students.

This activity can be the source of valuable reflections upon the nature of dramatic tension and the way audiences are emotionally positioned. Students may also reflect on the way in which performers need to exert control and adjust what they say and do in order to make the situation comic, tragic, sad or absurd. They should also consider how tension is heightened for the audience by careful use of timing and positioning.

④ Tension in context

The way a drama is structured contributes to the tension experienced by an audience. Although a play or film might start with a shocking image, tension needs to be built up. Timing is crucial. By relating back to the games described above, students will recognise that a sudden release of tension tends to provoke laughter and this may not be appropriate. On the other hand, it is equally possible to over-egg the cake and build up the tension so much that the situation feels clichéd and the audience want to cry out, 'Just get on with it!'

In the structure described below, students' attention is drawn to different kinds of dramatic tension and to ways of creating and conveying tension to an audience to provide different reactions.

Setting the fuse

1 The students work in threes on the following script extract, two acting and one directing. The rehearsed scene should:

- show that each character is suffering tension
- show that there is a tension between the characters
- build up a tension for the audience.

EXTRACT SCENE ONE

JEN	*(waking from a nightmare)* No! No! Who are you? It's you. I've seen you . . .
TREV	For God's sake! Shut up, will you? You're dreaming again.
JEN	What? What? *(coming round)* Oh. Sorry.
TREV	Every flippin' night! I have to work in the morning you know.
JEN	It's not my fault.
TREV	What was it this time?
JEN	Same one. *(Then, more to herself than Trevor)* Big explosion. Bodies. A woman's face. She's looking straight at me . . .
TREV	You want to get some therapy. Or jack in that job. If you can't take it, get out. Either way, let me get some sleep. Where are you off to now?
JEN	Downstairs. It's not easy for me either, you know. You try doing what I do when you're only getting a few hours' sleep each night.
TREV	*(rolling over and pulling the blankets up)* Take something.
JEN	Pig.

2 Two or three groups perform the scene, and the class then compare the techniques used, focusing on:

- what sort of tensions the characters were experiencing
- how the actors conveyed this through their use of voice and gesture.

3 The students are given the next extract (below) to work on, with different groups being given different constraints. If stage lighting and sound equipment are available, the permutations of how the scene is presented are numerous. For example:

- character sits with back towards audience so that they cannot see what the actor is doing; the actor is lit from above by a narrow white spotlight
- character faces the audience while working but appears to be talking to themselves; lighting is from the front but dim
- character addresses the audience directly while they work; they are lit from below by a floor flood
- only the bottom half of the character's face is lit, by a dim red table lamp
- audience only hears character's amplified voice through darkness.

It is also interesting to contrast the effect of having the scene played by both male and female performers.

EXTRACT SCENE TWO

VOICE   The last clip. Battery. Now, insert the detonator. Tape. Set the timer. Gently. Gently.
Just one flick of the switch and it's set.
It's what they've been asking for. Innocent lives. That's what they'll say. In the paper. On the telly. 'Innocent lives were lost.' But they're none of them innocent. They let it happen to others. Now it will happen to them.
Gently into the bag with you.
Now, let's go shopping.

4 Groups share examples of how they tackled the task to compare and contrast different ways of creating dramatic tension. They discuss how tension would be further created for an audience by having Scene Two following on immediately from Scene One. What connections are made and what expectations set up?

5 Scene Three (opposite) requires a slightly larger group. The task here is to rehearse the scene so that an audience:

- focuses on the tension of the relationship between Jen and Lucy
- is also aware of the presence and actions of the Woman (stage directions for this have deliberately been left out so that groups can decide on them for themselves)
- becomes aware of what will happen next, although the characters of Jen and Lucy remain unaware. This is an opportunity to explain one manifestation of dramatic irony.

A café area in a shopping mall.

JEN   You're not coming home then? (*Silence*) It's not helping me, you know, you just upping and going like that.

LUCY   Yeah, well it's helped me. You let him push you around if you like but I've had enough.

JEN   So what do you expect me to do? Just jack everything in and go? Look at you. What sort of a job do you think you're going to get looking like that? What sort of a life are you going to have?

LUCY   Well, I'll not be getting a job that stresses me out like you.

JEN   At least I've got a job.

LUCY   Which you hate.

JEN   It's not always like this. You shouldn't have left. Yes, I've got some stress. I'm not sleeping too well just lately. (*Pause*) I don't want to lose you. (*Silence*) Oh my God, look at the time! I'll be late on my shift. Must go. (*Suddenly looking up*) Excuse me . . . hey, excuse me . . . you've left your bag..

LUCY   What is it? Mum? Are you OK? You look . . .

JEN   It's nothing. Look, that woman just left her bag . . .

LUCY   Do you know her or something?

JEN   No. No, I don't know her. Look, I must go. Just hand the bag in at the counter – I'm sure she'll come back for it in a minute. I'll see you later. (*She goes. Lucy watches her, then moves over towards the bag.*)

6 As a whole class the students read and briefly discuss Scene Four.

WOMAN   It's done.

MAN 1   Were you seen?

WOMAN   No one saw me. Everything went as you said. Make the call. They've got ten more minutes – then we're out of here. Me and you. We'll have done what we said . . .

MAN 2   (*entering*) What do you think you're doing?

WOMAN   We're going to make the call. Then we're off.

MAN 2   Very cosy. Just one problem – it's already gone off.

WOMAN   It can't have.

MAN 2   It did. It's been on the damned radio already, along with a description of a woman seen leaving the bag. It's a good description.

7 By this time the students will probably have built a pretty clear picture of what sort of story is unfolding. Rather than spending time rehearsing Scene Four it is more productive to keep the focus on the way in which the order and content of the scenes is introducing different lines of tension and raising questions for the audience. Students' discussion can be focused through use of prepared worksheets or discussion of an overhead transparency. For example:

STORYLINE	TENSIONS	QUESTIONS
Jen wakes from a nightmare. Her husband is unsympathetic.	She is distressed by a strange and frightening dream.	Why is Jen so stressed? Is the dream a premonition?
Someone is making a bomb.	It's a delicate task. One slip and BOOM!	Who is this person? Why are they doing this?
Jen meets her daughter. She sees a Woman leave a bag. She tells Lucy to hand the bag in.	Jen wants Lucy to come home. She won't. ? ?	Why has Lucy left? Who is the Woman? ?
A Woman says she has done a job. She prepares to leave. Man 2 tells them a bomb has gone off.	? ? ?	What is the relationship between the Woman and Man 1? ?
?	?	?

8 Students work in pairs to write or improvise a scene which could answer a number of questions such as 'What is the relationship between the Woman and Man 1?' They are given the five options listed below in order to consider:

- which would be most believable
- which would fit in best with the scenes worked on so far.

Options:

1 Woman and Man 1 are professional terrorists being paid for the job.
2 They are husband and wife. Their daughter was killed by a bomb. This is a revenge attack.
3 The Man is Trevor. He and the Woman are lovers. The bomb is intended to kill Jen.
4 They are both agents of an evil organisation planning world domination. Their target is Lucy, who is an undercover agent for MI5.
5 . . . any other possibilities?

The purpose of this part of the structure is to draw the students' attention to the balance that needs to be kept in order to make drama successful. Too many lines of tension, or over-stretching any one of them, can make the play comically implausible. It is useful to invite students to name any films, television dramas or stage plays where they feel this was the case, and perhaps ask them to say why.

Tension and genre

A development of the last activity is to consider the apparent genre of this play, and therefore what sort of tensions are acceptable and believable. This discussion is introduced by revealing Scene Five:

EXTRACT SCENE FIVE

JEN	Over here, cubicle three. Staff, take a look at the man in five . . .
NURSE	Another two are just coming in, doctor. One male, early thirties, lacerations. One female. She must have been very close when it went off. She's lost both her arms. Severe injuries to face, chest and abdomen.
JEN	Let's take a look at her.

1 After reading this scene the class discuss:

- who they think the injured female is
- what evidence they would use to support their case
- what sort of dramas the play reminds them of
- why it does so.

2 In threes, the students draw on the work done so far to find an effective way of staging Scene Six. If a stage gun is available it is productive to explore the option of actually firing it as opposed to leaving the ending ambiguous as in Pinter's *The Dumb Waiter*.

EXTRACT SCENE SIX

MAN 2	So what do you suggest? She walks out of here and she'll be picked up straight away.
	And don't be telling me she won't talk. You know what to do.
MAN 1	I can't do that.
MAN 2	And I told you not to get her involved. (*Hands Man 1 a revolver*) Just do it.

In reflecting on how to tackle this scene the students must answer a huge range of directorial questions. Is the Woman present on stage? Perhaps she is seen by the audience listening to the conversation but the men are unaware of her presence (dramatic irony and overtones of Polonius behind the arras!). Are the men standing or sitting? Should Man 2 shout or be quietly menacing? Does Man 1 say his line to Man 2 or to himself? What does Man 1 do when he is handed the gun? At what point should the scene end?

⑤ Structuring a unit of work on dramatic tension and irony

One of the limitations of spontaneous improvisation and role-play work is the difficulty of building in tension and irony. These elements of drama need careful crafting. Working with specially written or established scripts allows students to focus more specifically on how tension and irony is created and to what effect. This being the case, there is an opportunity to introduce students to a wide range of drama. In this particular unit students learn something about Greek tragedy and the devices it employed to heighten tension for the audience. The unit also allows the students to experience tension at first hand through the careful and focused use of the teacher in role. By placing the students in role as citizens of Thebes, a congruence between what the students feel themselves and what the characters in the story feel is achieved.

● Researching the context

Students will find it helpful if the names of the key characters are displayed (that is, Creon, Antigone, Ismene, Polynices, Eteocles, Haemon). Teachers might also take advantage of the opportunity to create a wall display on Greek theatre showing images of masks, the auditorium at, say, Epidaurus and a glossary of key terms such as chorus, orchestra, skene and tragedy.

Students working at this level should be encouraged to research further into the topic by, for example, using library or Internet resources to find out about:

- the origins and social functions of Greek theatre
- conventions of the Greek theatre such as the use of mask, chorus, protagonist, antagonist
- the surviving plays and their writers
- the story of Oedipus and the city of Thebes, and how it has been the subject of a number of plays.

They can present their research in group seminars.

Engaging with the dilemma

1 The teacher narrates the background: a war has taken place. Two brothers, princes of the city of Thebes, have fought and died on opposing sides. The city is in mourning. Control has been taken by Creon, the uncle of the two princes.

2 The class imagine that they are standing along the walls of the city looking out at the carnage of the battlefield beyond. The teacher asks individuals to say aloud what they see in order to build a shared mental image of the scene.

3 The teacher enters in role as a messenger bearing Creon's proclamation that one of the princes, Eteocles, will be afforded a state funeral with full honours on account of his trying to defend the city. Meanwhile, Polynices, who died in his attempt to overthrow the city, will be left rotting in the sun.

4 The class discuss the implications of this proclamation, in or out of role as the teacher decides. Either way, the dramatic potential of the situation needs to be identified and reflected upon.

5 The students share their knowledge, or are told about, the nature and function of the Greek chorus.

6 Working alone, in pairs or in small groups, the students formulate a line that members of a chorus of citizens of Thebes might say in response to Creon's proclamation. These are gathered together on an overhead transparency and the class decides on an appropriate order.

7 The students go back into role and speak their lines in turn.

8 They are then given more background information concerning the princes' sisters, Antigone and Ismene. Antigone loved both her brothers equally and mourns them both. Ismene does not love either one less than Antigone does, but she feels that life must go on and that Creon will be a strong leader.

9 The students are encouraged to look further into the different dramatic re-tellings of the story of Antigone and its origins in Greek history as a research task. At this point they can usefully start to consider the psychology of the characters.

10 In groups of three, students improvise the scene in which a messenger or servant tells Antigone and Ismene about Creon's proclamation.

This activity is reflected upon in terms of how tension might be built up in the scene for an audience.

11 The class divides into three equal-sized groups representing Creon, Antigone and Ismene. Each group considers what they want or do not want to happen as a result of meeting. The meeting is organised with three individual students playing the key roles and using the techniques of forum theatre (pages 145–7). The rest of their group may stop the scene at any time and advise them how to proceed in order. The aim of the activity is not to resolve the problem but to inspect the different arguments.

Reflection on the forum once again focuses on how tension was developed through what the characters said and did.

12 The three groups create tableaux depicting the different aspects of their given character. Each group crafts a short statement about themselves and what they think and feel about each other and the situation they are in. The tableaux and statements are shared.

13 The students decide for themselves what different arguments might run through Antigone's head as she considers whether or not to break Creon's ruling and bury Polynices. Those who would urge her to bury her brother stand in a row, those who would urge her not to form a row opposite. The students are encouraged to formulate a line of dialogue which is:
   • appropriate to the chorus of citizens of Thebes
   • likely to add to the dramatic tension by the way it is delivered.

14 The teacher, in role as Antigone, walks through the two rows of students to hear the two choruses.

15 The students adopt the role of soldiers. The teacher, also in role as a soldier, tells them that someone has attempted to bury Polynices. Who will be prepared to tell Creon, knowing how furious he will be? The class (including the teacher in role as a soldier) improvise the scene.

16 The teacher should ensure that a situation arises in which the soldiers write their names on a slip of paper in order to draw lots as to who will tell Creon. It is worth taking time on this in order to deliberately build up the tension. At this point, the tension is double edged in that what the students will be feeling as themselves will be congruent with what the soldiers would be feeling – that is, whose name will be drawn?

17 In pairs, or as a whole class, the students improvise the scene in which Creon is told.

18 The teacher narrates the next part of the story, revealing that Antigone is caught red-handed trying again to bury her brother.

19   The whole class work in role as the chorus, with the teacher in role as Creon, to improvise the scene in which Creon tries to decide what to do with Antigone. What sort of advice does the chorus offer?

20   The students work in pairs. One is Creon, the other his son Haemon, who pleads with his father to spare Antigone's life. The students suggest how sympathetic suspense could be added to this scene. If they do not suggest it themselves, they need to be told that Haemon is in love with Antigone. How could this knowledge be used to heighten the tension in the scene between father and son? What could Haemon threaten if Creon does not back down?

21   The students speculate on what happens at the end of the play.

22   The class work in small groups on the last scene of Sophocles' play and discuss its dramatic effectiveness, paying particular attention to the use of tension and irony in the story.

23   Students are asked to read the whole text as homework and to complete an evaluation on the unit in essay form, focusing on how form can be used to build tension.

After working through this structured improvisation, the students should reflect on the relationship between the tension the fictitious characters would feel and the tension they personally felt as player-participants in the fiction. Such a discussion should help students focus on the enduring qualities of classic texts such as Antigone.

Tension in the text

By way of seeing their own work in a greater context, students might profitably explore, in a practical way, the potential of a scripted version of the Antigone story. Declan Donolan's 1999 translation of Sophocles' play clearly presents the Sentry (the soldier who tells Creon that Antigone has attempted to bury Polynices) as a comic, slightly bumbling and sympathetic character to contrast with Creon's stern authoritarianism. Rehearsing this extract will offer students deeper insights into how playwrights sometimes craft their scripts to create dramatic tension and irony in quite unexpected ways. Jean Anouilh's use of the story as an allegory for Nazi-occupied France may also be drawn upon for a deeper study of dramatic tension, most notably when the context in which Anouilh was writing and the play was first performed are taken into account.

Unit planning sheet for drama

Unit title *Antigone*   **Time scale** 3 × 100 minutes or 5 hrs

AIMS

- to extend students' understanding and practice in heightening dramatic tension
- to introduce students to performing Greek drama.

SUGGESTED ACTIVITIES

- introduction to Greek theatre/Greek tragedy through discussion, feedback plus sharing of visual and other recorded materials plus recap on the critical nature of tension in drama (connections with particular forms used in television etc.) plus KS3 work
- warm-up activities using 'undercover agents'
- brief scenarios given for paired improvisations – building of tension – responses – how tension was heightened
- research activities (questions and issues) raised in preparation for homework on Greek theatre
- research findings shared through seminar groups
- whole-group improvisations – teacher in role as narrator/messenger, students as chorus – setting context plus edict
- discussion on dramatic potential of scene – suggestions for key lines
- scene re-created and refined following reflection and feedback (students may use thought tracking etc.)
- further research on the psychology and context of Antigone and Ismene – findings shared
- small (3) group improvisations – messenger or servant informing Antigone and Ismene of Creon's proclamation – focus on building up of tension during the scene – sample scenes shared and feedback given
- forum drama – 3 groups, one each to focus on Antigone, Ismene and Creon – possible arguments explored
- further discussion/reflection – how was tension developed through what characters did and said in forum?
- image/tableau – groups each depicting aspects of their character plus a statement about themselves – reflection
- conscience alley/chorus of *Antigone* focus on dramatic tension through language, pace and tone
- ritualistic selection of soldier/sentry to inform Creon of Antigone's deed
- paired improvisations of scene when Creon is informed of Antigone's act
- comparison with extract of same scene from Sophocles' play – students experiment with different interpretations of role of sentry to see if any one form provides additional tension and irony to play
- improvisation with teacher in role as Creon and whole group as chorus – advising
- paired work as Haemon pleads with Creon to spare Antigone's life (students to use different approaches to increase tension)
- whole-class prediction/speculation of what could happen at the end of the play
- reading of whole play (homework × 3)
- written evaluation on unit focusing on how form can be used to build tension.

EVIDENCE OF LEARNING (CREATING, PERFORMING, RESPONDING)

Creating Are students:
- experimenting with different approaches to heighten tension successfully?

Performing Are students:
- showing understanding of the motivations and behaviours of Antigone and Ismene in their improvisations?
- demonstrating that they can focus and engage audience through the effective use of form?

Responding Are students:
- identifying key characteristics of Greek tragedy through their research and in seminars?
- showing understanding of how form can be used to build tension in drama?
- critically evaluating how the structure of scenes studied contribute to dramatic effect?

INTENDED LEARNING OUTCOMES

By the end of the unit the students should know and understand:
- principal characteristics of Greek tragedy
- how an audience can be focused and engaged through the use of form.

They should be able to:
- apply specific approaches to heighten tension
- apply their knowledge of the psychology and context of two key characters.

RESOURCES

- sufficient relevant extracts from *Antigone* by Sophocles for whole class
- photographs, texts, reference documents on Greek theatre, chorus, production programmes of *Antigone* and masks (if available)
- computer with access to Internet, e.g. www.temple.educ/classics/dramaterms.html

COMMENTS/EVALUATION POINTS

- Levels 6–Exceptional Performance
- Ideally use this unit during a term when visit can be made to a performance of a Greek play.

Investigating how plays are written, performed and received is a fundamental part of drama education. Considering how drama is notated forms part of the National Literacy Strategy. Being able to realise a playscript in performance is an essential part of GCSE and A level syllabuses in the subject. Progression in drama involves students:

- understanding how plays, in their scripted form, are different from other forms of literature

- being able to interpret scripts from different perspectives and for different purposes

- learning how to notate their own ideas using the conventions of dramatic writing.

The practical ideas in this chapter may be used to introduce and develop the skills essential to working with scripts.

① Introduction

Younger students are increasingly being given opportunities to tackle scripts as 'briefs for performance' rather than as pieces of literature. This involves regarding the script as something to be interpreted and developed by a production team who will tackle the different challenges involved in bringing it to life, or realising it, in performance. The approach represents something of a sea change from 'traditional' classroom-based practices in which plays tended only to be taught as part of the English curriculum, while drama focused more on improvisations and role-plays. With drama now playing a more identifiable part in the National Curriculum for English and the National Literacy Strategy, drama teachers have opportunities and responsibilities to ensure that students progress in their knowledge and understanding of drama in its written form.

Methods that may be appropriate in the study of other forms of literature are not necessarily helpful in the study of dramatic writing. For example, whereas reading a novel may be a fulfilling and pleasurable solo activity, most students find it difficult to get a sense of the play in action by reading it on their own. An alternative is to read the play around the class, but this can take far too long and stumbling and droning delivery will only result in increasingly uninterested students. Setting comprehension tasks or critical essays is unlikely to provide students with an insight into how directors, designers and actors go about interpreting the script and communicating the narrative to an audience. The end result of applying inappropriate and unimaginative methods to the study of plays is, of course, to turn many students away from reading them and to limit their ability to discuss them effectively in dramatic terms.

In contrast to the desk-bound study of plays, the 'practical approach' might be taken to imply working towards an actual production. This is often impossible because of time, space and technical restraints and sometimes undesirable because the learning outcomes of working on a production are so highly differentiated. For example, a student playing Lady Macbeth may understandably be so concerned to get her bit 'right' that innumerable other points of interest are simply blocked out. Conversely, students with minor acting parts or technical responsibilities may be in a better position to gain an overview of the process of production. In reality though, as the first night approaches, opportunities for learning about the play through reflective discussion tend to dissolve in the furious rush to iron out a myriad of practical problems.

Any viable alternative to both the desk-bound and the stage-bound model of teaching dramatic literature needs to offer:

- ways of getting the students to engage with the text from the first encounter
- ways of getting them to see the text as a whole as quickly as possible
- ways of encouraging them to consider their personal responses to the text
- methods which will help them see the characters and narrative as dramatic creations, rather than as real people and situations
- ways of regarding the text as an incomplete experience, the meaning of which they – as readers, actors, directors and audience – will have a hand in creating.

② Introducing scripts through scripting

All too often students' first experience of a script is when they are given a complete, and probably quite sophisticated, play to read. What a contrast this is to the gradual way in which many children are introduced to poetry and prose fiction. In any event, a play is not simply a story told through dialogue. Students need to be taught how to see the words on the page as indications of what is actually happening on the stage. Students can learn a great deal about the way scripts work by reading, writing and playing around with very short pieces of dialogue. The activities outlined below are extremely flexible and can be adjusted to suit groups of widely different experience and ability in order to introduce some of the central concepts and challenges of working with scripts.

● Four-line plays

The four-line play device is an extremely economical way of teaching students about the basic clay of the art form. By sharing and discussing the different ways students have realised a short script, attention can be focused on how gesture, movement, spatial relationships, timing, pauses, use of voice and so on all contribute to the matrix of meaning.

Acting and writing out dialogue

1 The students are shown this piece of dialogue:

  A Good morning.

  B I beg your pardon?

  A It's a lovely day.

  B I'm glad you think so.

2 In pairs, the students try at least six different ways of acting this play out. They must not add any more dialogue but should look at what happens when they change the tone and volume of their voice, or add pauses and movement.

3 The students decide on a situation in which this conversation might occur. They might, for example, decide that A is a condemned prisoner being led up to the chopping block where B the executioner, is sharpening the axe.

4 Having decided on the context for the dialogue, the students rehearse it again and try to find ways of making it clear to an audience who they are and where they are without adding more lines. Their work is shown to an audience of classmates who comment on how successful they have been in making the situation clear. The teacher helps them to pinpoint how they have managed this.

5 Next, still in pairs, the students are asked to write a four-line play of their own. First they must think of a situation, then they write their four lines. When they have done this, they pass their play on to another pair but tell them nothing about the situation as they have imagined it. This new pair will rehearse the lines in their own way.

6 A further task can be set involving the students rehearsing a four-line play of their own and then trying to notate what they did in performance as accurately as they can. The script is again passed on: can another group of performers realise the script in exactly the same way? If not, why not? Just how important is it to be able to replicate performance?

When scenes created through this sort of constraint are shared, the class will have lots to talk about. In what ways did the performers imagine the scene differently from the authors? What does the activity suggest about the process of realising scripts in performance? What does it suggest about the problems involved in notating ideas in drama?

● **Stage directions**

Writing plays involves more than just putting down on paper what people actually say in real life. Hold a tape recorder up and record a group of people talking; when you play it back you will soon discover that people talk over each other or leave sentences unfinished and it is often a complete mystery as to what they are actually talking about. In real life, for example, people might be pointing at something which an audience listening to a tape would not be able to see. Playwrights get round this problem by giving stage directions.

From page to stage

1 The teacher reads just the dialogue from the extract overleaf, and asks the students what they make of it.

SHELTER	(*off*) Why not take the weight off your feet?
LINK	(*to himself*) Why not indeed.
	He sits in SHELTER'*S chair, then spots something under the table. He stoops to find a watch.*
	Can't be.
	Sees the inscription. Enter SHELTER, *noticing* LINK'*S discovery. He quietly closes the door behind himself.*
SHELTER	Found something?
	LINK tries to hide the watch.
LINK	(*getting up*) I've just remembered, I'm supposed to be meeting someone . . .
SHELTER	You all right son?
LINK	Fine. Yeah. I just . . .
SHELTER	(*pushing* LINK *back into the chair and losing the do-gooder voice*) Don't sound very fine to me. What have you got?

Stone Cold by Joe Standerline

2 The class are then shown the complete extract and discuss what function the stage directions serve. From this snippet alone, what impression do they get of the characters?

3 The students try the extract out, working in groups of three, with one taking the role of director to comment on, for example, use of timing, space and gesture.

4 They write another short script which attempts to convey the same sort of tone and atmosphere as the example. It should have no more than six lines of dialogue and must rely on some stage directions to make sense. As with the four-line plays, the finished scripts are passed on and rehearsed to see if they work in performance as the authors imagined. It is important that the players are not allowed to consult with the authors.

5 Students research the different ways stage directions are written by skimming through a selection of scripts and identifying directions which appear to perform different functions or address different members of the production team.

The whole point of the activity, and indeed the fun of it, is to realise how actors and directors interpret what playwrights actually write. Being able to identify and discuss the different interpretative lenses a script is seen through as it moves from page to stage is an essential ingredient of students' critical reflections on drama at examination level.

● Clues in the dialogue

Playwrights do not always rely on explicit stage directions to make the required action clear. Doing so can make scripts cumbersome and dull to read and it is often possible to work out more or less what is going on by paying attention to what is actually being said as in the following extract:

EXTRACT

MEG	Let's have some of yours.
McCANN	In that?
MEG	Yes.
McCANN	Are you used to mixing them?
MEG	No.
McCANN	Give me your glass.

The Birthday Party by Harold Pinter

▶ Words that speak volumes

1 The students read the above snippet of dialogue: what do they imagine the actors are actually doing here? In pairs, they act it out and then write out the script, putting in stage directions which make it absolutely clear who is doing what and how they are doing it.

2 The students share their ideas with other pairs to compare how similar their stage directions are and to discuss whether they are really necessary in order to understand the action, or whether they make reading the script more difficult in some way.

3   In pairs, students write a four-line play in which it is absolutely clear who is speaking, where the play is set and what is happening. These scripts are passed to other pairs who must realise them.

Just as lengthy stage directions can make scripts tedious to read and may sometimes be unnecessary, so over-burdening dialogue with too much contextual information can make characters sound unbelievable. Tom Stoppard's play The Real Inspector Hound *successfully lampoons this kind of strained writing. Students can have a lot of fun to a sound purpose by investigating the dividing line between dialogue which flows and convinces and that which jars and sounds false.*

● Utilising information and communication technology (ICT)

Some teachers are now beginning to see the possibilities of interactive whiteboards and other ICT facilities to help students work with scripts. ICT offers students the facility to edit, cut and paste, and annotate pieces of text without destroying expensive, and therefore precious, hard copies. A productive sub-text of this kind of interaction is the way it undermines the 'tyranny of the text'. The process of interpreting plays is as much about students finding form for their own beliefs and creativity as it is about trying to retain the integrity of the original writing.

● Writing dialogue

One of the most notable differences between the way students improvise dialogue and write it down is that improvisations tend to be very wordy, while written scripts are often extremely scant. There are some obvious reasons for this. Talk is cheap, but writing takes more time and effort. Another difference is that while improvised dialogue can capture the rhythms and cadences of everyday speech, written dialogue often feels stilted and very unnatural. One of the limitations of role-play and many improvisations is that they tend to invite students to work only within a vaguely naturalistic genre. Writing convincing naturalistic dialogue is extremely difficult. In order to improve the quality of students' written coursework and extend the range of the drama they create, they need to be taught how to use a few effective techniques.

Hearing between the lines

1 The students imagine a simple scene such as a time when they wanted to go out but an adult was telling them that they could not. The class are divided into two groups. Working in pairs, one half of the class are asked to write the scene. The other half improvise the scene for a set time (two minutes will be plenty) and, if possible, tape record it. Next, they either write down an extract of what they remember improvising or transcribe a part of the tape.

2 Pairs from one group join up in fours with pairs from the other group and share their work. What do they notice about the sheer number of words spoken in an improvisation? Do the scripted scenes flow in the same way, or does the language somehow seem false?

3 Students new to scripts of plays need to be shown that sometimes dialogue can come across as being more realistic when there are gaps and jumps between what characters are saying. The class read the following short extract and talk about how the two characters seem to be thinking about different things. They try to pick out those moments when the conversation seems to jump from one thing to another.

EXTRACT

IRIS	I'll give you sorry, my lad.
ALISTAIR	Ow ow ow ow ow ow!
IRIS	What else have you two been up to?
ALISTAIR	It wasn't me it was him!
IRIS	What have I told you about lies?
ALISTAIR	He said he'd torture me if I told.
IRIS	Nothing but trouble since he got here.
ALISTAIR	I tried to stop him, Mum – honest.

Two Weeks with the Queen by Mary Morris

Focusing on the idea that different characters will have different things on their minds when they are speaking gives the audience the impression that what is being said is only the tip of an iceberg. It is as if the playwright wants to give us the impression that there is a lot more to the characters behind what they are saying. The 'gaps' in between the lines are there for the audience to fill in.

- **Creative constraints**

  One way of getting students to create interesting gaps in their script-writing is to make them work to a very strict rule.

   Alphabetically speaking

1 The students write out the first sixteen letters of the alphabet down the side of a sheet of paper. In pairs, they write out a conversation between a teenager who wants to go out and an adult who says they cannot do so (either basing it on the previous activity or creating the conversation from scratch). The first line starts with an A, the second with a B and so on. For example:

  ADULT   And just where do you think you're off to?

  TEENAGER   But, Mum . . .

  ADULT   Can't you see you've caused me enough trouble?

  TEENAGER   Dad would let me go if he was here.

2 When they have finished their script they pass it on to another pair, who discuss how clear the action is just through what is being said and also decide how it should be staged. They then try out the scenes and, as a group, talk about how realistic some of them were, even though they were written to a very unrealistic formula.

   Patterns of long and short

  Another technique is to dictate the length of lines spoken. The technique involves the students writing short scripts in an agreed pattern of either 'long lines' or 'short lines'. So, for example, the agreed pattern may be:

  This technique can be very revealing of the structure and rhythm of dialogue.

A menu of constraints

All sorts of other constraints can be added to the two previous activities to give an impetus or focus to the work. Create a menu like the one below on which the students can draw – it can, of course, be as extensive as you please. Get the students to write a few lines of dialogue with constraints taken from the different columns, and to play around with different combinations.

Contrasting scripts arising from the menu above might be:

SETTING	CHARACTERS	TONE
police station	young child	comic
shop	police woman	menacing
sinking ship	alien	tragic

A   So mummy didn't pick you up at school like she usually does, is that right?

B   No.

A   But you went home on your own and found the front door open.

B   Yes, so I went inside and that's when I found her lying there.

A   I see.

A   Rose! Rose! We'll always be together my love, no matter what happens.

B   Whatever.

A   Nothing will part us. Not the sea, not the night, not death itself.

B   This is Zarg calling Mothership, Zarg calling Mothership. I've had enough of this now – it's cold and wet and this dress looks awful on me so beam me up right now.

A   Rose!

As with the four-line play, this is a simple yet extremely flexible technique that can be utilised to explore elements of genre and the way in which the rhythm of the lines carries meaning. It is extremely difficult, for example, to make some combinations menacing while equally hard to make others comic.

• Juxtaposition

Mixing and matching different types of writing illustrates how drama does not involve dialogue alone. Letters, news reports, one-sided telephone conversations, poems, songs and so on can all be used to communicate characters and situations to an audience. Juxtaposing monologues can create economical and deeply ironic pieces of drama.

▶ Monologues

1   The class read through the extract below and discuss how the drama works. They consider, for example, the contrasts between who the characters are and what responsibilities they have.

General Haig was Commander-in-Chief of the British Army in the First World War. The scene takes place on the eve of the Battle of the Somme, in which over 600,000 British soldiers lost their lives (20,000 on the first day). Far from 'driving the enemy into the sea', the battle moved the front line forward by less than eight miles. Given this context, the students should pay particular attention to the dramatic effect of the last stage direction.

EXTRACT

NURSE	The fields are full of tents, O Lord, all empty except for as yet unmade and naked iron bedsteads. Every ward has been cleared to make way for the wounded that will be arriving when the big push comes.
HAIG	I trust you will understand, Lord, that as a British gentleman I could not subordinate myself to the ambitions of a junior foreign commander, as the politicians suggested. It is for the prestige of my King and Empire, Lord.
CHAPLAIN	Teach us to rule ourself always, controlled and cleanly night and day.
HAIG	I ask thee for victory, Lord, before the Americans arrive.
NURSE	The doctors say there will be enormous numbers of dead and wounded, God.
CHAPLAIN	That we may bring if need arise, no maimed or worthless sacrifice.
HAIG	Thus to grant us fair weather for tomorrow's atttack, that we may drive the enemy into the sea.
NURSE	O Lord, I beg you, do not let this dreadful war cause all the suffering that we have prepared for. I know you will answer my prayer.
	Explosion. They go off.

Oh What a Lovely War by Theatre Workshop

A	B
A child is writing to Father Christmas saying what they want for Christmas.	A news reporter is giving the first details of an air crash.
A terrorist is dictating instructions on where and how to plant a bomb.	Someone is speaking to a friend on the telephone about their forthcoming holiday.
A doctor is filling in a report on a patient who is seriously ill.	A teacher is writing a report on a particularly difficult student.
A teenager is writing a love letter to someone they are too shy to talk to directly.	A character is writing their personal thoughts in their diary about the events of the previous week.

2   The students experiment with the idea of cutting monologues together. Working in pairs, they try to write a scene in which two characters are somehow involved in the same situation and speaking aloud, but not actually to each other, by using an idea from column A and one from column B in the table above.

3 Tools for text work

The written text of a play may be interpreted in different ways. A designer, for example, would be interested in different aspects of the text from an actor. A director who knows the constraints of a particular venue, is working within a set budget and is keen to attract a certain type of audience, will consider different questions. Students need to adopt a mind set which sees the script as something that will inevitably change when it is interpreted into a performance. Helping students realise that, in professional theatre, scripts are cut up, edited and changed around releases them from the intimidating and stultifying notion that the script is sacred and only has one 'correct' meaning.

Cutting and pasting

Working in pairs or small groups, the students are given an envelope containing several single lines of dialogue to re-construct in the form of a short play or scene. They will tend to want to know whether they have managed to match the original but that is not the point of the activity. Rather, discussion should focus on:

- what they perceived the atmosphere and tone of the piece to be
- where and when they thought the scene was set
- what they felt about the characters.

It is often the case that there is a good deal of agreement about these things even though groups will have re-constructed the text in different ways. The question to consider, then, is, how significant are any of the alterations in the order of the lines? What is it about the script that manages to carry more or less the same meaning forward even though the structure is changed? In other cases, of course, even the most minor change will have a radical effect on the meaning. Here again, the purpose of the activity is to identify why this is so.

Captions and images

Applying captions to images from a play does require the students to read the play, or extract, though not necessarily in depth. The aim of the activity is simply to write a brief caption describing each of the main events in the play. Brecht used this technique in the written text of many of his plays. Seeing the play as a series of different units serves as a good introduction to some of Stanislavski's ideas.

Having identified the 'stepping stones' that the play appears to be built on, the students then create a simple tableau for each one. The ultimate effect is to present a kind of simple 'cartoon' version of the play. Further work involving re-structuring the scenes into a different order highlights both how the plot is tied in with the structure and how re-ordering can change the meaning or dramatic effectiveness of the piece.

The flat book

This is a splendid way of helping students see a play's script as a whole and allowing them to engage with it. Each page of the script is pasted on a sheet of card and all the cards are then displayed on a wall (in the way Chinese newspapers are presented). Students are usually astonished at how small even plays by Shakespeare appear when they are presented in this way. Such a change in perception is very helpful as it makes the script look considerably less daunting.

Once displayed on the wall, students can 'plot' different themes in the play using map pins and coloured wool. For example, in *Hamlet*, one group might identify all those lines that deal with the mother/son relationship and link them together with one colour. Another group might choose to look at the theme of death and link together useful quotations with a different colour. The final effect of this work is to show the text as a working document. Older students who have used the activity have found that it is an excellent revision activity which helps them plan their critical essays.

④ Exploring dramatic characters

There is a delicate balance to be achieved between suggesting that characters in a play have a psychological reality of their own, and treating them just in terms of the function they serve in the narrative. While trying to avoid fatuous questions such as the apocryphal 'How many children did Lady Macbeth have?', speculating on details of a character's life can be a creative and helpful activity. Students must understand, however, that the way a character is portrayed on paper is open to interpretation, the result being that no two productions of a play will show the characters in exactly the same light.

A number of techniques may be used to explore how characters are developed, how they can be played, how they relate to each other and how they might be viewed by an audience.

- *Video clips*: showing the class a number of short clips of the same scene from different filmed versions of plays is an excellent and quick way of reminding them that their personal response to a written text will affect the way they might go on to play a character (see pages 263–4).
- *Role on the wall*: students draw a simple outline to represent a character and then add notes on, for example, what they know about the character from the text (perhaps placing these inside the outline) and what they assume about the character (perhaps placing these outside the outline). Their personal response to the character, notes on the character's relationship to others and details of the character's personal history are other ideas which can be used.
- *Hot-seating*: students ask one of the characters (played by either the teacher or another student) questions about their attitudes. This technique is especially productive if the questions are asked from another character's point of view.
- *The character pot*: students sit in a circle and a character is selected. One student crosses the circle and addresses another as if they were that chosen character; that student then approaches a third student and so on. So, for example, if Macbeth is the focus of the study the first student might say 'You really think a lot of yourself, don't you?'. The second student could say, 'I expect meeting the hags was a bit of trauma. Do you think the experience unbalanced your mind in any way?' The technique can be made more sophisticated by insisting that the statement or question is made from another character's point of view (as in hot-seating) or by allowing the character the right to reply.

- *Imaging relationships*: groups are asked to physically show the tensions and relationships between characters. A chair is placed in the middle of the room to represent a character and, selecting other characters in the piece, students adopt an appropriate position in relation to the chair. For example, the character's mother might stand next to her son; an enemy might crouch behind the chair with hands ready to throttle him; a jilted lover might stand to one side and at a distance, looking over her shoulder at him. The activity can lead to a useful discussion about how relationships in the play are perceived and how stage space can be used to convey this.

- *Find yourself*: students are given or choose lines from the play which they deem typical of a character. The task is then to mill around the room saying the line and listening carefully to the lines being said back. The game is to try and identify which other students have lines spoken by the same character but at a different moment in the play. This is an intriguing activity and reveals a great deal about the way in which playwrights give characters an identifiable voice through use of register and rhythm.

- *Conscience alley*: this is a way of exploring what might be going through a character's mind at a moment of crisis. The students form two lines and think to themselves what the character might be thinking as they ponder their course of action. The teacher or another student walks down between the two lines and listens to different voices and arguments as the students say out loud what they think might be going on in the character's head.

- *Re-setting the lines in a new context*: students are given an extract to study for genre and style. They select no more than four consecutive lines from the extract and hide them in a new scene of their own devising. The task inevitably demands that they assimilate the style and language of the original.

- *Packing up*: students imagine that a character is moving house. A box or case is placed in the middle of the circle and one by one, in role as the chosen character, the students pretend to pack the box, speaking aloud what they are putting in and what the significance of that might be.

- *The family album*: if a character had kept a series of photographs of key moments in their life, what would those photographs show? The students make still images of those moments (which may come from the play or beyond it).

- *Centring*: this rehearsal technique is a particularly useful activity for students of all ages and can be employed in many contexts. The underlying idea is that a character is ruled by a particular centre. Students walk around the studio space imagining, for example, that the 'centre' of their character is based in their forehead, or on their left knee, or in the small of their back. How does simply imagining this change the way they walk? It may be suggested that the 'centre' has a colour and shape. How does a character walk if their centre is a medicine ball in the belly (Sir Toby Belch)? What if it is a little sparkling thing on the end of their nose (Sir Andrew Aguecheek)? Or, by way of contrast, a very tight knot in between the buttocks (Malvolio)?

  Students can be asked to decide on a particular centre and to explore how this suggests a certain type of person to them as they move around the space, or try to sit or mime certain actions. Other students could ask a character questions and set them tasks: 'Sit down', 'Answer the telephone', 'Make a cup of coffee'. By watching carefully, the observers try to identify where the actor has placed the character's centre and what shape and colour it is.

  This technique can be used to explore the performance style associated with certain genres such as *commedia dell'arte*. It is a particularly useful adjunct to mask work based on archetypes.

- *Writing in role/creative extension*: students are asked to produce creative writing from the perspective of a character in a play, or to relate the events of a play in a different sort of format. There are all manner of devices which can be employed to generate lively pieces of writing but not all of them successfully provide greater insights into the way plays work and dramatic characters are constructed. For example, one recently trialled Key Stage 3 Standard Assessment Task asked students to write in role as Juliet's Nurse explaining to her employers, the Capulets, what her role was in the young lovers' relationship. A student who understood how, in production, the Nurse could be shown as duplicitous and self-preserving, might reasonably write an answer in which she denied all knowledge of any relationship – not an approach, unfortunately, that would have gained many marks against the given assessment criteria for the task.

⑤ Exploring plot and structure

A good deal can be learnt about aspects of scripts such as genre, style and characterisation by experimenting with very short extracts from plays. Inevitably, it is more difficult to study plot and structure through extracts. If students are studying a whole play it is essential that attention is paid to the way the whole thing hangs together and progresses. Nevertheless, there are active and imaginative alternatives to plodding through the text with the students and attempting to dictate to the class what the play means and how the playwright has put over that meaning.

- *The quick read*: the class is split into small groups. Give each group a different section of the play to read. Their task is to note, on slips of paper, the main events of that section even though at this point they will not know how those events relate to the overall narrative. This leads on to . . .

- *Mapping*: this involves each group re-telling the rest of the class what happened in their section of the play in chronological order. The slips of paper are laid out on a long sheet of paper. Lines are drawn between events that seem to relate to each other. In this way the class can very quickly achieve an overview of the narrative line and the main characters. An example of the first part of a map of Noel Greig's play *Final Cargo* is shown on page 241.

- *Cloze*: this exercise involves the students filling in blanks in the text. The blanks might indicate key words or whole phrases. In drama, the teacher might, for example, hand out an extract of a script from which all the original stage directions have been removed. The task would then be to discuss what sort of directions would be needed to make sense of the remaining dialogue.

- *Scenes we'd like to see*: students write a brief description of a scene that might be inserted into the play. The description is passed to another group who improvise it.

- *The set next door*: this is a similar activity to the one above but takes Tom Stoppard's approach from *Rosencrantz and Guildenstern Are Dead*, in which characters on the edge of the action improvise new situations (based on the premise that 'Every exit is an entrance somewhere else').

- *Re-constructing passages*: students are given a short section of text which has been cut up into individual lines. The task is to re-assemble the scene. The sophistication of this task obviously depends upon the complexity of the scene chosen. With younger groups the focus is most likely to be on narrative sequences whereas older groups could focus on the language style of different characters or the action implied in the lines.

- *Hot spots*: students pick out a line or action that seems to mark the most tense moment in a given scene. Discussing how dramatic tension is achieved is a very important element of working on plays. Tension has many forms and can only be really understood in the context of the whole play.
- *Time and tension lines*: students make a graph to show how the tension of the play changes for different characters, and indeed the audience, as it progresses.
- *The Reader's Digest proudly presents . . .* : using the notes created from the mapping activity, or captions given to different scenes, students present a highly edited version of the play through still images, short improvisations and use of selected lines.

6 Attending to elements of design

Set, costume, make-up, lighting and sound design are optional areas of study in many drama examination syllabuses. Certainly, students going on to study drama at AS and A level will need a firm understanding of the way design elements contribute to the meaning plays have for an audience. Although teachers may feel themselves to be less than expert in some areas of theatre design and technology, there are a number of tasks that can be set for individual or group study. Encouraging and facilitating greater engagement with information and communication technology gives students greater insights into contemporary professional practices and deepens the understanding of how the written text is transposed into a performance text.

Over the course of a drama programme in secondary school, students might reasonably expect to have an opportunity to:

- design the costumes of different characters
- design and make models of settings for scenes or whole plays
- design posters and programmes using information communication technology (ICT) wherever possible
- explore the possibilities offered by computer technology in set and lighting design
- find and record appropriate music for a soundtrack on tape or compact disc

- ascribe different colours to scenes according to where they are set and what atmosphere they convey, and use this as the basis for writing lighting plots
- produce extracts of the play on cassette or video recorder to explore how the different media are constrained; schools are rapidly becoming better equipped with technological hardware allowing for still or moving images to be edited on computer
- storyboard short extracts for filming
- photograph actors or set models to show how different lighting effects change and enhance dramatic meaning (here again, digital cameras are extremely useful).

7 Responding to scripts

The types of questions one can ask about a play are fairly limited, although as students progress in their knowledge and understanding of drama they should be expected to tackle basic areas in more and more detail. Through oral and written work, an assessment can be made of students' knowledge of content, form and context. A list of questions that it is useful to pose about plays seen in performance is given in chapter 3.4 (*Discourse in drama*) on pages 143–4. Many of these can be used to guide students towards a deeper appreciation of the written text.

In the case of some plays, students can discuss how the play should be performed but generally it is more productive to speculate on how it might be performed by asking:

- To what extent does the play reveal something about the context in which it was originally written and is now being received? How will this guide decisions about how to put the play on?
- How do we understand the actions that a character is taking or the relationship that characters have with each other?
- Does the story have any metamorphic or symbolic value? Is it working at more than one level?
- What particularly interests us about the play? What aspects do we want to emphasise?

- **First responses**

Questions and tasks geared towards exploring what students feel and think about a play produce richer responses than bald comprehension questions, which all too often suggest that there is just one right answer. Activities following a reading of a play or seeing one might include:

- re-telling the story in pairs or groups
- identifying moments of surprise and delight
- noting questions which were raised but unanswered by the play
- tackling a cloze activity in which the story is re-told with certain words missing (see page 230)
- re-telling bits from a new perspective, for example, how would one of the main characters relate the events of *Hamlet* to someone outside the world of the play?
- sketching a map of the location
- making a storyboard of some scenes
- sculpting a physical image in groups of what the play meant overall
- creating two images – one that captures the tone of the play at the start and another contrasting one for the end
- using movement to suggest the way the tones and rhythms of the play change through the play.

- **Written tasks**

Drama can be a powerful stimulus for creative writing and to some extent setting creative extension tasks can give new insights into some aspects of the storyline and the characters, for example:

- writing newspaper headlines and the first paragraph of news stories
- letters from or to characters
- epitaphs and obituaries
- prayers spoken by characters
- using acronyms to make statements about the themes or as a constraint for imagined conversations
- diary or filofax entries
- school reports for key characters, for example:

Prince Hamlet is making good progress in some areas of the curriculum. He shows progress in fencing and works well with a small group of friends. At times he can appear surly and aggressive (especially to some of the girls). His work in technology has been hampered by his confusion about the differences between hawks and handsaws.

The object of all of the activities described above is to give students new insights into scripts in an imaginative and engaging way. However, there is a grave danger that tasks such as these become too peripheral to the actual text and do little to extend the students' ability to respond critically to drama. As with any work that is designed to help the students progress, the objective of the task needs to be considered carefully. Is it to stretch the students' knowledge of the play, or to exercise their own creativity *per se*?

⑧ Structuring a unit of work around a playscript

• *Final Cargo* by **Noel Greig**

Final Cargo is a powerful play by a contemporary playwright that could be used with a strong Year 8 group and is certainly suitable for groups in Year 9 and above. Ostensibly the play concerns the captain of a small ship who is told by the owners to take the boat to a scrapyard. In order to have one last voyage, though, he accepts an illegal cargo of toxic waste. Personal and ecological tragedy occur when the ship collides with a Greenpeace vessel that is tracking the cargo. *Final Cargo* is a moving and poetic play which offers a number of interesting dramatic challenges in terms of characterisation, staging and style. Through its use of metaphor and allegory it may be seen as dealing with themes such as love, greed and political corruption.

The unit outlined below is designed to help a group of students aged 14+ to learn strategies for understanding, rehearsing and presenting scripted work. The unit leads the students into the play in a highly structured way. The techniques espoused serve as either a foundation for smaller groups to organise and focus their rehearsal of scenes from the play, or a basis upon which to build devised work of their own on themes or ideas drawn from the text.

1 The whole class discuss the work of Noel Greig, drawing out key features of his use of form and style, for example the use of metaphor and allegory in *Rainbow's Ending* (pages 183–4).

2 The class are shown a colour transparency of the front cover of a copy of the play (page 236) and asked to jot down what they actually see.

3 They discuss what the images on the cover imply about the play itself and analyse why the publishers might have chosen the various typefaces on the cover.

4 Working individually, students then write a short personal prediction about the underlying themes of the play.

5 The group stand in a circle and, in turn, are given one line from the opening scene, which they must memorise (see pages 237–8). The teacher reads the opening stage direction, then the group recite their lines in a variety of ways, for example angrily, as if they were a naughty joke or a vicar's sermon, or sadly.

Playing with the lines in this way helps students see the text as something they can manipulate. After trying out different ways of reciting the lines the group should decide on an appropriate style and tone. Keeping their eyes closed in order to concentrate on the sounds of the words, the scene is spoken aloud again. A discussion can then take place regarding how the visual images conjured up by this opening scene appear to connect, albeit tacitly, with the images on the cover.

A shark: forever hungry. What's it eating? 'Shark' can mean money-grabber.

Author: is this a personal signature? Type suggests a 'real' person.

Noel Greig

FINAL CARGO

Title: 'Cargo' links with the ship. The fish are on top of the ship! Has it sunk? Why 'Final'? Money suggests a successful trip.

Money from all over the world. International problems? World finance?

Ship looks old. It's dirty and rusty. What's the nature of this 'final' trip and what's the cargo?

Looks like an oil slick. Pollution? Does this link with money-grabbing?

Nelson

Type suggests handwriting. A 'personal touch' – plays are written by people, for people.

The SKIPPER, in a small pool of light. He has a small, battered tin globe, with all the time-zones, meridians, etc., on it. He spins it. The OWNER enters.

SKIPPER   (*pointing to the small, battered globe*) Put your finger down, anywhere. Bet your bottom dollar I've been there.

He spins the globe. The owner puts his finger down.

Been there. Cancer, Capricorn, Equator, parallel, I've seen the lot.

OWNER   Safe home in harbour now.

SKIPPER   I'm not worn out yet. Nor me, nor boat.

OWNER   She's pooped.

SKIPPER   My boat?

OWNER   My boat.

SKIPPER   Yours by property, mine by feeling.

OWNER   Time's up for that old tub.

SKIPPER   No . . . never.

OWNER   The firm recognises all you've done . . . (*hands him a package*) You'll have a tidy pension, too.

The SKIPPER takes out a watch on a chain from the package.

We're calling her in.

SKIPPER   And me? I'm to tick off my days?

OWNER   Her time's up.

SKIPPER   She's not a boating-lake dinghy, with a ticket and a number . . .

OWNER   Woodwork's all gone to pot . . .

SKIPPER   A bit of care . . .

OWNER   Brasswork comes off in your hand . . .

SKIPPER   Bit of love and affection . . .

OWNER   Money's tight. Her days are done.

SKIPPER   Like me?

OWNER   You'd never manage the new ones.

SKIPPER   I've seen them. That's not ships. That's floating factories, floating coffins.

OWNER   That's the modern world. Brass and wood is history. Come round next month. You can supervise the breaking up.

SKIPPER   Break her?

OWNER	Strip her to the bone, sell off her parts. You'll get a bonus.
SKIPPER	Just one last sailing . . .
OWNER	Out of the question . . .
SKIPPER	A short trip . . . anything.
OWNER	I might be owner, but I've shareholders to answer to. No. She's had her day. She's done. You too. (*He goes*)

RUTH sits on a deserted shoreline with a tiny baby in her arms. She rocks it and sings to it. We can hear the sound of the sea not too far off.

RUTH (*singing*) They went to sea one night in June
The skipper, the pilot, the cook and the engineer.
They sailed away when the moon was full
And the sky was like velvet
And the stars shone out bright and clear.

(*She talks to the baby*) Oh, you'll have such adventures my little child. I'll take you in a boat with me. We'll sail right round the world. Do you know when's the best time for setting sail, eh? Dawn or dusk. Like now, like right now. When it's neither night nor day. (*Points up to the sky*) See. There's the day going and there's the night coming. They're both with us, looking down at us. Taking care of us.

DAY and NIGHT both appear. They are looking at another, larger spinning globe of the Earth. It is lit from within and is very beautiful.

DAY Little planet. She spins in space. She lives, she breathes. All that blueness, greenness, not like those other planets, Jupiter and Mars and whatnot. They're all dried up and dead. Not her. She's got her water, all stocked full and fat with fish. She's got her forests, all drenched with rain, her plains all teeming with livestock, her great slabs of ice, her roaring torrents, her valleys of flowers. And spinning, always spinning. Just for me to watch.

Final Cargo by Noel Greig

1 The class split into small groups and are given a section of the play to read aloud, simply by taking a line in turn. For a class of thirty, the play can be split into six equal parts and given to groups of five students. The students should not to try to 'cast' such readings as this is time consuming and can lead to some students claiming ownership of parts while others feel they have no vested interest at all.

2 After reading their section, groups are asked to:
   • write on slips of paper the key events of the section in terms of what happens, where, when and to whom (these notes need to be kept safely)
   • choose a line each which seems to capture the essence of one of the major characters.

3 The students walk around speaking their chosen line and listening to others. After allowing a few minutes, they join up with anyone they think is playing the same character as themselves.

4 Having formed groups of characters in this way, the students briefly share details of what their character was like in the different parts of the play.

5 The 'character groups' then make a collective still image which shows how their character comes across in different parts of the play.

This is an effective way of getting the students to share what they know so far about the play, thus building an overall picture of the entire storyline. It is usually quite remarkable how easily different characters group together and listening to the chosen lines will reveal why. It can be useful for the students to discuss this.

The activity reveals how some characters develop through the course of a play while others appear to stay the same throughout. Any anomalies in the way students have tried to group themselves need to be quickly sorted out but can nevertheless lead to a fruitful discussion regarding what it is about the chosen lines that allowed individuals to find each other in this way or indeed mistake each other's characters.

Physicalising the text

1 The original 'reading groups' are re-formed and given a short while to remind themselves of what happened in their section.
2 They consider how the section they have read connects with other things they now know about the narrative and characters.
3 The key moments that were previously written on slips of paper are then used as stepping stones for a presentation of the section.

It may be that there is insufficient time to actually move towards a practical presentation at this point. If so, the class might consider how such a presentation could employ tableaux, mime, narration etc. If time does allow, the presentations are best shown in the order in which they occur in the text. In this way, the whole play is presented in a highly edited form.

Mapping the structure

Each group lays out their slips carrying the key moments of the play on a long sheet of paper. In this way the story of the whole play becomes even clearer, as does its narrative structure. The mapping technique is an extremely useful way of ensuring that everyone knows the story and sees the way themes are introduced and developed in the play by linking different moments in the narrative. A representation of the first part of such a map is shown on page 241.

Identifying the issues

The students share their responses to the play as it now appears to them. A focus for the discussion might usefully be the extent to which it met with their initial predictions as based on an analysis of the front cover. What surprises were there? What questions have been raised?

As homework students can be given a group task of researching one of the key issues of the play such as love, greed, the environment, politics. They need to present how the author has used form to depict these themes and could be asked to state the extent to which they think he has been successful in giving them new insights.

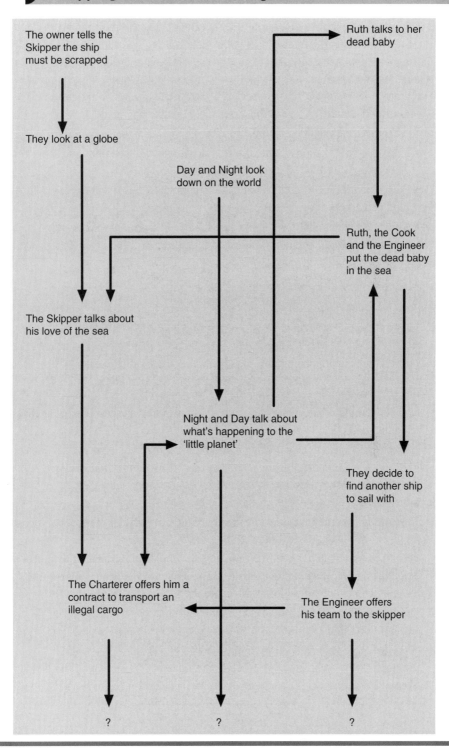

The owner tells the Skipper the ship must be scrapped

Ruth talks to her dead baby

They look at a globe

Day and Night look down on the world

Ruth, the Cook and the Engineer put the dead baby in the sea

The Skipper talks about his love of the sea

Night and Day talk about what's happening to the 'little planet'

They decide to find another ship to sail with

The Charterer offers him a contract to transport an illegal cargo

The Engineer offers his team to the skipper

?   ?   ?

Extension work on *Final Cargo*

From this point the teacher might lead the class through a number of the activities described earlier in order to explore the problems involved in staging the play, developing and performing the characters and tackling the technical and design challenges. Of course, it may be decided to take the play on to a full or workshop production. Associated with such a project would be opportunities to:

- design the set, lighting, sound, and front of house material
- consider how casting can be used to add new layers of insight into the themes explored in the text
- adopt and adapt different rehearsal techniques to deepen characterisation and achieve impact
- reflect on how to address drama to a specific audience and work within spatial, temporal and financial constraints.

The students' own interpretations of a play such as *Final Cargo* may also be used to generate new work, as in the next activity.

Creating new work

1 The class brainstorm what resonance the play has for them personally. What undertones, themes and issues does it raise for them?

2 In groups, the students select one or perhaps two of these resonances as the stimulus for a piece of drama of their own.

3 Each group tries to evolve the synopsis of a story that would serve as a vehicle for their chosen theme or issue. This may be a story that they already know, or their own invention (Noel Greig actually based the story of *Final Cargo* on 'The Rime of the Ancient Mariner').

4 The groups experiment with ways of telling the story orally, writing it out in prose or notating it in the form of a storyboard.

5 The students reflect on the structured exploration of *Final Cargo* (or whatever play they have worked on), especially the mapping device, and consider the order in which they will unfold their narrative.

6 Another useful strategy is to reflect on the different theatrical strategies employed in the original text and to try and write or devise a scene from a new story in the style of the play studied. This activity can raise interesting possibilities in the employment of formal devices and their appropriateness to the content.

Practical work such as this can produce very creative and deeply reflective
written work including, for example:
- *character studies written from an objective point of view or in role*
- *process diaries in which the students record the decisions they are taking*
  and their thoughts and feeling about the work as it unfolds
- *critical commentary on how the techniques being employed in the devised*
  work are drawn from, relate to or develop those used in the play studied.

Unit planning sheet for drama

Unit title *Final Cargo*   **Time scale** 2 × 100 minutes or 3 hrs 20 mins

AIMS

- to prepare students for independent work on realising a script in performance
- to prepare students for devising their own scripts and productions based on a specific theme.

SUGGESTED ACTIVITIES

- discussion on work of Noel Greig already experienced and key features recalled (e.g. use of metaphor in *Rainbow's Ending*)
- anticipating the text work – focus on images presented on the cover through focused group discussion and feedback – connections to be made with previous work in drama on semiotics
- whole-group activity 'playing with' individual lines from text – emphasis on how style and delivery can change meaning; reflection on what is appropriate and what and why visual images are suggested by opening lines (connection with first activity)
- encountering the text – students work in small groups each focusing on one of 5 or 6 different sections of play – (specific tasks to guide focus given)
- tracing the characters – students work as whole group identifying major characters – findings shared and key characteristics discussed
- students work in character groups to create image of character – responses and analysis given to each group – thought tracking and out-of-role questions can be used by students
- physicalising the text – students work in original groups (encountering texts) – reflection on information and understanding preparation for performance of key moments
- key moments shown in text order, using form determined by individual groups (tableau/mime/narration)
- mapping section – clarifying narrative structure, story and themes
- identifying the issues – students reflect on initial and current responses to the text and the issues it raises
- research by students of key issues raised in the play – power, environment, politics – emphasis must be on their connection with the play/final reflection/evaluation on approaches used by playwright
- whole-class discussion and agreement on form to be used for presentation of scenes – using scripted dialogue, mime, documentary drama, tableaux etc. (with consideration of purpose/connections with issues and themes – if audience, time and resources available)
- play can be developed into independent performance (further performance unit) whole class/groups using design process – staging, technical resources, character interpretation, rehearsal process, performance and evaluation.

EVIDENCE OF LEARNING (CREATING, PERFORMING, RESPONDING)

Creating Are students:
- developing their ideas with others in using practical approaches to the play, with particular emphasis on analogy and metaphor?

Performing Are students:
- physicalising the development of key characters, events and themes during the course of the play successfully?
- selecting and using appropriate form to interpret identified scenes?

Responding Are students:
- showing understanding of the playwright's use of structure to communicate the central themes and issues of the play in their discussions and as they experiment with sections of the play?
- critically evaluating how the structure of scenes studied contribute to dramatic effect?

By the end of the unit the students should know and understand:
• some different practical approaches they can use in approaching a new text
• how the playwright has effectively structured the play to communicate specific complex issues.

They should be able to:
• independently explore key characters, events and themes through practical drama activities
• explore and make effective use of analogy and metaphor
• select and use appropriate form to interpret identified scenes.

RESOURCES

• copies of *Final Cargo* by Noel Greig for whole class (including cover)
• selected single lines from opening scene of text printed on separate sheets (one per student)
• technical resources as identified by students.

COMMENTS/EVALUATION POINTS

• Level 6–Exceptional Performance
• This unit should be taught immediately prior to the unit on the independent work for scripted performance.

Drama is a social art form. It involves people working together to explore, interpret, and find a way of commenting upon the human condition. Drama draws on the world as it is experienced by humans for its content. It provides a perspective on this through its form. Progression in drama implies an increased ability to:

- explore events through use of a range of dramatic strategies
- reflect on the relationship between fact and fiction
- understand and make use of metaphor to gain new insights and clarify issues
- investigate how the written, aural and visual texts of a drama can be manipulated in order to focus an audience's response.

This chapter considers drama's capacity to comment and reflect upon the contemporary world by considering the philosophical and aesthetic relationship between content, form and context.

1 Introduction

Drama can be a critic of society and a force for social change. Throughout the entire history of Western drama, the power of playwrights to draw attention to injustice and absurdity has all too frequently led to their imprisonment and even execution. It is not always the case, however, that writers fall foul of authority because they tackle issues head on. The use of metaphor, for example, can intensify the critical power of a drama.

Sometimes social or political comment has been made by the production of a play at a particular time and in a particular place. To take a famous example, the 1601 production of Shakespeare's *Richard II* was used to inflame the Earl of Essex's supporters who, having attended a specially commissioned performance, rose up against Elizabeth on the following day. In more recent times, the production of Timberlake Wertenbaker's *Our Country's Good* by prisoners of Her Majesty's Government in 1991 was seen by some as a poignant indictment of an uncaring and rapidly decaying administration.

In discussing the critical and redemptive power of drama, students' attention can be drawn to television drama's capacity to bring about change. The housing charity Shelter was founded after the screening of Jeremy Sandford's *Cathy Come Home* in 1966, while Jimmy McGovern's dramatisation of the events surrounding the 1989 Hillsborough disaster was effectively responsible for a re-opening of the case for compensation for the families of the victims. Conversely, dramatisations have been criticised for misrepresenting actuality through their fictionalised portrayals of real people and events.

Drama can certainly be a means through which society can celebrate as well as criticise itself, though it is perhaps a sad paradox that because of the medium's propensity for drawing attention to what is rotten, there is never a shortage of material for new drama. Drama is a powerful medicine, but like all medicines, used without due care and attention, it can as likely poison as cure. It is for this reason that drama students need to have a sound understanding of the relationship between fact and fiction and how, in the art form of drama, one may inform and shape the other.

② I heard the news today . . .

Director Jean-Luc Godard once said, 'You can start with fiction or with documentary. But whichever you start with, you will inevitably find the other.' Or perhaps, as Melvin Burgess writes in his personal introductory note to the novel *Junk*: 'This book isn't fact; it isn't even fiction. But it's all true, every word.'

Raymond Williams's concept of a 'dramatised world' is an especially important one for any teacher interested in helping their students understand how our perceptions are influenced and shaped by a conscious manipulation of form. Even the seemingly objective news bulletin is, effectively, a fictionalised version of actual events in that any film footage used is edited and was most likely shot in order to reflect predetermined principles. Bulletins are of course scripted with particular target audiences in mind and stage managed to maximise their impact. This may imply that the makers of news programmes are cynical in their choice and representation of items. However, their clarity of purpose and judicious selection of communicative strategies can offer valuable lessons to drama students wanting to progress in their ability to convey, through drama, what is discovered in reality.

In drama, it is in the interchange between the objective, unfeeling world 'out there' and the subjective, feeling world within each of us that meanings are made, interpreted and developed into new expressions of experience. Progression in drama thus encompasses the developing ability to engage with and articulate personal responses to complex personal and social matters.

- **News headlines**

  Working on news headlines can help young people find ways of using the spoken and visual language of drama economically and purposefully. The headline device is used in a number of plays as a kind of modern equivalent to the *Greek Messenger*, in order to impart information to the audience about events elsewhere which are of significance to the drama being portrayed. A clichéd device in films is to have a sequence of newspaper front pages spinning out of the screen in order to quickly tell an audience that time has passed or a number of important events have happened in the lives of the characters. On-stage methods might include headlines simply being shouted out and commented on or a character turning on the radio just in time to hear an important bulletin. Students might usefully consider the use of irony in their exploration of such scenes noting, for example, how a piece of tragic news can be underlined when it is received by people having fun. Conversely, comedy can be created by having a potentially earth-shattering event taken preposterously lightly.

 News impact

1 Students brainstorm all the different ways that important news events can be quickly communicated to an audience and try to remember examples of films, television and stage dramas that have used these techniques.

2 In groups, they are given a short amount of time to devise a scene in which a news item has a profound effect on the action. This might range from, for example, an item in the local newspaper about the unexpected death of a popular local character to a radio announcement of a meteor heading towards Earth.

3 The class work on short extracts of plays, such as the ones opposite and overleaf and consider why it might be important for the theatre audience to have such contextual knowledge and whether the news being spread is, in itself, dramatic.

4 In groups, students choose a current world event and employ some of the techniques introduced in the examples to put them into a dramatic context.

Two newsboys run across the stage.

FIRST NEWSBOY   Special! Austria declares war on Serbia!

SECOND NEWSBOY   Extra! Russia mobilizes! Russia mobilizes!

Two girls cross the stage pushing a tandem bicycle.

FIRST GIRL   Russia mobilizes?

SECOND GIRL   Ja, and Papa says France must stand by Russia.

FIRST GIRL   Oh! Is that good?

Two German businessmen pass with bowler hats and dispatch-cases.

FIRST BUSINESSMAN   I understand that we have ordered Russia to demobilize within twelve hours. The point is will France remain neutral?

SECOND BUSINESSMAN   Russia is asking for time.

FIRST BUSINESSMAN   Where did you hear that?

SECOND BUSINESSMAN   It's all over town.

FIRST BUSINESSMAN   War's off, then?

SECOND BUSINESSMAN   Yes. War is off.

FIRST BUSINESSMAN   Good. Otto, Otto, the war is off.

Oh What a Lovely War! by Theatre Workshop

SANDRA	Shut up a minute. They're saying someat.
	She reaches towards the radio.
	Momentary blackout. The scene lit, with overhead spot, on the radio. The actors freeze.
RECORDING ANNOUNCER	The Prime Minister. The Rt. Hon. Winston Churchill.
CHURCHILL	Yesterday morning at 2.42 am at General Eisenhower's headquarters, General Jodl, the representative of the German High Command, and the Grand-Admiral Doenitz, the designated head of the German state, signed the act of unconditional surrender of all German Land, Sea and Air Forces in Europe.
	Followed by the cease fire.
	Blackout.
	Lighting as before. The group sit, silent, unmoving.

Touched by Stephen Lowe

In addition to providing a springboard for an exploration of the content which lies behind any given headline, focusing on the style of the news bulletin gives students the opportunity to work in a register which must necessarily be lucid, economic and appreciative of a specific audience.

This is an activity which can be productively used with students across the secondary age group. In preparation for it the students could watch a number of different news programmes for homework.

1 Students select from a choice of headlines provided by the teacher and discuss what the underlying story behind it might be. Some possible examples are to be found below.

'OUR HELL' BY VICTIM'S MOTHER

WHY MOUTHY MELISSA GOT GOBSMACKED

Tiger rips off child's arm in spectacular circus horror

Police quiz 'happy hubby' over disappearance of wife

CAN'T SAY, WON'T SAY!

Prima donna treads the boards – with two left feet

'He was my idol – yet all I could give him was a cup of tea'

2 They prepare three short scenes such as might be shown on either a children's television newsround or the main evening news:

Scene One: The studio presenter formally introduces the story and hands over to ...

Scene Two: An on-the-spot reporter who gives further details and perhaps interviews someone involved before handing back to ...

Scene Three: A specialist who makes a comment about or gives an analysis of the story.

3 The presentations are recorded on video.

Playing back the video will inform a discussion around the different presentation styles and language used and their appropriateness to the target audience.

Headline stories

This activity, which is more challenging than the last, involves students dramatising events by using news headlines alone.

1 In the first instance, a range of newsworthy events – either real or fictitious – of global, national or local significance are suggested. For example:

- first humans land on Mars
- Royal Family in financial difficulty
- scandal on the local council.

2 Groups of students then prepare a way of telling the story through headlines alone, for example:

- Local leader to reveal far-reaching new election promises!
- Opposition candidate calls for investigation into shady deals.
- Town's top businessmen pledge support for council leader.
- Low-life informer spills beans on top politician!
- Council leader retires: 'I want to spend more time with my family' he says!

This activity can serve as an example of how dramatic irony can be used to make a comment. Extension work to this end could involve students composing different extracts of writing to surround the central narrative – for example, radio broadcasts, interviews with key characters, telegrams, one half of a telephone call – and then juxtaposing them.

This activity shows how a more structured approach to building a drama from a newspaper headline might work.

1 The students select one headline from a large selection (the teacher should choose headlines that the students are unlikely to be familiar with).

2 The group suggest what picture might go with the chosen headline. The characters are carefully positioned one by one. The students must explain and justify their choices regarding use of space, gesture and facial expression at every stage.

3 The students then suggest some speech balloons and thought bubbles which might fit the picture (perhaps ironically).

4 Some of the characters in the picture are hot-seated to find out more about their relationships with each other and their part in the news item.

5 The students discuss what scenes in the characters' lives could be shown to help an audience understand more about how the story came about. Small groups work on and share these scenes.

6 Finally, individually or in pairs, students write another short newspaper item as a postscript to the first. What has happened to the characters?

A discussion around why some headlines are seen as having more dramatic potential than others is very useful. The depth of this discussion will, of course, depend on the age group and the teachers' objectives for undertaking the activity.

❸ Staging reality

Any attempt to convey the drama of real-life situations through the use of dramatic form raises a number of problems. Most obviously, there is a need to condense the time scale. This inevitably means that details and perhaps important characters are edited out of what is presented to a public audience. While such decisions are made in order to clarify the issues, the process of dramatisation implies that actuality is mediated. Dramatists have tackled this problem in a number of ways. Alan Bleasdale's series *Boys from the Blackstuff* and *GBH* are examples of the way in which the medium of television offers one possibility of exploring contemporary issues in depth over an extended period of time. A number of Brecht's plays employed allegory to reflect and comment on contemporary issues, while Dario Fo has used farce and heightened comedy to satirise current affairs.

Both these methods relate to the strategies used in other plays such as John McGrath's *The Cheviot, the Stag and the Black, Black Oil* or Alan Plater's *Close the Coalhouse Door*, which variously used caricatures, narrators, songs and cabaret to critique social and political concerns.

Other examples of these strategies being used to document, explain and explore issues can be found in the work of theatre-in-education companies. In Belgrade TIE Company's 1980 documentary-style play *Example*, the controversial case of Derek Bentley was examined. Bentley was infamously hanged in 1953 for the murder of a policeman, despite it being acknowledged at the time that Bentley was not directly responsible for the death. His sister Iris campaigned tirelessly for an official pardon but this was only granted by the Home Secretary in 1998. The same company drew on Japanese theatre forms to illustrate the catastrophe of mercury poisoning in Minamata Bay in *Drink the Mercury*. Lin Coghlan characteristically used a poetic voice to draw attention to the human cost of the leisure industry in *A Feeling in My Bones*, and in *Bretevski Street* she drew on the structure of a soap opera to explore the absurdity of the way close neighbours turned on each other in Bosnia.

Researching dramatisation

Students working at a higher level in drama, and possibly embarking on a process of dramatising a real event, will benefit from researching into how different practitioners have gone about similar projects. This research could include:

- using resource books and the Internet to gather definitions of and words related to terms such as:
  - documentary
  - living newspaper
  - agit-prop
  - parable
  - allegory
  - happening
  - cabaret.
- finding out about particular companies and playwrights associated with the above types of theatre, for example:
  - 7:84
  - Caryl Churchill
  - Michael Hastings
  - David Hare

- Living Theatre
- Michelene Wandor
- Monstrous Regiment.
- logging the different dramatic techniques employed in plays dealing with social and political issues
- reading Jean-Paul Sartre's essay *Myth and Reality in the Theatre* (1966). This essay coined the term 'theatre of fact' which was subsequently used as a name by an English community/theatre-in-education company.

Courtroom drama

In some notable cases, overtly theatrical and literary devices have been dismissed in favour of simply staging edited versions of actual events. Court proceedings have frequently lent themselves to replication in the theatre or on television. This is partly because there is already something intrinsically theatrical about a courtroom with its use of costume and careful stage management and the deliberate attempts by advocates to provoke certain responses. The televising of the O. J. Simpson murder trial was an extraordinary phenomenon in which a world-wide audience was witness to life imitating fiction or vice versa, without being quite sure which it was they were witnessing.

More usually, the drama of the courtroom serves as the raw material for a re-creation of the drama in a mediated form. One example that contributed to public awareness and disapproval of the South African apartheid regime was *The Biko Inquest* by Jon Blair and Norman Fenton. Another is the 1999 dramatisation of the inquiry into the way in which British police handled the investigation of the racist murder of black teenager Stephen Lawrence. Some of the problems of attempting to stage reality in this way are articulated by Richard Norton-Taylor, who edited the transcripts of the inquiry into a play he entitled *The Colour of Justice*.

The Lawrence inquiry consisted of 69 days of public hearings. The transcripts of the inquiry amount to more than 11,000 pages which I have distilled into about 100 – less than one per cent. Inevitably, I have had to make brutal choices about which witnesses and which exchanges to include.

I set out to include the most telling exchanges for a theatre audience, many of which did not hit the headlines at the time but which reflect the interlocking threads which ran throughout the inquiry – police incompetence, conscious or unconscious racism and stereotyping and the hint of corruption in the background. And I have included exchanges which reflect the personal tensions between the police and the Lawrence family . . .

Above all, I wanted to select evidence to the inquiry which presented as fair, balanced and as rounded a picture as possible. But if it contributes to a greater understanding of all the issues involved, it was, I hope, worthwhile and valuable.

Editor's Note, *The Colour of Justice* by Richard Norton-Taylor

▶ From real life to drama

1 Using the extract above as a primary source, students are asked to:
- identify the different logistical problems of staging a re-creation of a courtroom drama
- identify the way in which, in this particular case, the dramatist had a specific intention
- speculate on the way in which the editing process would be likely to position an audience in relation to the evidence presented
- discuss the way a consideration of what is dramatically effective may have influenced Richard Norton-Taylor's editorial decisions.

2 In the light of their discussions on the points above, students work in small groups to:
- discuss their personal responses to the two extracts on pages 257–62
- stage the two extracts
- consider the way the extracts used elements of the dramatic form to make the script effective when realised
- consider the likely effect on an audience of re-creating these scenes from an actual trial
- consider what the intention of the dramatist might have been in editing the original transcript in such a way.

These two brief extracts exemplify many facets of the power and problematic nature of drama. On the one hand, simply having the opportunity to see one of the most important judicial inquiries of recent times re-created demonstrates the power of drama to capture, comment on and perhaps influence public opinion. However, the extracts also illustrate that in order for drama to have such an effect, the conscious, judicious and sensitive manipulation of form must be exercised.

The inquiry into the way the police investigated the Stephen Lawrence case came about as a result of a Police Complaints Authority report which stated that there were 'significant weaknesses, omissions, and lost opportunities in the conduct of the case'. Amongst these was the assignation of an un-named police officer to 'protect' Duwayne Brooks, who was with Stephen at the time of the murder. The officer was subsequently discovered to have had a spurious relationship with the father of one of the men accused of Lawrence's murder. The father, Clifford Norris, was allegedly known to be an influential and dangerous criminal. The transcript makes for uncomfortable reading in its own right. For the drama student, the way in which Michael Mansfield QC, Counsel for the Lawrence family, 'positions' Mellish is an object lesson in the purposive use of language. In a different vein, Norton-Taylor's choice of where to close the scene offers the chance to discuss the dramatic effect of careful editing.

EXTRACT

From the evidence of William Mellish, formerly Detective Superintendent, 11, 15 and 16 June 1998

LAWSON	We are now leaving what might be called the first investigation and going into the second, which was conducted by Mr Mellish.
MACPHERSON	Mr Lawson, on behalf of the inquiry, will question you first.
MELLISH	Yes, sir.
LAWSON	Mr Mellish, we are grateful to you for volunteering your assistance to the inquiry. It is right, is it not, to say you were not involved in the investigation that was carried out by the Kent police.
MELLISH	That is correct.
LAWSON	No complaint or allegations having been made against you or relating to the second investigation?
MELLISH	No, sir.

LAWSON	Mr Mellish, it was in the middle of 1994, was it not, that you assumed the mantle of Senior Investigating Officer?
MELLISH	Yes, sir.
LAWSON	Can I ask you in the most general terms, your own experience of racism within the Metropolitan Police Force?
MELLISH	I would say there is some racism in some officers, in a minority of officers.
LAWSON	Over your last ten years, did it get better, get worse, or stay much the same, would you say?
MELLISH	I would say much the same.
LAWSON	Your investigation – you decided to take an entirely fresh approach? No-one had been prosecuted to conviction.
MELLISH	Yes.
LAWSON	You were aware this was racially motivated?
MELLISH	Yes, sir.
LAWSON	By virtue of Duwayne Brooks' evidence of the shout of, "What, what nigger" before the gang attacked?
MELLISH	Yes, sir.
LAWSON	Your belief that this was a racially motivated murder was hardened up as a result of the use of intrusive surveillance methods?
MELLISH	Yes, sir.
LAWSON	You knew that David Norris' father was Clifford Norris, wanted for a large-scale drug importation and that his presence in south-east London could have a significant intimidatory effect, both on witnesses and sources of information, including any supergrass, and that it would be profitable to bring about his arrest?
MELLISH	Yes, sir.
LAWSON	You seemed to arrest him quite quickly.
MELLISH	There was a point where David's birthday was coming up and we hoped that old man Norris would come and visit the boy. We searched the dustbin of David Norris and his mother received a birthday card from the husband which was our first indication that he was in the country and was in communication.
	We did surveillance on mum and the boy and we were very lucky. She went down into the country and visited some oast house cottages near Battle, Sussex. We carried on observations and Norris went in for a drink. My sergeant got

Section 3 ● Progression in practice

	in the pub and gave me a positive ID: it was Norris. I sought permission for an armed operation. The next morning Norris stopped for breakfast at the local cafe and was arrested.
LAWSON	Thank you. That came about thanks to a combination of surveillance operation, looking in a dustbin, and a bit of luck?
MELLISH	Yes, sir.
LAWSON	Your report refers to loaded firearms, handguns, sawn-off shotgun, and another weapon, an Uzi?
MELLISH	An Uzi machine gun.
LAWSON	And a large amount of ammunition?
MELLISH	Yes, sir.
LAWSON	I will move on, if I may. Intrusive surveillance – that included inserting the video-audio probe into the flat occupied by Dobson? The probe was inserted, in effect making the film?
MELLISH	Yes, sir.
LAWSON	Of what Dobson and his mates, including some of the other suspects, including some Acourts, were saying amongst themselves and doing in the flat?
MELLISH	Yes, sir.
LAWSON	You have described an edited product of that probe revealing amongst that group of young men 'a propensity for violence and the carriage of knives and raving bigotry'?
MELLISH	Yes, sir.
MANSFIELD	Can I go to MET00510149. It is also PCA00450286. There it is.
	The first thing that we see is that, despite Dobson's denials in interviews, he plainly is associating with the very people, one of whom he denied knowing, namely David Norris?
MELLISH	Yes, sir.
MANSFIELD	The purpose of the exercise was to produce evidence against the suspects of motive?
MELLISH	Yes, sir.
MANSFIELD	And that it did in abundance, did it not?
MELLISH	On racism, yes, sir.
MANSFIELD	Can I extend it. It is beyond racism. It is racism conjoined with an obsession to extreme violence?
MELLISH	I would agree with that. I think I would add to that, 'with knives'.

MANSFIELD	There are vast tracks when often Neil Acourt is toying with knives of the very kind that it is thought by the pathologist inflicted the injuries on Stephen?
MELLISH	That is correct, sir.
MANSFIELD	There is another feature – the toying with knives. We can see before they leave through a door in the rear, they will go to the window sill, pick up a knife and they will put it in the inside of their trousers so it cannot be seen whilst they are walking along?
MELLISH	Yes.
MANSFIELD	In addition to all of that, Neil Acourt can be seen on more than one occasion actually demonstrating what I am going to call the modus operandi of this particular stabbing in the Lawrence case.
	There are some racially obscene comments throughout the whole of this recording but perhaps the high water mark is when Neil Acourt is heard to say words to the effect: 'I reckon that every nigger should be chopped up, mate, and they should be left with nothing but fucking stumps.'
	Then later David Norris indicates he would like to, 'go down Catford and places like that with two submachine guns and I am telling you, I'd take one of them, skin the black cunt alive, torture him, set him alight.' In relation to comments like that by all of the four suspects, is it right to say consideration was given to prosecuting these men for incitement to racial hatred?
MELLISH	Yes, sir.
MANSFIELD	It is the Public Order Act 1986, section 18 (2). May I just read it so that it is clear to the public why no action has been taken. 'An offence under this section may be committed in a public or a private place, except that no offence is committed where the words . . . are used . . . by a person inside a dwelling and are not heard or seen except by other persons in that or another dwelling.'
	That was seen to be providing a real practical problem in bringing a prosecution based on this recording?
MELLISH	That is true, sir.
MANSFIELD	Can I just ask, the officer we are calling XX. This is becoming like a Pinter play with surreal references. There is an officer named there in relation to Clifford Norris.
MELLISH	I am pretty sure he was on the Flying Squad at Tower Bridge with me when I was in charge. I was aware that XX had met a criminal in bad circumstances and was disciplined.

Section 3 ● Progression in practice

MANSFIELD	Neil Acourt was extremely conscious of the fact that something had happened in his room. There is a lot of concentrated interest on the plug and socket. Somebody had tipped them off?
MELLISH	I don't think so. The people at my end were people of utter integrity. There is another possibility which has always been [in] my thoughts on the subject of how and why they suspected from the very first day, if I may give it to you.
MANSFIELD	Yes?
MELLISH	A day or so after the murder, David Norris is involved in it and gets hold of his father. The father sits the boys down wherever, somewhere in London, somewhere out of London, and gives them a very firm lesson in why they must keep their mouths shut, which they have done ever since.
	Gives them a very firm lesson in methods of interception.
MANSFIELD	Right?
MELLISH	On technical and telephone. These 18 year-old spotty thugs were using the telephone box in the public street and not their own telephone. They had to be briefed by somebody, that is my point.
MANSFIELD	In relation to the Old Bailey trial, the private prosecution, had you known that XX had, in fact, been consorting with the father of one of the suspects – that is Clifford Norris – presumably you would have thought it quite improper, unwise, undesirable, whatever term you may use for him, that is XX, to have anything to do with protecting, helping, or guarding the main eye witness, victim, Duwayne Brooks, in this case?
MELLISH	What you say is correct.

The Colour of Justice by Richard Norton-Taylor

This is the last scene of the play, just as it was the last episode of the inquiry. In this sense, there is a congruence of purpose to the words spoken by both the real Sir William Macpherson of Cluny and the actor portraying him. In both cases, the intention is to find a way of formally closing a public event in a way that respectfully marks the death of Stephen Lawrence, whose murder inquiry was, in itself, a synecdoche for the pervasion of racism in Britain. The means by which the theatre audience are induced to share the emotional responses of the audience present in the original inquiry are worthy of detailed analysis.

EXTRACT

Closing statement by Sir MacPherson of Cluny

MACPHERSON Thank you very much. Ladies and gentlemen, that concludes the evidence which will be heard by the Public Inquiry in connection with matters arising from the death of Stephen Lawrence. I should indicate, however, that the future holds much activity and much work still to be done.

Finally, it seems to me right that we should end as we started with a minute of silence to remember Stephen Lawrence and to couple with that our congratulations, if that is the right word, on the courage of his parents.

Would you stand with me for a minute's silence.

A minute's silence.

Thank you very much for your attendance today.

The End.

The Colour of Justice by Richard Norton-Taylor

---

❹ Guiding concepts in dramatisation

In their book *Theatre Studies: An Approach for Advanced Level,* Simon Cooper and Sally Mackey introduce and discuss the term overall design concept (ODC). They stress how formulating an underlying concept of what is being communicated to an audience is essential if the different elements of production are to be coherent. Their choice of term emphasises the importance of drama's visual text in communicating meaning: stage settings, lighting and costume are the most obvious aspects of this. By way of giving an example of an overall design concept at work they discuss the collusion between director Trevor Nunn and designer John Napier on Andrew Lloyd

Webber's *Cats*, the set for which shows the world from a cat's perspective by enlarging everyday human objects such as tin cans and lorry tyres.

The overall design concept will similarly guide the way actors suggest relationships between characters through the use of space (proxemics). The choice of music, the exact nature of sound and other technical effects, characters' voices and gestures and so on will all contribute to the discourse, that is, the discussion that lies at the heart of the drama. How such discourse is interpreted and what it ends up meaning to an audience are also a matter of context. That is, where and when is the drama produced and at what audience is it primarily aimed?

An effective way of illustrating how an overall design concept affects every aspect of a drama, and so comments upon a particular issue, is to use clips from filmed versions of plays. Film Education, for example, provide a number of extremely useful study packs which include teachers' notes and video compilations. One such focuses on *Hamlet*. Students do not necessarily have to have a detailed knowledge of *Hamlet* to see how scenes from contrasting productions emphasise different things in order to convey particular meanings.

Comparisons

1 Having been briefly reminded of the basic story, the students read the opening scene of Shakespeare's text then watch the opening sequence of four different film versions of the drama:

   1. Laurence Olivier   UK   1948
   2. Grigori Kozintzev   USSR   1964
   3. Tony Richardson   UK   1969
   4. Franco Zeffirelli   USA   1990

2 These opening sequences are wildly different. Students reflect on:
   - what they actually saw and heard
   - what the overall tone of each sequence was
   - what their personal 'gut level' response to the different images was
   - what different expectations of the film were being set up by the directors
   - how justifiable they think it is to call films *Hamlet* when they seem so very different from the original stage text.

3   The class consider other filmed versions of plays they have seen and discuss how they differed from the play. They may also be able to discuss how stage productions they have seen have similarly interpreted the text in ways they did not expect.

4   The students are shown four quotations. Each quotation reflects the overall concept of the play being explored in one of the four films of *Hamlet*. From their experience of the opening sequences, they try to match the quotations to the different films.

   • 'This is the tragedy of a man who could not make up his mind.' Olivier, 1948
   • 'He sticks in the wheels of government . . . they grind him up. Yet he all but broke the machine.' Kozintzev, 1964
   • 'Hamlet is the sarcastic, constipated type who feels he ought to have gone South and got on in the world.' Richardson, 1969
   • '*Hamlet* is about people and relationship. What matters is the modernity of feeling.' Zeffirelli, 1990.

5   The students are given a number of slips of paper on which an event from Act 5 Scene 2 of Shakespeare's play is written. For example:

   • Hamlet and Laertes fight
   • Gertrude drinks from the poisoned cup
   • Hamlet stabs the King.

   In pairs or small groups, they consider which of these events they would focus on if they were to make a film version of the play, and which they would be tempted to leave out. They speculate how Olivier, Kozintzev, Richardson and Zeffirelli might have shot the sequence of events in order to reflect their overall concept of the play.

It is interesting to note the manner in which these different film versions reflect their historical and social context. A-level students could profitably spend time on the Internet researching the different directors and the context in which they were working (though the Teachers' Notes provided by Film Education may provide as much material as is needed to illustrate the notion of the overall design concept).

Zeffirelli's Hamlet, played by Mel Gibson, seems in some ways to be a model of re-constructed Western man: tender, anxious, appealing. Richardson, directing in London at the end of the hopeful yet hedonistic 1960s, presents him as an angry young man, raging at the corruption yet apparent immovability of the old order. Kozintzev's Elsinore is an imposing grey fortress peopled by slaves and whispering, watching courtiers: an allegory for the Soviet Union at the height of the Cold War, perhaps?

A sound grasp of the way playwrights, directors and performers work within an overall concept is essential for students working in the later secondary years. A study of how a play such as *Hamlet* may metamorphose and be used to comment on context can be the basis of further work on the dramatisation of real-life events.

⑤ Structuring a unit of work around a real event

When introducing this unit as part of the GCSE Drama and Theatre Studies coursework, it may be helpful for students to recall the stages of the production process and identify the key roles and responsibilities. Students can share and discuss their individual interests and particular skills and agree the different tasks and roles that will be involved in this new project.

● The case of Ruth Ellis

Ruth Ellis was hanged for the murder of her lover on 13 July 1955. She was the last woman to be hanged in Britain. The case attracted considerable attention at the time. 50,000 people signed a petition for a reprieve of her death sentence and interest in the story has been frequently renewed. The release of a statement concerning the murder weapon in 1973 began to cast doubts over the safety of the conviction. A film, *Dance with a Stranger* in 1984, and a BBC documentary, *A Life for a Life* in 1999, both attracted wide media coverage and gave new insights into the character of Ruth Ellis and some of the questions that surrounded the crime.

In many ways, the case seemed an open and shut one. The evidence appeared straightforward:

- On 9 April 1955, Ellis had been waiting for her lover, David Blakely, to pick her up. It was Easter Sunday and Ellis had wanted to go to Hampstead's Easter Fair with him.
- Furious at him for not turning up, she went in search of him to the Magdala Tavern in Hampstead, where he was drinking with friends.
- She waited for Blakely to emerge, took out a revolver and shot him four times at point blank range.
- She was found by the police to be completely calm.
- When asked in court what she had set out to do that evening, she replied, 'It was obvious that when I shot him I intended to kill him.'
- She claimed that she had been given the gun about three years before, by a man in a club whose name she could not remember.

These bare facts suggest that Ellis was simply a cold-blooded killer, a perspective adopted by the account of the murder printed overleaf.

Waving goodnight to other regular customers, the two men left the bar and went out to Blakely's grey-green Vanguard van, parked at the kerbside immediately by the pub door. Gunnell waited by the passenger door while Blakely went around to the driver's side and – juggling with the flagon of beer he was carrying – searched in his pockets for his car keys.

Neither at that moment had noticed a slight, determined, platinum blonde walking down the hill, past a newsagent's shop, towards the pub. But she was observing Blakely carefully as she walked, and she called his name – 'David!' Blakely, still having difficulty in finding his keys, took no notice and showed no sign of being aware that the girl was approaching him.

Finally, she stood beside him and as Blakely looked up he saw her swiftly open her handbag and take out a heavy Smith and Wesson .38 revolver. She raised the gun and pointed it straight at Blakely, saying nothing, making no other movement. For a moment the scene was frozen as in some sinister tableau, the blonde appearing to be making an effort to hold the bulky revolver, the man staring mutely at her with the beer flagon still cradled in his arm.

Then, as if at the movement of a switch, the tableau sprang to life. Blakely turned and began to run towards the back of the van but, before he reached it, the woman fired two shots in quick succession. Blakely, who had assumed the stooped posture of a man fleeing for his life, reared up, slammed into the side of the van and stumbled forward again, appearing to reach out towards his friend Gunnell and screaming, 'Clive!'

Gunnell stood absolutely still, hypnotized by disbelief. But still the woman came on, walking in steady pursuit of Blakely, whose blood was already smeared along the Vanguard's side. 'Get out of the way, Clive,' she shouted and relentlessly followed Blakely, who had now stumbled round the other side of the van and was trying to stagger away.

Again the woman fired and Blakely reacted with a sharp half-spin of his body, lurched sideways, and fell full-length on his face with his head parallel to the bill-boards outside the newsagent's shop. The blonde walked towards the inert form and fired more shots directly into it, until the emptied six-chamber gun clicked uselessly.

Crimes of Passion, Treasure Press

1 The students read the account of the murder and break it down into a sequence of captions, for example:

a) Blakely and Gunnell exit from pub.

b) Ellis walks towards them.

c) Blakely fumbles for keys unaware of her approach.

d) She moves on towards them . . .

2 They re-enact the murder through a series of *tableaux* based on these captions.

3 The series of *tableaux* are presented again but this time words and phrases from the account are used as a voice-over for each image. The phrases are read in a way that emphasises and heightens the sense of drama. For example:

a) (*cheerily*) Waving goodnight to the other customers, the two men left the bar . . .

b) (*sinister*) Determined, the platinum blonde walked down the hill . . .

c) (*cheerily*) Still juggling with the flagon of beer he was carrying, Blakely searched for his keys . . .

d) (*sinister*) Observing Blakely carefully, she called his name . . .

Through this activity the effect of the emotive language of the account is brought to light. The students will be able to reflect on how the 'bare bones' of the event can be presented in order to steer an audience towards making a particular judgement.

Identifying perspectives

From the dramatist's point of view the story of Ruth Ellis provides a rich vein for exploration. The newspaper article about her on pages 268–71 offers a distinct contrast to the account given on page 266.

1 Students read the newspaper article and compare the way it depicts Ruth Ellis with the impression left by the account in *Crimes of Passion*.

2 They pick out a number of images that could be shown in tableau form and that would give a completely different perspective on the crime from the one they previously worked on.

3 The students consider how Ruth Ellis's story might be re-told as:

- a crime of passion, focusing on the obsession and jealousy Ellis and Blakely had for each other

'I will always be haunted by the look Ruth Ellis gave me as the hangman led her off to die'

JAILER WHO BEFRIENDED HER REVEALS KILLER'S FINAL THOUGHTS

The Mirror, 27 November 1999.

Eveyln Galilee shook with fear as the hangman expertly flicked a rope around Ruth Ellis's wrists.

As Ellis calmly left her cell to begin the final walk to the noose, she flashed a look at Evelyn – her constant companion of the past three weeks – that the warder would not forget.

"It was a look of pity – *she* felt sorry for *me*," says Evelyn, now 69. "She looked at me and mouthed; "Thank you" and she went out. That was it."

But that wasn't it. Evelyn who had grown incredibly close to Ruth, the last woman to be hanged in Britain, has been haunted ever since by memories of those last few days.

She still wakes up sweating and screaming at the image of the petite platinum blonde being led to her doom by legendary executioner Albert Pierrepoint.

Today, as Ellis's sister Muriel Jakubait, 77, launches her campaign to reopen her case, Evelyn has finally broken her 44-year silence to reveal Ruth's final thoughts and prison-cell confidences.

Both women are convinced had all the facts been known during Ruth's trial, her conviction for gunning down lover David Blakely on Easter Sunday, 1955 would have been reduced from murder to manslaughter.

Evelyn's revelations coincide with a BBC documentary tomorrow in which Muriel paints a dark picture of the girls' childhood – a background which was never revealed in court. She tells how their father Arthur Nielson, an unemployed musician, sexually abused his daughters and threatened them with violence if they ever revealed his vile secret.

"While my mother, Elizabeth was away working, he'd force me to sleep with him." recalls Muriel.

When Ruth was just 11, her father began sexually abusing her, too. For years, Muriel blocked out the pain of their physical and mental torture.

But she believes the systematic abuse and succession of failed relationships had a bearing on Ruth's mental stability.

It's a belief backed by former warder Evelyn, who at 27 was just a year younger than Ruth when she befriended her. Ever since she has felt guilty she did not do more to stop the woman she described as "a beautiful Dresden doll" from going to the gallows.

Now Evelyn feels the time is right to banish the ghost which haunts her dreams.

"On the anniversary of Ruth's death, I have a very vivid dream about her. I can see her face as clearly as if she was standing here in front of me now. And I always wake up bathed in sweat just as Albert Pierrepoint enters her cell." Speaking from her home in Brandon, Co Durham. Evelyn recalls how the dream takes her back to July, 1955.

Then she listened to Ruth often reflecting on the day when, in a fit of drunken rage, she emptied the barrel of a Smith & Wesson revolver into David Blakely.

In her official statement, Ruth said she had waited for Blakely to collect her and take her out on April 9, 1955. When he failed to show, she took a gun "given to me about three years ago by a man whose name I do not remember".

She stated that she took a taxi to the Magdala Tavern in Hampstead where Blakely was drinking. She waited for him to come out – then fired at point-blank range.

But Evelyn, wringing her hands at the memory of it, says: "It wasn't that clear-cut. It was presented as black and white but there was an awful lot of grey.

"I know Ruth had been provoked to the degree where she just snapped and I wish I could have stood up for her.

"She told me that on that day, Blakely had promised to take her and her son Andre to the Easter Fair on Hampstead Heath. It was a big event and the boy had been looking forward to it all day. He and Ruth sat on the doorstep waiting for Blakely. After several hours, he had still failed to show so she took her son back inside and he cried himself to sleep.

"Ruth must have knocked back half a bottle of Pernod – that was her drink. She told me her son was heartbroken and as she felt his disappointment, her anger grew.

"She said that before she started drinking she had a visit from a man. She wouldn't name him but the feeling I got was that it was Desmond Cussen who was hot on her.

RUTH took Cussen as a sugar-daddy lover to make Blakely jealous and, although she did not implicate anyone in the murder, it is widely believed that Cussen gave her the murder weapon.

Evelyn says "This friend, as she called him, gave her a gun which was loaded. She'd never handled a gun and wouldn't know how to load it.

"He told her he had seen Blakely in a pub in Hampstead with a couple of women – that's why he hadn't come to pick them up.

"Ruth had told me she had still not recovered from the shock of miscarrying Blakely's child. He had beaten her up badly three weeks before and her son found her in a pool of blood. She told me that's when she lost the baby.

"Well, at that moment, I believe she just snapped. She went looking for Blakely with the gun in her handbag. But she refused to allow any of this to come out in court.

"I was bound by the Official Secrets Act and was not allowed to say a word of what she had told me. That's why I feel guilty – maybe I should have done more to help.

"If this case were being heard today, there is no way a murder conviction would stand."

Prior to Ruth's arrival Warders at Holloway prison had been briefed to expect a brassy, troublesome prostitute.

"Instead," says Evelyn, "in came this fragile girl, a Dresden doll. She was my age and tiny – no more than 5 ft – and so very slim.

"Her skin was like porcelain. They had taken away her false nails, eyelashes and glamorous clothes and put her in baggy prison issue clothes.

"But they could not strip her of her dignity. Not once did she break down, scream or cry. Ruth had this acceptance of what she'd done and felt the punishment fitted the crime. And her eyes . . . they were bewitch-ing, the most beautiful violet-blue, the colour of forget-me-nots.

"People talk about Elizabeth Taylor's eyes but Ruth's were even more stunning.

"They were honest eyes – not the evil eyes of a killer. Her hair was platinum blonde and what amazed me was in those three weeks we were together, not once did her roots come through.'

BUT what really sticks in Evelyn's mind was Ruth's obsession with a green, 6ft-high screen which ran almost the full length of the back of the cell.

"She kept asking me what was behind the screen. I think she knew what it was but she kept badgering me to have a look.

"I told her I wasn't allowed to. But one night when she was doz-ing, I sneaked a look. My heart froze.

"It was the door hangman Albert Pierrepoint would come through when it was time for her to go."

Ruth was hanged at 9am on July 13, 1955. Recalling it, Evelyn says "At 8am, she was given her final breakfast of scrambled eggs. Even on that last day she wasn't allowed the dignity of eating with proper cutlery or plates.

"She had to use plastic because they thought she might use the crockery as a weapon.

"The breakfast tray was taken away. Then the deputy governor came in with the chaplain and they sat at each end of the table. Ruth was in the middle and I was standing up.

"She was sitting with her back to the screen which hid the door. Nothing was said and then we heard footsteps and we knew that door was going to open any minute.

"Ruth used to wear those blue diamante glasses because she was short-sighted. At that stage she took them off and passed them to the deputy governor. She said very coolly. "I won't need these any more. Thank you."

"A door opened, then more footsteps and another door opened. Then the door behind the screen flew open – and there was Pierrepoint, his assistant and two male prison officers.

"Ruth jumped out of her chair at the sound, knocking it over. Pierepoint was very reassuring, if you can say that of a hangman. He said to her, 'It's all right, lass. It's all right.' He kept to the back of her so she wouldn't see his face, picked up the chair and told her to sit down again. He said, 'Put your arms behind the chair'.

"He flicked his hand and a rope snaked onto her wrist and within seconds she was tied up with her hands behind her back. I thought that was so unnecessary and inhumane. That was when she said 'thank you' to me and left."

E VEN in her final days, Ruth did not forget her caring warder. Shortly after her death, Evelyn received a posthumous gift – a gas cigarette lighter she had once admired.

It was the first of its kind and cost £17 – a small fortune in the Fifties. Today it is one of her most treasured possessions.

Evelyn told how Ruth's sparse cell had two chairs, a desk, a table and a window which was so high, it was impossible to look out.

Ruth slept on a narrow, iron bed with a naked lightbulb directly above her head.

It was kept on day and night and Ruth would plead with the warders to turn it out so she could sleep at nights. Evelyn says "One day I smuggled some cardboard into the prison and with another warder, we made a little lamp-shade.

"It made a huge difference to Ruth and she was really touched by this simple act.

"The Governor was aware of it but turned a blind eye because he liked Ruth. We all did. She was a model prisoner."

Ruth was buried in a common grave with two other killers in the grounds of Holloway. Poignantly, it was an area where nothing grew.

"I could not bring myself to visit her grave because it upset me too much." says Evelyn. "One day a warder told me I had to visit. She practically dragged me there.

"I stood and looked and there on the centre of her grave was a tiny violet – the same colour as her eyes.

"The tears just rolled down my cheeks and I thought, 'Ruth, I think you've gone to Heaven, because you were never a bad person.'"

- a sordid sex scandal. Ellis has been described 'a bar hostess' and 'a scheming prostitute' who 'seduced the luckless yet debauched young aristocrat' (in fact, Blakely was the son of a Sheffield doctor who quickly frittered away his £7,000 inheritance on drink and an attempt to become a motor racing driver)

- a thriller. Why was Ellis so reluctant to provide background details about the gun she used? Was there someone else involved that she was trying to protect? In fact, there is now considerable evidence that the gun was given to her by Desmond Cussen. Cussen may even have driven Ruth to the scene of the crime. Ellis did not mention any of this at her trial; had she done so it could well have been that Cussen would have been tried for incitement to murder and Ellis convicted of a lesser offence such as manslaughter

- a social tragedy. Was Ruth Ellis the victim of an unhappy background? Since the trial it has emerged that she was abused by her father and beaten by Blakely. In the context of the 1950s, were these sorts of details ignored? shied away from? seen to be further evidence of Ruth's 'bad character'?

The group discuss which of these, or other, options they would prefer to work with, and why.

A number of factors will have a bearing on such a choice. The students' own values and sympathies in terms of the story itself will play a part, but so too will their recognition of the potential its dramatisation would have to explore underlying issues. They will also need to consider the nature of the audience that will, ultimately, be witness to any dramatisation.

▶ Applying an ODC

1 By way of fixing on and illustrating their overall concept for a dramatic interpretation of Ruth Ellis's story, the students set about arranging an installation that could serve as an opening image. The activity involves collecting a number of objects together and finding ways of arranging them in a space and against a carefully chosen backdrop so that they project certain meanings (see page 77). Objects which might play a part in the installation could include:
   - a handgun
   - a pair of handcuffs
   - a bottle of Pernod and a glass
   - a judge's wig and black cloth
   - a racing car's steering wheel
   - a hangman's noose.

2 Having experimented with positioning the objects in different ways, the image is lit in a variety of colours and from different angles.

3　How might meaning be added to the image by having carefully selected music playing?

4　How might the central characters of Ruth Ellis, David Blakely and Desmond Cussen be introduced into this opening image in a way that captures something of the students' overall concept for the drama to follow?

From this foundation there are a number of ways of developing the drama. Different types of dramatic writing such as monologue, reportage, chorus, verse, narration may be employed to animate and elucidate. Background research might reveal other evidence worth placing into the context of a devised drama: Ruth Ellis's will, actual headlines from the time, Albert Pierrepoint's account of the hanging (Pierrepoint was the hangman, who retired shortly after this case).

● The purpose of progression?

In the opening chapter of this book it was proposed that a drama curriculum should endeavour to:

- introduce students to a wide range of dramatic texts and forms and encourage students to interpret them
- help students understand the cultural and historical context in which drama originates and is performed
- facilitate experimentation with different ways of performing and recording drama
- introduce different performance styles and match these to the texts studied
- teach students how to respond critically to written texts and both live and recorded performances from a variety of cultures, genres and styles
- help students review how their own explorations of ideas in drama match the ideas of other practitioners and commentators
- teach students how to speak and move with fluency and clarity of intention
- improvise around the central themes of a stimulus in order to gain greater insight into its dramatic potential
- enable students to work towards a formal presentation of both scripted drama and drama of their own devising.

There are many, many true stories as intriguing and powerful as that of Ruth Ellis and an infinite number of fictitious ones that can give us new insights and somehow change us and the world in which we live. To be able to tell those stories effectively through drama surely constitutes progression.

Unit planning sheet for drama

Unit title Ruth Ellis   **Time scale** 6 × 100 minutes or 10 hrs

AIMS

- to enable students to produce a piece of original devised theatre based on a factual event

RESOURCES

- newspaper articles on Ruth Ellis including *Mirror* article 1999
- account of events from *Crimes of Passion*
- book *Ruth Ellis My Mother*
- video *Dance with a Stranger* (Mike Newell, director, 1984) or *A Life for a Life* (BBC documentary 1999)
- last letter written by Ruth Ellis
- music (selection, but including *Dance with a Stranger*)
- handcuffs, handgun, judge's wig and black cloth, racing car's steering wheel, hangman's noose
- access to Internet, video camera, recorder and monitor, lighting and sound equipment.

SUGGESTED ACTIVITIES

- introduction to unit through discussion on production process – connections with previous work – key roles and responsibilities identified. Group consider individual interests and skills and agree possible tasks/roles
- very brief outline of events surrounding Ruth Ellis given to set context, then video of *Dance with a Stranger* or *A Life for a Life* shown
- students discuss immediate responses and reflect on feelings evoked
- account of the murder (from *Crimes of Passion*) read by students, who develop sequence of 8/9 frames depicting the murder (no spoken words) working in groups of 3/4
- frames presented again, but with written captions that emphasise the sense of drama
- groups reflect on frames and captions, considering how the style and language of the author have been dramatised. Connections made with other dramas where audience is steered towards particular judgement
- contrasting account of the events shared
- students consider (whole group) use of different genres to depict the events (as a thriller etc.)
- students work individually (homework) recording why they think particular genre should be used for the story, justifying their choice in terms of personal perspectives and values and considering dramatic potential and implications for staging
- choices shared and preferred concept established
- decisions re choice of characters that are to be included – possible further research and writing in role

EVIDENCE OF LEARNING (CREATING, PERFORMING, RESPONDING)

Creating Are students:
- independently working effectively with others during the whole research and creative production process?
- developing original and imaginative interpretations of the material?
- making an effective contribution to the production by carrying out their role/responsibility with imagination commitment and expertise?

Performing Are students:
- using and manipulating form to appropriately and effectively create the scenes?
- using theatrical elements and performance skills effectively – e.g. lighting, sound, space, tension etc.?
- engaging the audience throughout the performance.

Responding Are students:
- effectively communicating their ideas through the integration of form and content?

By the end of the unit the students should know and understand:
- how drama can be structured to achieve an intended effect
- how to select forms that are appropriate for the material and its intended purpose
- how to use dramaturgy to enhance production with attention to details including mood, atmosphere and historical accuracy

They should be able to:
- adopt key roles for an independently managed performance (director/designer etc.)
- work with others in negotiating, researching, devising, staging a production based on a factual event
- create an original and imaginative piece of theatre that engages the audience and achieves the desired responses
- effectively record the development of the work at all its stages in individual working notebooks.

SUGGESTED ACTIVITIES (CONTINUED)

- creation of installation to serve as opening or closing image (connection with KS3 and 4 work on semiotics) – use of stage lighting and sound to depict planned mood, atmosphere and meaning
- with overall concept in mind, students consider appropriateness of introducing central characters to image
- further research into life of Ruth Ellis and the case history plus attitudes towards women and capital punishment at the time
- group works independently, using variety of drama techniques to explore content and additional research (e.g. character motivation)
- drama devised following decisions re form and style to be used
- students adopt roles and responsibilities, agreeing and recording decisions, including design process and rehearsal schedule etc. (students to work independently in own time as well as in two double lessons, using teacher as resource only)
- performance for GCSE students (Y11)
- students lead discussion with GCSE students, following performance – focus on responses and insights gained
- whole-group evaluation focusing on whether the performance had prompted the responses they intended and whether the development and performance of the drama had provided them personally with new insights about the Ruth Ellis case and the effectiveness of the form they had chosen to use.

COMMENTS/EVALUATION POINTS

Links to GCSE, A/AS level work
- preparation for a group project
- application of skills within a performance
- groups working independently from teacher for major part of process
- research work and links with other playwrights who have tackled similar complex events.

References

1.1 The drama curriculum

Clipson-Boyles, S. *Drama in Primary English Teaching*. David Fulton, 1998.

DfEE/QCA. *The National Curriculum for England*. DfEE, 1999.

Hornbrook, D. *Education in Drama*. Falmer Press, 1990.

1.2 The drama curriculum in context

DfEE. *The National Literacy Strategy: Framework for teaching*. DfEE, 1998.

Hertrich, J. *Internal Report on the Inspection of Drama*. Ofsted 1999.

Ofsted, *The Arts Inspected*. Heinemann, 1998.

Arts Council Working Group on Drama Education. *Arts Council Guidance on Drama Education*. ('Drama in Schools'). Arts Council of Great Britain, 1992.

Ofsted. *Inspecting Subjects and Aspects 11–18*. Ofsted, 1999.

2.1 Planning for progression

National Curriculum Council. *The Arts 5–16: A Curriculum Framework*. Oliver & Boyd, 1990.

Hirst, P. *Knowledge and the Curriculum*. Routledge & Kegan Paul, 1974.

Fleming, M. *Starting Drama Teaching*. David Fulton, 1994.

Fleming, M. 'Progression and continuity in the Teaching of Drama', in *Drama*, vol 7. No 1. 1999.

3.2 Shaping the dramatic eyesight

Meek, M. *How Texts Teach What Readers Learn*. Thimble Press, 1988.

3.3 Working with the voice

Langer, S. *Feeling and Form*. Routledge & Kegan Paul, 1953.

3.4 Discourse in drama

Postman, N. *Teaching as a Subversive Activity*. Cambridge University Press, 1975.

3.7 Finding the form

Boal, A. *Games for Actors and Non-Actors*. Routledge, 1992.

3.9 Dramatisation

Cooper, S. & Mackey, S., *Theatre Studies: An Approach for Advanced Level*. Stanley Thornes, 2000.

Further reading

In addition to books mentioned in the text, teachers will find any of the following useful.

- **Planning and teaching the drama curriculum**

Bolton, G. *New Perspectives on Classroom Drama.* Simon & Schuster, 1992.

Fleming, M. *The Art of Drama Teaching.* David Fulton, 1997.

Hornbrook, D. *Education and Dramatic Art.* Routledge, 1997.

Hornbrook, D. *On the Subject of Drama.* Routledge, 1998.

Neelands, J. *Beginning Drama 11–14.* David Fulton, 1998.

Nicholson, H. *Teaching Drama 11–18.* Cassell, 2000 .

O'Neill, C. *Drama Worlds.* Heinemann, 1995.

- **Practical classroom activities**

Kempe, A. *The GCSE Drama Coursebook.* Stanley Thornes, 1997.

Kempe, A., & Warner, L. *Starting with Scripts.* Stanley Thornes, 1997.

Mackey, S. *Practical Theatre.* Stanley Thornes, 1997.

Marson, P. et al *Drama 14–16.* Stanley Thornes, 1990.

Owens, A., & Barber, K. *Dramaworks.* Carel Press, 1997.

O'Toole, J., & Haseman, B. *Dramawise.* Heinemann, 1986.

- **General reference texts**

Aston, E., & Savona, G. *Theatre as a Sign System.* Routledge, 1991.

Birch, D. *The Language of Drama.* Macmillan, 1991.

Dawson, S. W. *Drama and the Dramatic.* Methuen, 1970.

Devlin, D. *Mask and Scene.* Macmillan, 1989.

Esslin, M. *The Field of Drama.* Methuen, 1987.

Hartnoll, P. *A Concise History of the Theatre.* Thames & Hudson, 1968.

Hodgson, T. *The Batsford Dictionary of Drama.* Batsford, 1988.

Johnstone, K. *Impro.* Methuen, 1979.

Kelsall, M. *Studying Drama.* Edward Arnold, 1985.

Reynolds, P. *Drama: Text into Performance.* Penguin, 1986.

Styan, J. L. *Drama, Stage and Audience.* Cambridge University Press, 1975.

Index